WITHOUT TRADITION
2 PARA – 1941-45

Born in London in 1924 Robert Peatling followed family tradition by becoming an apprentice compositor. On the outbreak of war he joined the Air Training Corps and became an ARP messenger going on to enlist in the Army in 1942 and becoming a Sherman tank wireless operator. A year later he volunteered for parachute training and joined 2 Para and fought with them at Arnhem. Evading capture, he fell in with the Arnhem resistance group and was with them for seven months until liberated by the Canadians. He was recommended for a Mention in Despatches. On return to England he was an instructor at the Parachute Regiment Depot until demobilisation.

Returning to the printing trade he joined the Daily Mirror in 1951 and stayed until his retirement in 1984. At the same time he became a SSAFA caseworker and devoted much time to the Scout Association, rising to be a Commissioner.

Now retired and living in Dorset, Robert was until recently Secretary of the Wessex Branch of the Parachute Regiment Association and now serves on the Committee.

WITHOUT TRADITION

TRADITION

2 PARA – 1941-45

Robert Peatling

Pen & Sword
MILITARY

First published in 1994 and reprinted in 2004 by
PEN & SWORD MILITARY
an imprint of
Pen & Sword Books Limited
47 Church Street
Barnsley
S. Yorkshire
S70 2AS

ISBN 1 84415 111 5

A CIP record for this book
is available from the British Library.

Printed and bound in Great Britain by
CPI UK

For a complete list of Pen & Sword titles please contact:
PEN & SWORD BOOKS LIMITED
47 Church Street, Barnsley, South Yorkshire, S70 2AS, England.
E-mail: enquiries@pen-and-sword.co.uk
Website: www.pen-and-sword.co.uk

Dedication

To every man who served in the
Second Battalion The Parachute Regiment
and took part in the parachute operations described
but especially to our Commanding Officer
John Frost, CB, DSO and Bar, MC
who led all four drops into enemy territory

Introduction

ON RETURN from the prison camp in 1945, Captain Duncan McLean, our Adjutant spent a few happy months at the War Office compiling a short history of the Second Battalion The Parachute Regiment. It was a 44 page Octavo booklet that sold for two shillings.

Forty-five years later in 1990, General Frost suggested to me that he would like to see the history revised with much more detail. Being the Editor of our Parachute 2 Club newsletter I had already spent much time at the Public Record Office collating Honours and Awards to the Battalion and reading the War Diary for items to report.

The Roll of Honour had been produced by me some years earlier, so I gladly undertook the work.

The title of the book is taken from the fact that all men left their parent Regiment, many steeped in 300 years of tradition to volunteer for an unknown parachute unit Without Tradition.

General Frost had wanted to write a Foreword but unfortunately when the time came he regrettably was unable to manage that task. Nevertheless he was, until the end of his life, interested in all that was happening and gave his approval to the outline of chapters.

The history of the Second Battalion closely follows the wartime history of Major General John Frost and I am so sorry he is unable to enjoy the finished work. I have greatly enjoyed its production.

Robert Peatling
February 1994

36 Park Lane
Wimborne Minster
Dorset BH21 1LD

THIS IS YOUR LIFE 1977 – John Frost is watched by Jean, son Hugo and two sisters. 2 Para men were invited to contribute to the programme. *Photo: Thames TV*

Foreword

THIS IS the story of 2 Para, from 1941 until 1945 and of some recollections which Bob Peatling has compiled through individual personal accounts from all the different operations.

My husband had the great honour of commanding the Battalion at Bruneval, North Africa, Sicily, Italy, Arnhem and post war in Palestine and he felt very strongly that the history had not been fully recorded in North Africa where they suffered enormous casualties. Bob Peatling has put this right, but very regrettably too late for Johnnie to read and appreciate.

I felt very honoured to be asked to write the Foreword, which as the author says, is very much a tribute to the "Colonel".

Johnnie was immensely proud of everyone in the Battalion and to the end of his life 2 Para was very close to his heart.

Jean Frost
Northend Farm
1994

Acknowledgements

MY THANKS are due to all members of the Parachute 2 Club for permission to use their personal stories in this history of Number 2 Parachute Battalion, as it was originally designated. In many cases their stories add a light touch to the serious business of war.

I wish to acknowledge the kindness shown by the following individuals. Dr Glyn Bayliss of the Imperial War Museum gave permission to quote from that fine authoritative work 'Airborne Forces' by Lt Col TBH Otway, DSO. I have reproduced a map from the book and give acknowledgement to the Crown copyright, Imperial War Museum for the photographs used. Chris v Roekel willingly helped.

Major A Digby Tatham Warter, DSO, gave approval for his unique Arnhem battle report to be used together with the story of his achievement of bringing 138 men back through enemy lines one month later.

I have been unable to contact Group Captain Maurice Newham, OBE DFC to get his permission to use the story of the first Battalion jumps at Ringway, I hope he approves.

George Millar immediately gave approval to my request to use an extract from his book The Bruneval Raid. He had been captured in North Africa, escaped to England and returned to France by parachute as a secret agent. Dave Brooks gave me tremendous encouragement to finish the book. Fred Radley ex 3 Battalion sent me much information on the African campaign. John A Hey's Arnhem Roll of Honour was of inestimable value as were David Buxton, Major John Dickson and The Commonwealth War Graves Commission in the compilation of the Roll of Honour.

Roger King helped with his research at the Public Record Office on the Pigeon Post and John Wallace. Mrs Diana Andrews at the Airborne Museum and Mrs Pat Blake at The Parachute Regimental Association gave me every encouragement. Mrs Patricia Reid gave me the loan of her late husband's collection of papers on Bruneval to sort through.

Terry Farmiloe of the Typesetting Bureau and Dennis Ross of Wimborne Print were unstinting with their professional knowledge and I thank them. The only person I wanted to write the Foreword was General John Frost, it was not possible and I am delighted that his widow Jean Frost gave us that honour.

Contents

Maps

Illustrations

CHAPTER ONE

Enthusiastic early days

OUR STORY starts in September 1941 when volunteers for parachute duties were called for from the British Army. An extra two shillings a day (10p) pay was offered and hundreds answered the call. Experience showed that only one man in three possessed the necessary morale and physical fitness to become and remain a parachute soldier.

Hardwick Hall near Chesterfield was chosen as the army training centre and RAF Ringway at Manchester was responsible for teaching the parachuting technique. Who were these volunteers? They came from the Guards, Light Infantry, Line Regiments, Sappers, Gunners, Drivers, Medics, Craftsmen and Ordnance. They were English, Irish, Scots, Welsh, Canadians, Poles, Italians, a German Jew and one of Scottish descent from Argentina.

History shows that this mixture was a success, the rivalry between different regions and Regiments was an enormous asset. Every man felt hand picked, the officers, more so.

Men of the Second Battalion were involved in five operations behind the enemy lines, over two hundred were killed in action. It is rare to find a man who served with us who was neither wounded nor taken prisoner of war. In every chapter you will read of the thoughts of the men who went to war and how they coped with the difficulties.

Throughout October, officers and other ranks continued to arrive and the difficulties of forming an entirely new type of battalion from scratch, and with no nucleus, became apparent. The Battalion was one of the first three of its kind ever to be formed. Initially a shortage of equipment and scant knowledge of what equipment a parachute battalion should have, and a lack of experience in tactical use of parachute troops, were further handicaps.

However, all these disadvantages were overcome, in the first place by intense keenness on the part of all ranks and, secondly, by a desire to make a show in a new branch of warfare. There was plenty of scope for individual ideas on all subjects, and at the end of November, 1941, the Battalion strength was 32 officers and 552 other ranks.

During these first three months, intensive training was undertaken by each company in turn prior to carrying out qualifying jumps at

Ringway. Lieutenant Colonel EWC Flavell MC, had been selected to command the No. 2 Parachute Battalion and with his Adjutant Captain JD Frost arrived at Ringway in January 1942 to carry out their parachute training.

Their first jumps were made, as usual, from the balloon and they both landed quite safely. With the feeling of satisfaction and exhilaration which always follows this achievement they both expressed the desire 'to get on with it' and make another jump straightaway.

This time they were not so successful. Possibly through over-confidence or lack of concentration they both landed awkwardly. Flavell strained a ligament which delayed the completion of his parachute training by three months and Capt. Frost strained a knee. Fortunately in his case the injury responded well to treatment and he was able to resume training within a few days.

It was well that he did so, for it enabled him to take almost immediate promotion to the rank of Major. Instructions were received from the Brigade Commander that a company of trained parachute troops from No. 2 Parachute Battalion were to be sent to Tilshead Camp on Salisbury Plain to carry out combined exercises with the Navy and the Air Force. Capt Frost was appointed to command C Company, which was almost entirely composed of Scotsmen, and sent him off on the assignment. There was no inkling at that time of the reason for the exercises and they were assumed to be merely routine practice to co-ordinate the work of the three Services.

There was much cross posting of Officers at this time. Major Alastair Pearson was 2ic for one week before he was claimed by Lt Col Down for the First Battalion. Major Hope-Thompson was posted to form the Fourth Battalion. Major Gofton Salmond became 2ic in January. Later on in January, the now famous yellow lanyard was issued to all ranks for the first time.

Advance jumping training was being carried out by all companies, and difficulties in training and welding together a team were occasioned by so many officers and other ranks being sent away on courses. In the end, however, this policy paid a handsome dividend.

Martin Willcock . . . . *jumps before the first official course*

ON THE 8th September 1941 I saw that volunteers were required for Airborne Forces (Parachute duties) and so I put my name down, having looked through the minimum medical requirements.

On the 26th September 1941 I received a telegram instructing me to report to Hobart House in London at 10.00 hrs for an interview on the 27th. In the afternoon I was interviewed by a Lt Col Flavell, who I found out afterwards was selecting Subalterns for the 2nd Parachute Battalion which was being formed and which he was to command. I had no idea how I had fared. In the adjacent room another Lt Col was selecting his Subalterns for the 3rd Bn. I like to think that I picked the right room to be interviewed.

I returned to my Unit the following day. On the 29th I heard that I had been accepted, and then events moved at a bewildering speed. I was instructed to report the next day to the 2nd Parachute Bn. at Hardwick Hall Camp near Chesterfield. I got on the train at St. Pancras and met up with 2 other Subalterns and whilst rather naturally our conversation was a little guarded, when we all got out at Chesterfield it was obvious where we were all heading.

On the 1st October the CO spoke to all of us, 6 Subalterns and about 20 NCO's were detailed to go on a parachute course at Ringway that afternoon. We arrived at Ringway about 4.30 and settled in. The next morning there was some delay for our first parade in the gym as Mass was being said for a Pole who had been killed three days before! I rang my mother to tell her what I was doing, and for the first and only time in my life she hung up on me!

The next 7 days were taken up with PT, talks, films and synthetic training. We expected to make our first balloon jump the next day but this was cancelled due to the weather. The following day was full of hopes and disappointments. After breakfast we were told during PT that we would be jumping by balloon. So a quick change and out to Tatton by bus, only to be told it was cancelled and that we might make our first jump from a Whitley – and so back to Ringway where we waited and hoped. There was no decision till after lunch when we put our parachutes on and were all set. Again it was cancelled on account of the wind. We waited until about 4.30 when we changed into PT clothes and got on parade – only to be told we would be jumping after all. So we changed once again, put on our harness and waited. One stick went and when the plane returned we marched out full of hope. On arrival at the plane all was cancelled – the plane was U/S! And so it was not surprising when night ops and night jumping were also cancelled.

Next day, Saturday the 11th, after morning PT we were told once again we would be jumping. We hurriedly changed, collected our chutes, formed up and got into the plane. We took off and circled over Tatton. I was No. 4. It must be the real thing this time! Nos. 1 and 2 jumped and we waited expectantly – and then we got the wash out signal! It did not seem possible to be so near to jumping and then not to do it! And so we returned and carried on with normal training. I forget now why, on this occasion, jumping was stopped but I expect it was on account of the wind.

Sunday was a day of rest and so Peter Nauomoff and I walked to Wilmslow Church for the Harvest Festival Service.

On Monday the 13th October we went to Tatton Park and did two balloon jumps. We had been warned that we would drop about 180 feet before the canopy fully develops and this takes about 2 seconds. On my first jump I distinctly remember thinking to myself – 'It's about time this bloody thing opened!' which of course it did – and in due course I landed quite safely. The second jump was even easier and I landed on my feet. I thought this is a piece of cake – that afternoon taught me otherwise. The man I most admired was an NCO whose name I do not remember – he refused the first time but went up a second time and had to be pushed out. He had to be pushed out on his third attempt and after that he was alright and I believe he got his wings in due course. After lunch we returned to Ringway to make our first Whitley jump. I was No. 1 in the third plane and in my enthusiasm went too early causing some consternation in the aircraft! I landed with a bit of an oscillation and the shock of hitting the ground so hard taught me not to take jumping too lightly.

On the 14th and 15th we did 2 further drops without any problems that I can remember. On the 20th the news media descended on Ringway. Cameras and Newsreel cameras took pictures of us doing synthetic training from every angle. In the afternoon we did a drop for them at Tatton park either in pairs or sticks. Later we all watched the 1st Bn do a massed drop of about 60 men – I think every available aircraft was used. Anyway the weather was good and they took lots of photos. Some of us found ourselves in the national press a few days later.

On the 21st we made two more attempts to make a further jump but the weather stopped it. On the 23rd we were issued with our wings although we had only done 6 jumps. This was because the next day we would return to Hardwick and be dropped in the Park before the as-sembled 2nd and 3rd Bns and it was felt that as we would be making our 7th and qualifying jump it would be appropriate for us to land qualified. We thought this was a nice gesture.

On the 24th we fitted 'chutes etc. in the morning, but we were unable to go before lunch. We emplaned at 1.45 and taxied out to the take off point, but then returned as one engine was U/S. We got into another aircraft and took off about 2.25 – about 25 minutes after the others. I was No. 8 and thus I was the last to land. Thus we completed our course – at least most of us did.

Looking back on it it seems incredible that none of us had had any medical examinations and we made our first three jumps 14 days after joining the Battalion. Guinea pigs – I suspect!

Besides Peter Nauomoff, the only other Officer on this course whose name I remember was Lieut. Fitzpatrick – known as Fitz P. He sub-sequently left the Bn to join 4 Para which was then being formed under Lt Col Hope Thompson.

We were a mixed bunch from every regiment in the army – or so it seemed. But the one thing that we all had in common from the Col to the Private – was that we had JUMPED – a unique experience which we would never forget and one which made us all feel the Battalion was something rather special and we were proud to belong to it.

GROUP CAPTAIN Newman tells of the first jump course of the newly formed Brigade to arrive for training at Ringway on a special train from Chesterfield to Heald Green station on Saturday the 1st November 1941.

Seventeen officers, two warrant officers, twenty-two sergeants and two hundred and twenty-eight other ranks tumbled out on to the platform laughing and joking and wondering in their hearts what it was going to be like. Every man was a free volunteer, character and courage were innate in them, for not only had they shown the desire to meet and fight their King's enemies but they were willing to challenge the unknown perils of parachuting in order to hasten the day of combat.

Short days and the notorious November weather would add to the difficulties. In fourteen days, if all went well, those men would be leaving Ringway after having completed their training.

A group of men were sent to the Drop Zone at Tatton Park to watch demonstration parachute descents carried out by the instructors while others were given flights in the Whitleys to gain experience. In the afternoon the programmes were reversed and the intervals were filled in with lectures and practice on the synthetic training apparatus.

The following morning the men were aroused at five o'clock as the preliminary to a working parade at seven fifteen. The raw coldness of the dark November morning was slightly relieved by the brisk march of a mile or so from the pupils' camp to the RAF messes where they had their food. It is a Service custom to allow plenty of time to get ready for parades, and by seven fifteen cold feet and blue noses had returned as discouraging associates for the ordeal of jumping from the balloon. Each man carried his own parachute and had been warned that dreadful things might happen if he failed to take the utmost care of it.

After numbering off the men in the order in which they were to jump, the instructor would make a show of checking the equipment and then, having received the O.K. from the ground, order Action stations No. 1 in a manner which brooked no refusal. This was followed almost immediately by the word GO roared with such imperative urgency that the pupil's subconscious reaction almost invariably impelled instantaneous compliance with the order.

As the parachutist descended, the instructional role was taken over from the ground and directions were shouted through a megaphone. The words of advice were not always heard or acted upon, however, because the quickly succeeding emotions sometimes induced a dazedness from which the pupil scarcely recovered during the twenty seconds or so that it took to reach the ground.

The days sped by – balloon jumping was completed and followed by aircraft. Everyone was in high spirits and the experiences were almost as novel to the instructors as they were to the pupils. At the end of twelve days one thousand seven hundred and seventy-three parachute descents had been made – no one had been killed – and the first course was completed. Only two men on this course found themselves unable to screw up the necessary determination to make the seven jumps and they were returned to their units. The coveted badge with its blue wings and white parachute was presented to each man and hastily sewn on to uniforms. Parties into Manchester were quickly organized with the instructors invited as honoured guests by their erstwhile pupils.

Everyone was gay and in the mood to celebrate. Everyone, that is, except the twelve men, out of the two hundred and sixty-nine that I had met at Heald Green station less than a fortnight before, who were lying on their backs in hospital beds with broken legs or fractured spines.

Alex Reid . . . . *tells of his introduction to parachuting*

'VOLUNTEERS REQUIRED for Airborne Troop'. So read the announcement on Coy detail of the London Scottish Battalion. To escape the deadly monotony of Army life on the home front, I handed my name to the Coy Orderly Sgt, and promptly forgot all about it.

Several months elapsed when to my astonishment I, in company with 9 others was ordered to report to the 2nd Para Bn C Coy. The day after my arrival at Coy I was detailed to attend a course of jumping at the training drome.

For the first 3 days our training was a never ending succession of PT cross-country running, road walking, unarmed combat, boxing etc. In fact everything calculated to reduce men to physical wrecks in the shortest time! The next 2 days were devoted to learning how to make a correct landing, by jumping from towers at heights varying from 6' to 14'. Also how to make a correct exit from aircraft. For this we used the fuselage of an old Whitley raised on trestles about 8' off the ground. In our sticks of 10 we sat 5 each side of the hole – odd numbers forward and evens aft. Action stations is given by means of a red light and No. 1 drops his feet into the hole. On the light turning to green, out he goes, followed in rapid succession by the rest of the stick. A good stick can leave the aircraft in about 10 seconds, and when they land the distance between the first and the last man is approx. 500 yards. so you see that one man hesitating for only 1 second spreads the stick out another 50 yds. I should add here that the slower the stick the longer the last men are without arms. This we practiced numerous times on the mock up. Then came parachute control and how to collapse a chute on landing, a very difficult feat in gusty weather.

The parachute used is opened by a static line. This line is fixed in the plane to the envelope containing the 'chute and as the man drops out, the weight of his body pulls the 'chute from the envelope and he becomes airborne.

On the 6th day we were warned for jumping. With very mixed feelings, I fitted my 'chute, marched over to the Whitley and took my place in the stick. On the first flight only 2 men were dropped at a time, the first being the instructor, the plane then circles and drops the next 2 and so on. The engines were ticking over whilst we fixed our static lines, and then, with a mighty roar the Whitley taxied over the drome and took off.

Everybody looked a bit on edge, and I hope I didn't looks as scared as I felt. On came the Red light followed about 5 seconds later by the Green, out went No. 1 and then No. 2. We all sat back licking our very dry lips whilst the plane circled to drop the next pair, out they went and then came my turn. The chap before me made a clean exit, I swung my feet into the hole, glanced down, strictly against instructions, and saw the earth about 500' below, shut my eyes and just went. The next agonising few seconds seemed very confused – I dropped through space, the slipstream hit me with terrific force and swung my feet above my head – I instinctively grabbed for something and found that the canopy had opened and I was gently swinging in the air. The utter relief I felt up there on my own, the quietness after the noise of the aircraft and the realisation that my troubles were over is an experience I shall always remember. But were my troubles over? The ground seemed to be rushing up towards me before I thought about landing, but keeping my knees and feet together in the approved manner, I hit the deck, rolled over and released myself from the harness. Gazing upwards, I watched the rest of the boys descend. I felt very shaky at the knees, but that soon passed and the evening saw the 10 of us cheerfully celebrating our first descent.

Devizes January 1942. A section of Jocks unaware of the planned operation attend a photographers to show their newly won wings. Privates Judge, Conroy, McCann, Heywood, Higgins. Front row, L/Cpl Fleming, Cpl McKenzie, later won the DCM and MM, Sgt Muir and Pte O'Neill.

Hugh Levien .... *the first Intelligence Sergeant of 2 Para*

MY PERSONAL record shows that on 4th September 1941 I travelled from Beverley, to Chesterfield, leaving my 10th Bn. The Queens Own Royal West Kent Regiment. At Chesterfield railway station we were ferried to the camp at Hardwick where there were many newly-built red brick huts lined along partially constructed roads.

As a Sgt I was one of the first in the queue to report and was welcomed by a Major full of jocularity who enquired what Regiment I was from, in spite of the fact that we all had our own cap-badges. He made a most offensive remark, mispronouncing the County, accompanied by an inane cackle. On being told that I had been the Intelligence Sgt of the unit I came from, he said something like 'Oh, I think we still have a vacancy for one of those chaps in the 2nd Bn. You had better trot down there and see how you fit in.' So I followed his directions and was duly taken on in that capacity with Dicky Ashford at the Intelligence Officer.

I didn't really have any duties, and made out my own programme, which mainly consisted of joining a squad undergoing intensive PT and synthetic training under qualified parachutists. I was pretty fit at the time and so coped without undue strain. I moseyed around Bn HQ a bit each day to make sure I kept up to date with what was going on, and after parades if I still had the price of a few pints I fairly often took the free transport provided into Chesterfield. As soon as I discovered that C Coy was to be the first to go to Ringway I got myself a temporary posting to that Coy. We were still all wearing our separate forms of Parent Unit headgear and Regimental cap-badges, collar-dogs etc. On November 6th I went with C Coy to Ringway and did my qualifying jumps, and a couple more formation drops with schemes at the end. Sometime shortly after, Capt Ashford took over as Adjt and Lt Peter Nauomoff was appointed as the new IO.

In January 1942 I was again at Ringway and doing a jump at Tatton Park with a rising wind which would normally have caused cancellation but as I was in the last stick of the Company to drop it was allowed to go on. I had the misfortune to land during a gust of wind swinging me violently, with my insteps astride a railway line, and broke my left leg and 4 bones in that ankle.

By the time I managed to work my way back to the Bn it was August and they were stationed at Bulford.

Alex Reid .... *has now completed his jumps*

IN FEBRUARY 1942 we shared camp at Tilshead with the newly formed Glider Pilot Regiment – a god-forsaken camp if ever there was one. I shared a bunk with Sgt Jimmy Sharp (also known as Shorty – short in stature but very great as a soldier). Conditions in the camp were terrible. I had a touch of flu, and one night I was lying in bed trying to keep warm when a Sgt burst in brandishing a sten gun. He departed shouting

'Shorty, Shorty'. There followed an explosion, and I naturally thought he had shot Shorty. However, midst a lot of laughter and horseplay, Shorty and a bevy of Sgts arrived a little worse for wear, one of them clutching a massive chunk of cheese he had borrowed from the Mess. Sadly, I cannot remember the names, but I think Gibbie was one. I was more than a little apprehensive, for the early stens were unpredictable to say the least. Discussion arose as to whether the cheese should be shot off the rafters of the hut, but the cheese-bearer invited the sten-waver to shoot it out of his hand, whereupon the sten-man told him, 'don't be bloody daft I might hit your hand'. 'All right', replied the other, 'if you are frightened, let me shoot it out of your hands.' Such was the ale-inspired logic!

Training came to an abrupt end and the company moved off to Thruxton aerodrome for the Bruneval raid.

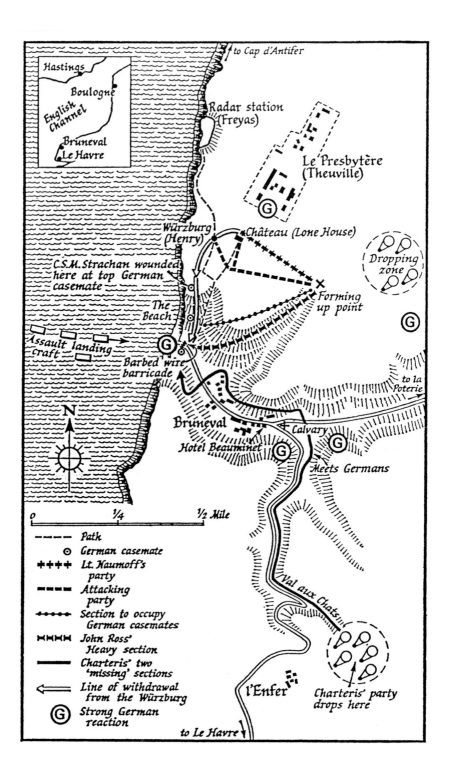

to Cap d'Antifer

Radar station
(Freyas)

Le Presbytère
(Theuville)

Hastings

Boulogne

English Channel

Bruneval
Le Havre

Würzburg
(Henry)

Château (Lone House)

Dropping
zone

C.S.M. Strachan wounded
here at top German
casemate

Forming
up point

The
Beach

Assault landing
craft

Barbed wire
barricade

N

to la
Poterie

Bruneval

Calvary

Hotel Beauminet

Meets Germans

0   ¼   ½ Mile

- - - - -   Path
⊙   German casemate
✛✛✛✛   Lt. Naumoff's
      party
▬ ▬ ▬   Attacking
      party
•••••••   Section to occupy
      German casemates
✕✕✕✕   John Ross'
      Heavy section
▬▬▬   Charteris' two
      'missing' sections
⟵   Line of withdrawal
      from the Würzburg
Ⓖ   Strong German
      reaction

Val aux Chats

l'Enfer

Charteris' party
drops here

to Le Havre

CHAPTER TWO

Into Action – The Bruneval Raid

THERE WERE good reasons for sending C Company to collect the Radar equipment from a hilltop site at midnight on a cold night in February 1942, HMS Delight, a destroyer was out in the Atlantic, 60 miles from France in bad visibility when dive bombed and sunk by German bombers. Our aircraft were being located when on bombing missions over France and shot down. The question being asked was, are the Germans more advanced with radar knowledge than us. Lord Mountbatten at Combined Operations decided to find out.

SECRET   **Not to be taken in aircraft**

OPERATIONAL ORDER 'BITING'.

Major JD Frost, Commanding C Coy. 2nd Parachute Bn.

From aerial photographs no sign of weapons heavier than MGs can be seen. Until recently these appeared to be sited for defence against seaborne invasion only, but in the last three months three blockhouses have been constructed on the North shoulder of the exit from the beach. These are all thought to cover the valley and are connected to each other by communication trenches, work on these still continues. This group will be called REDOUBT.

There appears to be a strong point at mount of the beach exit, consisting of Two blockhouses, Four LMG posts and a road block. This group is likely to be sited for all-round defence, it is connected to communication trenches to a further LMG post one hundred yards up the valley. This group will be called BEACH PORT, it is surrounded by wire two metres thick.

Further inland there is a house on the edge of a depression running North from the Valley. This being the main perimeter of wire, is surrounded by wire ten metres thick. This house is believed to contain two MGs and is permanently manned. This will be known as GUARD ROOM.

There are more possible LMG posts as shown on the model.

The garrison consists of 30 men under an NCO, five sleep in the GUARD ROOM and the remainder in the village in a house some 500 yards from the beach.

To the north of the valley is a lone building which will be known as LONE HOUSE, 50 yards west of LONE HOUSE is the main objective which will be known as HENRY, LONE HOUSE is believed to contain 20 signallers.

North of LONE HOUSE is an enclosure of trees and buildings, believed to contain a number of signallers, this will be known as RECTANGLE.

OWN TROOPS. 120 all ranks.

OBJECT:–

1. To capture various parts of HENRY and bring them down to the boats.
2. To capture prisoners who have been in charge of HENRY.
3. To obtain all possible information about HENRY and any documents referring to him which may be in LONE HOUSE.

METHOD. The force will be divided into three main parties, each party to be allotted a definite task.

No. 1. NELSON.

(i) **Task** – To capture and hold REDOUBT, BEACH FORTRESS and GUARD ROOM and to cover withdrawal of the remainder of the force to the beach for embarkation in ALC's.

(ii) **DZ** – NELSON will be dropped in the area due east of the track running north & south (model).

(iii) **Direction** – The aircraft will be flying from south to north.

(iv) **FUP** – The line of the track and the hedge running north & south in the re-entrant due East of the DZ.

(v) **Action** – OC NELSON will detail 3 light sections to approach as near as possible to the 3 objectives enumerated in the task paragraph. The heavy sections will move to and take up a position on the spur due east of the REDOUBT so as to cover the road leading from the village and give support for the assault on the GUARD ROOM and BEACH FORTRESS.

(vi) **Timing** – 1st NELSON stick will be dropped at 0015 hrs. The whole party will move to their objectives as soon as possible after forming-up.

(vii) **Co-ordination.** It is of vital importance that the enemy at LONE HOUSE and HENRY should be taken by surprise. Therefore NELSON will take every precaution to make no noise of any kind until either:

The attack on HENRY begins, or

Successive blasts on a whistle are heard, or it becomes absolutely necessary to fire on the enemy. However should any section Commander find it possible to occupy any one of the objectives silently, he will at once do so.

(viii) **R.E.** Immediately it is possible, Lieut Ross will move to the Beach with RE personnel and stores to:-

(a) Clear and mark a route through minefield (if any).

(b) Establish HQ and check point.

No. 2. JELLICOE, HARDY, DRAKE.

(i) **Task.** Move to LONE HOUSE and deal with HENRY. Immediately all material has been taken, information and prisoners captured, to withdraw to the beach and prepare to embark.

(ii) **DZ** – as for NELSON.

(iii) **Direction** – as for NELSON.

(iv) **FUP** – as for NELSON.

(v) **Action** DRAKE will move towards and take up a position west of the RECTANGLE in order to prevent enemy movement towards LONE HOUSE.

HARDY will move to and surround LONE HOUSE (Less RE party).

JELLICOE will move to, and surround HENRY (Less RE Party).

RE party will follow JELLICOE.

(vi) **Timing.** JELLICOE, HARDY and DRAKE will be dropped at 0020 hrs.

(vii) **Co-ordination.** On the sound of 4 blasts on the whistle, HARDY will force their way into LONE HOUSE, collect all enemy into a room on the ground floor and await further orders. RE party will commence their task with HENRY, JELLICOE will be responsible for their protection while doing so and will give any assistance they require.

No. 3 RODNEY.

(i) **Task.** To prevent with 2 sections any attempt by the enemy to attack HARDY from RECTANGLE and to support with 2 sections, NELSON, in the event of an attack from the village.

(ii) **DZ** as for NELSON.

(iii) **Direction** as for NELSON.

(iv) **FUP** as for NELSON.

(v) **Action.** RODNEY will take up position on the ground to the west of the FUP so as to be able to carry out both tasks. He must be able to reinforce either detachment in case of emergency.

(vi) **Timing.** RODNEY will begin dropping at 0025 hrs.

(vii) **Co-ordination.** No noise or firing until HENRY has been taken or the signal – 4 blasts on the whistle – is heard.

(viii) **RE and Signals.** OC Rodney is responsible for ensuring that RE and Signal personnel are guided to area of BEACH FORT, where they will be met by Lieut Ross and will then carry out their duties (see Signal Instructions).

WITHDRAWAL FOR EMBARKATION

1. Immediately HARDY have completed their task they will move to the beach by the most direct route.
2. JELLICOE and DRAKE will follow at 50 yard intervals.
3. However should OC RE have any doubts concerning HENRY, and should the situation warrant it, JELLICOE, HARDY and DRAKE will remain in position until a small party named NOAH arrive from the beach, inspect HENRY and complete their task. The withdrawal will then continue according to plan.
4. RODNEY will receive orders to withdraw by W/T or runner when HARDY etc. have reached the beach. OC RODNEY will however prepare to withdraw as soon as he sees LONE HOUSE area evacuated.
5. RODNEY will move by the most direct route.
6. NELSON will withdraw immediately RODNEY are clear of the beach.

BEACH CONTROL

1. OC parties are responsible for the disposition of their parties on the beach.
2. RE personnel will lay tapes to guide parties through the minefield (if any) Lieut Ross to ensure that guides are in position when required.
3. Section Commanders will report their sections present or otherwise to Lieut Ross, at the check point (BEACH FORT).
4. Parties will embark under orders from the Beach Control Officer – appointed by Lieut Ross.
5. The Beach Control Officer will ensure that parties get to their boats as quickly and vigorously as possible. He will ensure that each boat takes its correct load, and will inform the Naval Officer in Command as soon as the boat is correctly loaded, and ready to leave. He will give the Naval Officer all possible assistance.

GENERAL

1. No prisoners will be taken off, other than signallers.
2. Ammunition will be conserved as far as possible.
3. Sentries will be dealt with silently, whenever possible.
4. The password will be BITING.
5. It is emphasised that the whole operation fails unless HENRY is effectively dealt with and the parts required are captured. All ranks must be fully aware of this.
6. On the ALCs the senior officer or NCO is in command of all troops. He is responsible to the Naval Officer in Command of the ALC and will ensure that all orders given by the NO are implicitly obeyed.

INTERCOMMUNICATION

1. Officers. i.c. NELSON, HARDY, DRAKE and RODNEY will communicate with each other by:–
   (i) No. 38 W/T Sct.
   (ii) Whistle.
2. Signallers with RODNEY will communicate with the Naval Force by:–
   (i) D/F transmitter.
   (ii) No. 18 W/T Sct.
   (iii) Visual (torch).
   (iv) Very pistol.
3. The senior signaller will decide which equipment is to be used where two similar equipments are available.
4. Signals containers can be identified by a green light and will be painted with 4 black and white bands.
5. Signallers will RV with RODNEY in accordance with para.
6. On orders being given by O. i/c RODNEY to take up battle posn. signallers will accompany RODNEY.
7. Comn. will at once be established with the Naval Force by No. 18 W/T Set.
8. As soon as notification has been received that the beach is clear, signallers will leave RODNEY and proceed to the beach. No. 18 W/T Sets will be carried without being dismantled.
9. On arrival at the beach a REPORT CENTRE will be opened as near as possible to Check Point at BEACH FORT.
10. D/F transmissions will begin immediately on taking up posn. at check point. The drill for establishing D/F transmissions will be in accordance with Appx.
11. As soon as Naval craft are heard to be approaching, D/F transmissions will cease and the signaller i/c D/F apparatus will signal in the direction of the craft with a signalling torch using the white light.
    The signals to be sent on the torch will be the same as those sent on the D/F transmitter.
12. In the event of Comn. with the Naval force failing, signals will be fired by Very pistol **but only under order of o i.c. NELSON.**

Very light signals

To indicate the direction of the beach to the Naval Force:–

Two green lights will be fired, one to the right and the other to the left along the base of and below the cliffs.

ADMINISTRATION

1. Normal morning routine.
2. 1000 hrs. Pack containers – check weapons and ammo.
3. 1400 hrs. Containers to Thruxton.

4. 1700 hrs. Tea.
5. 1930 hrs. Move to THRUXTON by M.T.
6. 2030 hrs. Arrive THRUXTON.
7. 2100 hrs. Tea & refreshments.
8. 2115 hrs. Fit Statichutes.
9. 2140 hrs. March to aircraft.
10. 2200 hrs. All troops emplaned by.
11. 2215 hrs. First aircraft takes off.

John Frost, Major, Commanding C Coy., 2nd Parachute Bn.

REPORT ON SUCCESS OF RAID

Certain specialist personnel were required to deal with the RDF Station. Flight Lieutenant Priest was given a temporary commission in the RAF so that he could accompany the force and provide expert scientific knowledge if required; he was taken over in an ALC and was not allowed to drop by parachute, as his capture by the enemy could not be risked. In fact, he did not land but his knowledge was of great assistance.

F/Sgt Cox, RAF, a RDF specialist, was trained in parachute jumping at PTS Ringway, and actually dropped with C Coy. to assist in dismantling the RDF apparatus. His work was excellent throughout.

No. 13801753 Pte Nagel, 93 Pioneer Coy., a German fighting against Hitler, also joined C Coy. and dropped with them. His knowledge of the German language and of the psychology of Germans proved of great assistance.

All the above specialists were obtained through HQ Combined Operations.

The take-off and flight went exactly according to plan. Some flak was met in the area of St. Jouin and some damage was done to aircraft but not to personnel. This has been reported in detail by the Air Force Commander.

Two aircraft dropped their parachutists South of the dropping zone. Estimates of how far south they were dropped vary between 1500 yards and 3 miles. One aircraft dropped 15 minutes late. The remaining aircraft dropped their parachutists according to plan. All containers were dropped successfully and were found quickly. There was no enemy AA fire on the dropping zone and none of the parachutists were fired at as they dropped.

NELSON (less that part which had been dropped short) moved off unopposed to attack the beach defences. They were partly successful but could not complete their task owing to shortage of personnel.

HARDY and JELLICOE formed up and moved off according to plan. During this time a few shots were heard and it appeared that some of the enemy were aware of the attack. HARDY surrounded and took the House and found it empty except for one German in the attic – he was killed.

32

JELLICOE surrounded the Radio location set; the crew of 5 men offered little resistance but all were killed with the exception of one Luftwaffe man who was taken prisoner. From him it was learnt that there were 100 Germans in the Rectangle and approximately one company in the Bruneval area. The lighthouse at Cap d'Antifer had warned them that a parachutist raid was taking place.

In the meantime RODNEY and DRAKE had dropped. DRAKE moved to their positions near the Rectangle and when they received orders to withdraw threw grenades and opened fire on the enemy in the Rectangle.

Some of RODNEY were in the aircraft which dropped short and RODNEY were therefore slightly under strength. However, they took up their positions in reserve without difficulty.

After the RE and RAF RDF experts had taken what was required from the RDF set, HARDY, JELLICOE and DRAKE withdrew southwards about half way to the beach, when it was learnt that the beach defences had not yet been taken completely by NELSON.

The Company Commander detailed a party under Lieut Young from HARDY, JELLICOE and DRAKE to assist NELSON to take the remaining beach defences. This was done successfully and soon afterwards 2/Lieut. Charteris, who was in charge of that party of NELSON which had dropped short, arrived with 4 of his men and took over the beach according to plan.

RODNEY, who had been engaged with some enemy fire from the Rectangle, then moved to the beach under the orders of the Company Commander.

HARDY and all technical experts, with the equipment which they had collected, also moved down to the beach. The remainder of the company was arranged in defensive positions near the beach while contact was made with the navy.

This was done by No. 38 wireless set and a Very pistol, as the signallers with No. 18 set were amongst those who had been dropped short.

As soon as the ALCs arrived, orders were given for the whole company to withdrew and embark. This was done successfully with the exception of a small party, including the signallers mentioned before who had not yet reported to the beach.

At about 0300 hours it appeared from various vehicle lights that were seen that reinforcements were arriving just north of the Rectangle and possibly a counter-attack might have been put in at about 0330 hours. The troops actually left the beach at 0315 hours.

At 0815 hours a wireless message was received from Commander Cook that the operation had been successful.

Return sea voyage.

One MGB, with the RDF equipment and technical experts, returned independently at high speed and reached HMS Prince Albert off Spithead at 1000 hours 28th February.

The remainder of the force arrived at 1630 hours on 28th February, the sea being moderately rough most of that day.

No. 11 Group Fighter Command had fighters protecting the returning boats from about 0815 hours 28th February until they were all back. In consequence, no German aircraft interfered in any way.

Prisoners.

Three German prisoners were brought back in the boats, including one man of the Luftwaffe.

Casualties.

German casualties are estimated at a minimum of 40 killed.

Our own casualties were as follows. There were no casualties amongst 5 Corps troops in the boats, the Royal Navy or RAF.

Killed in Action

3252284 Pte McIntyre, H. D. McD   5347681 Pte Scott, A.

Wounded

2751640 CSM Strachan, G. Bullet wound in abdomen, may recover.
3195970 Sgt Boyd, J. Bullet wound in foot, looks well.
2929915 Cpl Heslop, G. Bullet wound in thigh, feeling well.
2879337 Cpl Stewart, V. Bullet wound in scalp, feeling well.
2037582 L Cpl Heard, R. Wound in hand, feeling well.
2928756 Pte Grant, W. Bullet wound in abdomen, very seriously ill.
3058375 Pte Shaw, H. Bullet wound in leg, not likely to continue.

Missing

2930416 L Cpl MacCallum, J.
2879968 Pte Sutherland, J. Badly wounded, left at farmhouse.
4745152 Pte Willoughby, J.
5951642 Pte Thomas, D.
4622613 Pte Cornell, G.
5047949 Pte Embury, E.

The operation was completely successful.

A preliminary report on the value of the RDF equipment captured is attached. Since that report was written, it has been ascertained definitely that all the equipment required was captured and brought in very good condition.

The prisoner of the Luftwaffe who was captured had spent some time previously in a German Concentration Camp and was willing to talk. As he is a RDF expert, the information he has given has been sufficient to complete the whole picture.

Composition of the Sections in the Whitleys

HARDY section:
Cmrd Major Frost
CSM Strachan
Sgt Fleming
Taylor
McLeod
L/Cpl Dobson
Hayhurst
F.Sgt Cox (RAF)
Halliwell RE.
Pilot: Sgt Clow

NELSON section:
Cmdr 2Lt Charteris
Sgt Gibbons
Cpl Hill
Branwhite
Venters
Sutherland
McCormack
Grafton
Laughland
Matkin
Pilot: WCmdr Pickard

RODNEY section:
Cmdr Lt Timothy
Sgt Forsyth
Cpl Walker
LCpl Johnstone
Stephenson
Hutchinson
Scott 335
Crutchley
Greenough
Millington
Pilot: S/L Meade

HARDY section:
Cmdr Lt Vernon RE
Sgt McFarlane
Cpl Heslop
Galey
Keyes
Gordon
McIntyre
Cpl Jones RE
Conroy
Nagel
Pilot: Sgt Hughes

NELSON section:
Cmdr Sgt Sharp
Sgt Tasker
LCpl Dickie
Wood
Sturgess
Coates
Henderson
Synyer
Gould
Barnett
Pilot: F/Lt Towsey

RODNEY section:
Cmdr Sgt Muir
D. Thomas
LCpl Fleming
McCann
Higgins
Judge
Cadden
Hornsby RE
Collier
Richardson
Pilot: P/O Mair

JELLICOE section:
Cmdr Lt Young
Sgt McKenzie
LCpl Burns
Flitcorft
Drape
McAusland
Wilson
Addie
Manning RE
LCpl Heard RE
Pilot: S/L Peveler

NELSON section:
Cmdr Sgt Grieve
Cpl Stewart
Sgt Ellis RE
Mitchell RE
Freeman
Creighton
Horne
Hughes
Fleming
Willoughby
Pilot: Sgt Pope

RODNEY section:
Cmdr Sgt Reid
Cpl Finney
Stirling
Buchanan
Lough
Graw
O'Neill
Harris RE
Flambart
LCpl MacCallum
Pilot: P/O Haydon

NELSON section:
Cmdr Capt Ross
Sgt Sunley
Cpl McLennon
LCpl Kerr
Shaw
Calderwood
Ewing
Heron
Grant
Thacker
Pilot: F/Lt Coates

DRAKE section:
Cmdr Lt Naoumoff
Sgt Lutener
LCpl Webster
Beattie
Herwood
Sgt Boyd
Murphy
Bond
Welsh
Williamson
Pilot: Sgt Gray

RODNEY section:
Cmdr Sgt Lumb
Cpl Campbell
LCpl Finlay
Eden
Sgt Bennett
Cornell
Embury
Stacey
Scott 681
Ward
Pilot: Sgt Cook

RE = Royal Engineer

Evening Standard

EVENING STANDARD February 28, 1942

FINAL NIGHT EXTRA

Amusements
Radio

BLACK-OUT: 7.3 p.m.—7.11 a.m.
NOON Blots 3.50 p.m.; Sets 6.56 a.m.

No. 36,654   LONDON SATURDAY, FEBRUARY 28, 1942   ONE PENNY

British Paratroops, Followed Up by Infantry, Wreck the Nazis Radio "Eyes" Across Channel

ARMY, NAVY & RAF RAID
N. FRANCE IN THE DARK

"It Was to Schedule and Very Successful"

In a combined operation, joint forces of the Royal Navy, of the Army and of the R.A.F. successfully attacked an important radio location post on the north coast of France.

THIS WAS ANNOUNCED TO-DAY BY THE ADMIRALTY, WAR OFFICE AND THE AIR MINISTRY IN A JOINT COMMUNIQUE, WHICH ADDED:

"Parachute troops of an airborne division were dropped by bombers of the R.A.F.

"The task was finished according to schedule and the parachute troops were supported in the latter half of their task by infantry and are being brought back by the Royal Navy."

First reports received in London to-day indicate that the raid was "very successful."

The operation was carried out to a strict time schedule dictated by the hours of darkness available. The paratroops were preceded by bombers and night fighters, which attacked airfields and gun posts. Their withdrawal was covered on land by the supporting infantry and from the sea by light naval craft. The R.A.F. maintained offensive patrols over the area until all the troops had been withdrawn.

It was stated that while the operation was a spectacular one, it must be regarded as small. Although reference is made to a combined operation, it did not necessarily mean that Commandos were used.

Berlin: "Raid Lasted Two Hours"

The Berlin communique to-day stated: "Last night a number of British parachutists landed on the north French coast. After overcoming a weak coastal defence, they withdrew two hours later by sea, under the pressure of German counter-measures."

COAL TO BE RATIONED ON MONDAY

Evening Standard Reporter

Coal will be rationed in London on Monday.

You will be restricted to a total of six cwt for the six weeks beginning on that day—one cwt a week—if you live in the London Civil Defence Region, which is approximately the same as the Metropolitan Police area.

This comprises the City of London the 28 Metropolitan boroughs. the county boroughs of Croydon. East and West Ham, the County of Middlesex, and parts of Hertfordshire Essex, Kent and Surrey.

You will not be supplied with coal during the next six weeks if you have more than half a ton already in stock on Monday. The order will not apply to boiler fuel or coke

700 STRIKE AT SMITHFIELD

About 700 Smithfield porters and warehousemen to-day continued a strike which began yesterday afternoon.

There are the employees of a number of merchants at the market. A member of one of the firms said: "The strike is not likely to affect housewives rations for the week-end have been delivered. Practically all the firms at Smithfield are involved."

Countess Refused

JAP INVASION FLEET FLEES FROM JAVA

The BIGGEST NAVAL BATTLE OF THE FAR EASTERN WAR RAGED THROUGHOUT MOST OF YESTERDAY AND TO-DAY IN THE JAVA SEA BETWEEN THE SOUTH COAST OF BORNEO AND SURABAYA, THE ALLIES' GREAT NAVAL BASE.

Allied squadrons have beaten back a strong Japanese armada, the Netherlands East Indies communiqué quoted by Associated Press, reported this afternoon.

Admiral Helfrich, described as "the modern Phone Girl

The chateau on the hillside, the DZ on the flat, a ravine and everywhere is covered with snow. The challenge, dismantle a Radar unit and get it down to the beach to meet the Royal Navy inside two hours. Photo: Alain Millett

George Millar has kindly consented to the following extract from his book 'The Bruneval Raid' to be included.

ON THE Monday morning C Company went through their normal routine. At ten o'clock they checked and cleaned all weapons and packed the containers, which were to leave for Thruxton Aerodrome at two. Ross had contrived, without breaking security with the Glider Pilot Regiment, to get the men a particularly good midday meal, and after it they were urged to have a siesta until tea, at five o'clock. And at tea-time a message came through from Division. 'Owing to adverse weather conditions' there would have to be a twenty-four hour postponement.

Each morning they repacked the containers, and each evening they unpacked them. The weapons were cleaned, recleaned, and cleaned again. Tuesday, Wednesday, and Thursday were exact repeats of Monday; and Thursday had always been named as the very last possible day in February for the raid.

Friday morning was bright and frosty. The wind seemed to have dropped. The clouds had gone. Frost expected a message from Division Headquarters instructing him to send everyone on leave. But the message was that the other arms involved had agreed to see what weather one more night would bring.

Stand-by again. For the fifth day running they went through the now tedious routine, breakfast, tidying up, containers packed. They all felt listless except, it seemed to Frost, Sergeant-Major Strachan, who was in high good humour and said he was sure they were going to have some fun at last.

At tea-time General Browning, immaculate as usual, arrived to wish them all luck. The raid was on.

When he had seen them off to the aerodrome in their trucks Frost sat down to dine with the glider pilot officers. He felt it hard to say nothing of the speculation and fears that galloped through his mind. He looked round him at the placid faces. Would he ever see them again? Lucky devils! Going soon to bed in their warm hut.

The Company was dispersed in huts round the perimeter. John Ross, John Frost and Sergeant-Major Strachan and Nagel, now to be known as Newman, visited each little party in turn. Some were fitting their parachutes, some having tea. There was a lot of talk, and one group was singing. It was a glorious night, an utter change in the weather; the kind of thing that only happens in England.

Flight-Sergeant Cox found the night scene dramatic. 'We were put in blacked-out Nissen huts. Inside it was warm and the light was yellow. Parachutes were laid out in rows on the swept floor and we each picked one hoping that the dear girl who'd packed it had had her mind on the job. These were dark 'chutes, camouflaged in greens and blacks. Until then I'd only used white or yellow ones. They pressed bully sandwiches on us, real slabs, and mugs of tea or cocoa laced with rum. We checked each other's straps and wandered about wide-legged, like Michelin men. It seemed brighter outside than in the hut, and bitterly cold. We were formed up in our tens, or jumping sticks as we had done so often in training. One saw then what it had all been about. It was reassuring to know exactly where to go and who with. Piper Ewing playing, and that has an effect on Scotsmen. It brings them to the boil – and they're excitable enough already. I'm not sure that the pipes are healthy. The piper was coming on our jaunt, but leaving his pipes behind.'

Piper Ewing played their regimental marches as they moved round the tarmac to the twelve Whitley bombers. Frost was exhilarated by the pipes and impressed by the airmen. 'They were a different breed, at ease, and dressed for what they normally did. By comparison we seemed a lot of clowns. I had a waterbottle of strong tea laced with rum, and I handed it round the blokes in my stick while we waited to emplane.'

'I was jumper number six in aircraft number six,' Cox remembers. 'We put on our silk gloves and crawled into sleeping bags for warmth. The Whitley's ribbed aluminium floor was fiendishly uncomfortable. Ahead we could hear a kite revving prior to take-off and then it was away. Others followed until it was our turn. The whole machine throbbed and bumped and dragged itself off the ground as though it had great big heavy sloppy feet. Nobody slept in that dim-lit metal cigar. We had some singing. We sang *Lulu, Come Sit by my Side if You Love Me*, and *Annie Laurie*. Then, by popular request, I gave them two solos, *The Rose of Tralee*, and *Because*. Somehow the engines made it easy to sing. They came in thrums, noisier one instant then the next.'

Corporal Stewart and two others had played cards all the way over. Stewart was winning as usual. He pulled out his wallet to put in yet another bank note and said generously that if he copped it on the raid the bloke next to him must take the cash and make good use of it.

When the cover was taken from the hole in the floor a piercing blast entered. Those who cared to look down saw the sea, gently moving in the moonlight. Suddenly they were over snow-covered land, bouncing and weaving in anti-aircraft fire. Frost dangled his legs in the hole. His bladder felt ready to burst from all the tea at Thruxton. He was so uncomfortable that he could not wait to get down. His companions were in a similar plight. He swore that he'd never get caught like that on any subsequent operation. Why had they not been told to keep off the liquids? Or indeed why hadn't he thought of it?

'Action Stations . . . GO!' One after the other they shot out. As soon as Frost's parachute opened he saw below him all the Dropping Zone landmarks, so well known from hours spent with the model. They were dead on target. He landed very softly in snow a foot deep. No wind. No German reception committee. The aircraft were swimming away over

France and there was flak from the main Radar station, probably firing at the last of the Whitleys coming in.

Having got rid of the Thruxton tea, 'not good drill but a small initial gesture of defiance' (Frost), they gathered at the line of trees. As they did so Timothy's RODNEY party were coming down in a sizeable cloud of parachutes. With such visibility, Frost knew, there was little chance of surprise, and anyway, presumably HENRY would have tracked them across the cliffs. The one good thing was that, even if a lot of Germans now knew that he and his Company were there, they would have no idea where and how they were going to hit. Everything seemed to be going so well that John Ross's news was a shock.

Ross and his heavy section, the organisational rearguard of the beach assault party had landed safely with their gear. So had another (Charteris) section of ten men, but it had a special task, and it left immediately to do it. The task was to take and hold the German pillbox (REDOUBT) on the north side of, and above, the beach. Should the pillbox be manned they would need surprise, luck and dash to take it. Having taken it, they were expected to act as a pivot for the whole withdrawal and also for the assault, but quite rightly remained in it according to orders. *Euan Charteris was missing with his other two assault sections, twenty men in all.*

Not for the first or the last time, Frost inwardly cursed the inflexible plan that had been thrust on him. This was exactly what he had feared would happen. Two aircraft had failed to deliver their parachutists. Perhaps they had been shot down, perhaps they had dropped them somewhere else. So?

He asked John Ross to wait for a few minutes to see if Charteris and his men turned up, and then to get on down to the beach defences and to do his damnedest with the heavy section. The main problems, HENRY and LONE HOUSE, must be tackled first as planned, and as soon as he could he would get Peter Naoumoff down to help Ross at the beach. Meanwhile Naoumoff and also Timothy's lot were needed to hold off any attack on the raiders at HENRY, either from RECTANGLE or from Bruneval village.

Within ten minutes of landing No. 2 Party had formed up into its four components. Naoumoff led his people off in the RECTANGLE (Le Presbytère) direction; Frost, with Newman at his heels, led his towards the plainly visible LONE HOUSE and Peter Young and his assault section made for the *Würzburg*, followed at a slight distance by the engineers and Cox, wheeling the trolley.

To Frost's astonishment, the front door of the house stood wide open. The hall was dirty, empty, quite unfurnished. He could just see that Young's party were round HENRY. Young and Sergeant Mackenzie and three others would have hand grenades ready, the pins out. The plan was to fling the grenades as soon as the whistle went, then charge in with their Stens. Frost blew his whistle four times and darted inside. The ground floor was empty, but shooting came from above. They ran upstairs and found only one German there, firing down at the tremendous shindy going on round HENRY. They killed him, and searched the rest of the house. It was empty.

Meanwhile Young and his men had overrun the *Würzburg* position and those Germans who could took to their heels. One of them scuttled towards the cliff edge, the moon-dazzle on the sea silhouetting him. There had been too much shooting, Young felt, and no prisoner had yet been taken. The German was chased and he fell over the edge of the cliff but managed to cling on and find footing. As he climbed back he was caught and taken to the Radar bowl. He was unarmed.

Dennis Vernon had left his own men and Cox kneeling in the snow. He went forward to reconnoitre and after a few seconds they heard thim call, 'Come on, the REs'.

Cox saw that the barbed wire round the pit was low and not much of a barrier. He thought it had probably been kept low to avoid electrical interference with the set. The firing from the big house had now stopped, mercifully, but more firing was coming from another direction, RECTANGLE. Major Frost soon appeared at the Radar pit and Newman was questioning the badly shaken German prisoner. He confirmed that he belonged to the Luftwaffe Communications Regiment, and that there were about a hundred of his fellows quartered across the fields at le Presbytère (RECTANGLE). They were fully armed for defence of the main *Freya* position and also of the *Würzburg*. Yes, he said, in reply to Frost's question, yes they had mortars, but were not in the habit of firing them much, they being signallers. Naoumoff and his section were responding steadily to the fire from RECTRANGLE, which was mainly directed at them and at the house, rather than at HENRY. Frost also heard firing from Timothy's lot, farther inland. His own group and Young's took up closer defensive positions.

Cox tore aside the thick black rubber curtain that shielded the entry to the Radar set. 'Hey, Peter!' he called to Newman. 'This thing's still hot. Ask that Jerry if he was tracking our aircraft as we came in.' The prisoner agreed that this was so. The *Freya* in the main part of the station had picked up the British aircraft far offshore. This set had picked them up at thirty kilometres. They had expected to be bombed, and had been getting worked up as the hostile machines came in low and virtually straight at them. The signaller pointed out that the site was 'extremely exposed'; on learning that the hostile aircraft were making directly for them, they had switched off in good time, and had taken cover.

Vernon began to take flashlight pictures of the *Würzburg*, while Cox made notes and sketches, using his hooded torch. The flashlights at once drew German fire, and Frost ordered him to stop the photography.

'Like a searchlight on a rotatable platform mounted on a flat four wheeled truck,' wrote Cox. 'Truck has had its wheels raised and is well sandbagged up to platform level. Paraboloid is ten-foot diameter and hinged so that radio beam can be swung freely up or down or sideways. Small cabin to one side shelters set's display gear and operator's seat. At rear of paraboloid is a container three feet wide, two feet deep, five feet high. This appears to hold all the works with the exception of display. Design very clean, and straightforward ... We found the set switched off, but warm. The top of the compartment taken up by the transmitter and what looks like first stage of receiver. Large power pack with finned metal rectifiers occupies bottom. Between the TX and the power unit is the pulse gear and the receiver IF. Everything solid and in good order. Telefunken labels everywhere which one sapper was removing with hammer and cold chisel. Just enough light to work by, with moon reflected off snow.'

Finding that there was no quick way of removing the aerial element in the middle of the bowl, Vernon ordered one of his men to saw it off. He agreed with Cox that the important material was in the consol, rather than in the display. They removed the pulse unit and the IF amplifier in a civilised way, using good tools on a well-maintained machine. They then tried to get out the transmitter. Cox had an immensely long screwdriver, but it would not reach the fixing screws. He and Vernon conferred, then the two of them grasped the handles and body of the transmitter while a third man put his weight on a crowbar. It was in a light alloy frame. It came away with a tearing sound, bringing its frame with it.

'A stroke of luck,' Cox says. 'When the equipment was examined later it was found that the frame which we in that somewhat hasty moment regarded as no more than an encumbrance, something we had not the time to detach from the transmitter, contained the aerial switching unit that allowed both the TX and RX to use the one aerial, a vital part of the design of a Radar set.'

Crowbars were used to rip out the last of the wanted components, and the engineers frequently had to use their torches. Enemy fire from RECTANGLE was getting heavier and more accurate. One of Frost's party, Private McIntyre, was killed near the door of LONE HOUSE. At last the REs were loading the trolley, Frost was glad to see. He had confidence in Vernon, and he felt that now, if they could only get away with the swag they had won the day. At the same time the battle situation was one of confusion. They had certainly stirred something up! There was firing from nearly everywhere. Heavy firing from down by the beach, with the odd white flare (which must be German) going up. That firing was mainly the deep stutter of a machine-gun, and it was being answered by one Bren. The firing from RECTANGLE had increased and had spread. Obviously the people there had deployed, and soon they would probably advance on HENRY and LONE HOUSE. Then there was an extraordinary amount of firing that seemed to come from the village itself. Had some of Timothy's men gone berserk and fought their way into the centre of Bruneval? Lastly there was a lot of noise on Timothy's front, but a runner had just come in from there. John Timothy said reassuringly that everything was under control except his No. 38 wireless set. That was the main trouble. Frost, except for whistle signals and runners, was without communications, and under the plan laid down he did not have a full complement in his Company Headquarters. As for the 38 sets, they seemed to be quite useless, and would not keep on net at all. The trolley was loaded. he sent a runner to call in Peter Naoumoff. He was to fall back through them and lead the way down to the beach. 'Remember the password, BITING,' he warned the runner. Young Naoumoff had been a supernumerary officer on training. Frost had allowed him to come on the raid because he had not the heart to disappoint him. He seemed to keep very steady.

Captain Ross waited until all Frost's group had left the forming-up place. Then he led his section across ground remembered from the model, and down to the road and the entry to the beach. The plan drawn up in England had envisaged a three-point initial attack. The assault section that had already gone out was to occupy the important hinge pill-box. Ross assumed that they *had* occupied it, as he had heard no firing from there. Ross and his heavy section were to be in reserve in the centre, nearest to the road entry to the beach, while Euan Charteris and his two assault sections were to sweep in from the south-east. As Ross slid from the trees down the hill towards the entry a white flare rose from GUARDROOM. He and the men behind him were at once pinned by machine-gun fire. Lying on the snow, Ross made out that the fire was coming from the inland side of the Villa Stella Maris (GUARDROOM) where, slightly above the road, the Germans had made weapon pits with trench communications. Several rifles, probably six or seven, were firing as well as the machine-gun. Ross's section replied with rifles and their one Bren. The section consisted of himself and his batman, one reserve sergeant, two signallers with a No. 38 set and a No. 18 set for contact with the Navy, two sappers with mine-detectors and a Rebecca radio beacon, two Bren-gunners and one runner. The Germans had an excellent field of fire, and they were hidden by the villa from the British section in the pillbox to the north. It had not been foreseen that the Germans might dig themselves weapon pits on the landward side. The heavy section was pinned down. The sergeant, dragging himself flat on the snow, managed to get to the thick barbed wire across the road, and tried to cut a way through. The Bren-gunners and riflemen kept firing. Ross would have given a lot to have in his section a mortar, even a two-inch one.

Mortars were in Frost's mind too, as he thought of his men

42

concentrating near and on the beach. So far he had heard no bombs, only rifle and automatic fire from the enemy.

In the centre of the withdrawal across the plateau and down the hill was the trolley. The two-wheeled affair took some controlling, being heavy-laden. As Naoumoff and his section withdrew through the main party Frost warned him that he would probably have to contact Ross and fight his way to the beach. Naoumoff got down unobserved but when the trolley party and its guards came to the German casemate high up on the north side of gully the machine-gun below caught them in full view against the snow and gave them a long burst. Company Sergeant-Major Strachan fell with three wounds in his stomach. Just then they heard John Ross clearly.

'Don't come down,' he shouted. 'The beach is not taken yet.'

Frost got Strachan behind the concrete jut of the casemate, put field dressings on his ugly wounds, and gave him a morphia injection. A runner came from John Timothy's party to say that the Germans were advancing from RECTANGLE and had already occupied LONE HOUSE. Frost accordingly told the trolley party to hold on by the casemate until the machine-gun below had been silenced, and taking every man he could, including sappers, he hurried back to the top to counter-attack in conjunction with Timothy's group. Whatever was happening down below at the beach, it was vital to keep the Germans above at a good distance. 'Fortunately,' he says, 'the threat did not amount to much. They hesitated and withdrew.' Frost left Timothy to defend the shoulder of the hill while he hurried back to the casemate and to take control of the fight for the beach. But he found that Vernon, Cox, and two sappers were on the move down, skidding and sliding on the frozen path. Sergeant-Major Strachan, shouting incomprehensible orders, was being half-carried, half dragged after the Radar booty. There had been a lot of shooting down below, but now there seemed to be silence. Frost dashed on down, leaving the trolley above.

When Ross saw the trolley party appearing on the skyline, and full in the field of fire of the Germans by Stella Maris, and called out to warn them, he realised that the distraction might be turned to account. His men found a knife-rest in the perimeter wire and pulled it aside to make an opening. At that moment Naoumoff and his section were about to rush through the wire and assault the German position they heard shouts and firing from the south-east. Charteris! The Scots voices raised in anger and triumph at reaching their objective came clear on the frosty air. The attack from the south-east had turned the enemy's position. The German machine-gun was abandoned and the defenders slipped out of their trenches and off to the southward, to the obscurity of the rough ground at the edge of the sea.

Pickard and the aircraft that immediately followed his had been caught in the worst of the flak. They had mistaken their landmarks and had dropped their two sticks of parachutists well south of Bruneval, indeed almost halfway between Bruneval and St Jouin. The twenty men landed with their containers in the Val aux Chats, near the small hamlet of l'Enfer. Euan Charteris was an outstanding young officer, remarkably intelligent and of the greatest promise. 'I don't mind saying that it was a nasty moment,' Charteris said. For when he picked himself up from the snow he saw at once that their pilots had made a mistake. Where were they? Fortunately they were able to watch the subsequent Whitleys flying in, well to the northward. They soon distributed the contents of their containers and Charteris's two scouts reported the narrow road leading to Bruneval, which, Charteris realised, lay between them and their objective. Putting himself at the head of his men he led them at a jog trot up the side of the road. As they neared Bruneval they saw other soldiers, but in the half-light they proceeded for some time un-challenged, and when a German joined their line thinking they were his own people he was killed silently. Then the challenge came and they had to shoot their way round the village. This was the firing that Frost heard while HENRY was being dismembered. But if the firing was confusing to Frost it was still more so for the German garrison, who had little idea where the 'commandos' were or what their objective could possibly be. Now fighting in the half-light, now hurrying on round the village in its sharp valley, now separated, now together again, Charteris's section shed a man or two here and there. The main party's firing was ahead of them now, and up over the hill on their right. Charteris led them at the double over the road from the sea to Bruneval and turned right-handed for the German defences and the beach. They paused to get back some of their breath, then, mad with relief at being at least where Orders had said that they should be, they charged forward with a wild yell. Their attack came, by a fluke, in conjunction with the attack from the other side of the valley. The three groups, Charteris's, Ross's, and Naoumoff's were through to the beach. At the door of Stella Maris Sergeant Jimmy Sharp caught a German telephonist coming out, and explained to him that he would be making a trip, 'nach England'.

But would he? Ross's two signallers seemed quite unable to make contact with the Navy on their No. 18 set, though they were still trying. The signallers who had been in Charteris's party and who also carried a No. 18 were both missing. As no contact could be made with the No. 18, Ross told his other signaller to keep trying with the No. 38 set. Meanwhile the sappers had set up the little portable radio beacon, the Rebecca, and said it was working properly. It was a gadget so new and so secret that it contained its own built-in demoliton charge. Its companion set, known as a Eureka, was in one of the landing craft. Whether the gadget was working or not, the parachutists doubted. Meanwhile Ross's two sappers checked the beach with their mine detectors getting negative results. And Ross himself at his report centre totalled the losses.

The Wurzburg Radar equipment photographed before it was brought back to England for the scientists to examine. Photo: German sources.

Below, another search of the prisoners before landing with two of the escorting infantry men watching. Eric Freeman has a captured German rifle over his shoulder to prove he had met the enemy.
Photo: Airborne Forces Museum.

45

There were two confirmed dead, Privates McIntyre and Scott, six missing, and six wounded who had all been gathered on the pebbles. Among them was Corporal Stewart, who had fallen, hit in the head, during the assault on the beach. He had called to his nearest friend, 'I've had it, Jock. Take my wallet.' Lance-Corporal Freeman took it and examined Stewart's head. 'Och it's only a wee bit of gash,' he said.

'Then give us back that wallet.' Stewart managed to get to his feet.

After consultation with Frost, John Ross fired one green Very light from north end of the beach and then another from the south. Frost 'with a sinking heart' called his platoon commanders, and began to organise the defences of an indefensible position. There had been reports from Timothy that headlights were approaching from the east and south-east. Before long the Germans were bound to appear in strength.

Bruneval was, for the light naval units, an easier target than the dark rocky beaches of Loch Fyne or the swelling cliffs round Lulworth. The trouble, as the Navy was only too well aware, was that the deadline for the raid had been extended and the landing craft would now approach a dangerous beach on a falling tide. Another difficulty was the weather itself which had become, frankly, unsuitable. By midnight the barometer was dropping sharply and the breeze was already fresh from the south-west, and increasing. While they waited in a state of increasing tension the flotilla of small craft saw enemy ships a mile or so to seaward, between them and England, two German destroyers and two E- or R-Boats. The Germans steamed very fast from north to south and apparently saw nothing. Soon after they had gone the white flares fired by the defenders of Stella Maris were seen. By two thirty-five the landing craft had closed to within three hundred yards of the beach when 'a blue lamp signal was seen followed by two green Very lights'. Two LCAs were ordered to close the beach, but as they started inshore Ross's signaller made contact with his No. 38 set and asked, without authority but understandably enough, that all the boats should go in.

The news of Bruneval, the first successful armed landing in German-occupied Europe, was a tonic for the Allies and a blow to German pride and confidence. Lord Haw-Haw, the English traitor propagandist, referred scathingly to Frost and C Company as a handful of redskins. And, possibly for security reasons, the decorations awarded to the parachutists were sparse, even by British Army standards.

From the purely military point of view, Combined Operations under its new leader, Mountbatten, had tackled something dramatic and difficult, and had carried it through well. Churchill was impressed, and his appetite for raids, always voracious, was whetted.

Only one of the Bruneval parachutists took part in the next raid, the extremely gallant and effective one on St Nazaire. 'Private Newman' had volunteered his services once more as German interpreter. He was taken prisoner, and spent the rest of the war in German hands. But so good was his cover story that his real nationality remained a secret, and he survived the war to become a prosperous business man in England.

German reaction at Bruneval during the raid was described in the following report, which revealed that the British could scarcely have chosen a worse night to attack . . .

German Document TSD/FDS/X.378/51, Cabinet Office.

At 055/28.2.42 (Time in England 23.55 27.2.42) the German *Freya* station reported aircraft NNE, range 29 km.

The parachutists were sighted by the Army and the Luftwaffe (ground and communications troops) at 0115. The landing was made south east of the farm and was carried out in complete silence.

All Army and Luftwaffe posts in the area were at once alerted. Scouts sent from the *Freya* position (near Cap d'Antifer) and the Luftwaffe.

Communications Station (at Le Presbytère) returned with information that the enemy was on the move south of the Farm (Le Presbytère) in the direction of the Château. The parachutist commandos had split into several groups and were converging on the *Würzburg* position and on the Château.

In La Poterie the reserve platoon of the First Company 685 Infantry Regiment had just finished an exercise shortly after 0100 when the parachutists were sighted. The officer commanding at once made contact with the Bruneval Guard; the Sergeant there had already alerted his men. The platoon reserve in Bruneval was ordered to occupy Hill 102 to the south east of Bruneval. The officer commanding la Poterie platoon then led his men in a westerly direction towards the Château.

On reaching the Farm buildings north east of the Château the German troops came under fire from the commando machine-guns, and from the west end of the buildings they engaged the British, who were already in possession of the *Würzburg*: Luftwaffe station near the farm. Here one of the commandos fell. This German platoon encountered fire from the left flank, but the commandos were nevertheless prevented from proceeding with their attack on the *Freya* position. The remainder of the Luftwaffe Communications Station unit quartered in the farm buildings took part in this action.

In accordance with orders, the platoon from Bruneval village divided into two groups and advanced on Hill 102. Outside Bruneval they came under fire from the commandos who had landed north of L'Enfer.

Although this platoon was unable to prevent the commandos from infiltrating between Bruneval and Hill 102, it was because of this platoon's action that individual commandos did not reach the boats in time, and were later taken prisoner. One wounded commando was also captured. It was only because the British objective was not known that this Bruneval platoon did not take part in the action at the Château.

CAPTURED: Three who missed the return boat on a snowy morning, MacCallum, Willoughby and Thomas. Bottom: A day later after interrogation in a villa on Avenue Foch. Photos: Alain Millett via H. Meiser and W. Bartig.

The Bruneval Guard, one Sergeant and nine men, had meanwhile taken up prepared positions guarding the coast. These (main) defensive positions were so built that they were effective only against attacks through the ravine from seaward. The commandos, approaching from north and north-east were able to get close to these strongpoints under cover of the woods. Thus the German guard positions were attacked from the high ground by heavy fire from three or four commando machine-guns. After one German soldier had been killed and another wounded the Sergeant was obliged to take up new positions. It was not until after one to one-and-a-half hours fighting that the commandos were able to get through the strong-point and the ravine to the beach. With them the commandos took a wounded German soldier and also the soldier who had been on telephone watch at the post. Here another commando fell, and one was wounded. The latter was assisted to the boats, which had come close inshore on the exchange of signal flares.

The commandos embarked just as strong German reinforcements reached Bruneval.

The platoon from La Poterie fought their way to the Luftwaffe Communications Station *Würzburg* as the commandos withdrew. It was learned that the Luftwaffe personnel there had put up a stiff resistance and, only after some of them had exhausted their ammunition were the commandos able to break through to the *Würzburg*.

One of the crew had been killed by a British grenade as he tried to set off an explosive charge to destroy the *Würzburg*. The commandos then dismantled parts of the set and also took photographs. On conclusion of this task they obviously intended to attack the *Freya* station. The skilful intervention of the La Poterie platoon, however, prevented this.

The operation of the British commandos was well planned and was executed with great daring. During the operation the British displayed exemplary discipline when under fire. Although attacked by German soldiers they concentrated entirely on their primary task. For a full thirty minutes one group did not fire a shot, then suddenly at the sound of a whistle they went into action.

German losses: Army, two killed, one seriously wounded, two missing. Luftwaffe, three killed, one wounded, three missing. British losses: two killed, one wounded (reached the boats), four captured.

POST WAR NOTES

Two of C Company Ptes Embury and Cornell were still at large in France when this report was circulated.

The following letter from M Maurice de la Joie was published on February 3rd, 1946 in the newspaper *Havre Libre*: 'We took in two English parachutists who had failed to get aboard their fast motor boats. After my sister, Mme Delarue had sheltered them for several days, we had them with us again. On March 9, 1942 we were arrested with them when about to cross the Line of Demarcation at Bléré, Indre-et-Loire. Condemned to death by a German Military Tribunal at Angers, we were taken to Paris, where we were imprisoned, my wife in La Santé, myself in the Cherche-Midi. In January, 1943 we were deported to Breslau in Silesia. Then my wife was sent to Ravensbrück, and I to Buchenwald. We both survived the war, but as invalids.'

All six of C Company taken prisoner survived the war.

Shaw recovered from his bullet wounds and rejoined the Bn. CSM Strachan also recovered and became the RSM and both ended up, together with Halliwell, Major Timothy, and Lt Col Frost as POWs at Arnhem.

The Second Bn. had put the first Battle Honour on the Parachute Regiment's standard.

Dick Scott . . . . *enjoys his rum, hit by the weapon containers*

DURING THE flight to Bruneval in Whitley, C for Charlie, we were about 10 minutes from the dropping zone sitting scared in our boots, when a water bottle was handed round for each to have a swig, it was pure Jamaican, given by a gentleman well known to C Coy and still with us. I was No. 6 and in the descent I was clobbered with the container and on landing I found my fighting knife had gone and my trouser leg was ripped down the seam.

We took up positions and I was placed with the bren gun on the left of the section facing the German camp. We were about 150 yards out and quite near to the radar post. There was some gunfire and then a lull. On the east side of the camp we could hear the Germans going away from the camp and were in a laughing mood. Then on the cliff-side tracers were seen attacking the radar post. I spoke to Crutchley and said I was having a go, but I can't boast of the result. Later I noticed six men in single file coming between the camp and us. There was no order to challenge so I fired a couple of rounds indirectly and they grounded. I thought if they were Germans we would get something in our backs when we withdrew.

After the withdrawal from the radar post, I knew that CSM Strachan was wounded by his behaviour, Grant was also in great pain and I was forced to shout at him to get moving to the boat.

I was the last to get aboard and it sped off much too quickly before the ramp was closed and we were in water nearly to our knees. There was a hand pump and we used our helmets to help bale out. On reaching the MTB our next predicament was to get the wounded CSM on to it safely for the boats kept parting until they were properly tethered. CSM Strachan kept calling for a drink, Corporal Fleming and I were left to manhandle him into the boat. When we got to sea there was a flashing light from the shore, it could have been an SOS from the one whose duty it was to guide latecomers to the beach.

50

Back home in Tilshead, everyone was cock-a-hoop and I was nursing two shiners and slight concussion. Not a sign of sympathy, and Sgt Forsyth had the impudence to say I must have made a bad exit and hit the aperture. We went on home leave to recover, I went to my local in Richmond, Yorks for a quiet drink and I overheard a conversation connected with piloting paras over France. I had to say I was one. He was a local boy whose mother I knew and was with Pickard on F for Freddie, his name was Broadley. He was later killed on a mission over Germany.

Sheffield Star – July 1948

RSM DIED OF RAID WOUNDS

STOMACH WOUNDS received by a Regimental Sergeant-Major during a raid on Bruneval in 1942 led to his death, it was stated at a Sheffield inquest today.

The inquest was on Gerald Alexander Strachan, aged 42, of Studley Road, Darnall, Regimental-Sergeant-Major in The Black Watch, who died following an operation. The coroner, Mr AP Lockwood, recorded a verdict of 'Death by misadventure.'

Mrs Ivy Strachan said her husband had served over 20 years with the Army and had been on Airborne operations during the war.

While on leave last Saturday, she said, he complained of stomach pains and was admitted to hospital. He was wounded in the stomach during the Bruneval raid and had said he was wounded during the Arnhem raid two years later, when he was taken prisoner.

Dr RH Canter said that under an operation an obstruction was dealt with successfully, but later a further obstruction developed.

The cause of death, he said, was shock due to paralysis of the ileus. 'On the assumption that Mrs Strachan's evidence of her husband having been wounded during a war operation in 1942 is correct. I am satisified her husband died as a later sequel to the injuries,' said the Coroner.

Bob Dobson . . . . *and the story of a prisoners expensive watch*

SGT GREGOR McKenzie and his section cleared the chateau of the enemy for Flt Sgt Cox to dismantle the enemy radar equipment. One of the operators in his rush to escape, fell over the cliff edge. Sgt McKenzie went after him and pulled him back to make him a prisoner. The orders had been no prisoners required except those working radar equipment. The German was so grateful at being spared he gave his wristwatch to the Sgt as a thank you present. Sgt McKenzie took the watch home on leave with him, had it cleaned and a new glass fitted, on return to the unit he was told to report to Company office and told it had been reported stolen by the German and it must be returned. Sgt McKenzie was not amused, it had cost him 5/- to be repaired. He would have liked to have found that German!

Major JD Frost MC at an aerodrome with the King and Queen watching the Battalion perform parachute manoeuvres in April 1942. Photo: IWM.

CHAPTER THREE

Preparing for North Africa

EARLY IN March 1942, the now familiar 'Pegasus' and 'Airborne' flashes came into use and were closely followed by the first issue of maroon berets.

Training during the next few months consisted of exercises between companies, co-operation with the Home Guard and long marches, examples of the latter being eighty miles in three days by A Company and 113 miles in four days by the Mortar and Signal Platoons. Later on A Company did fifty-four miles in twenty-four hours!

A good number of dropping exercises were carried out, one in April 1942, witnessed by the Brigade Commander Brigadier RN Gale OBE, being the first large-scale battalion jump to be carried out. Experimental jumps with varying types of equipment were also undertaken from Wellington aircraft. The culmination of all this training was Exercise 'Dryshod,' the first large-scale invasion operation carried out by the British Army, though it was on land in Southern Scotland.

Changes in command occurred in April 1942, shortly after moving to Bulford. The Brigade Commander left and Lieut-Colonel Flavell replaced him. Major Gofton-Salmond became Commanding Officer with Major RG Pine-Coffin as his Second-in-Command.

In May 1942, an inspection of the Division by their Majesties the King and Queen was closely followed by an inspection by the General Officer Commanding 1st Airborne Division.

In June 1942, Regimental Quartermaster-Sergeant Howe, Company Sergeant Major Strachan and Orderly-Room Quartermaster Sergeant Ellum were awarded Certificates for Good Conduct in the King's Birthday Honours List.

In mid-July, the Battalion moved into bivouac where field firing, battle drill and mess-tin cooking were carried out. Intensive training continued throughout August culminating in a battalion field firing exercise at Exford, during which pillboxes were attacked under heavy covering fire provided by light machine-guns and mortars. Detachments of Royal Engineers together with flame-throwers took part in the final assault.

Towards the end of September 1942, the Battalion began to mobilise for what ultimately proved to be the North African invasion. Although at that time it was not known that the Battalion was going to North

Brigadier EWC Flavell
(Middlesex Regt)
first Bn Commander.

Lt Col JD Frost
(Cameronian)
four difficult ops.

Major Phillip Teichman
(Royal Fusilier)
KIA North Africa.

Major Keith Mountford
(Middlesex Regt)
POW Sicily.

Captain John Measures
(Royal Fusilier)
POW Depienne.

Lieut Dennis Rendell
(Middlesex Regt)
POW Depienne.

Lieut John Timothy
(Royal West Kent)
won three MCs.

Lieut Richard Spender
(Royal Irish Fusiliers)
KIA, North Africa.

Lieut Martin Willcock
(South Staffs)
wounded NA, repatriated.

Africa, something was in the wind owing to hurried mobilisation and the fact that at very short notice it was found necessary to carry out jumps from American Dakota aircraft. In early October nearly 300 men jumped from Dakotas and despite fatal casualties, Lt Street and two OR's, this method of jumping was preferred by all ranks. At this stage, valuable assistance was received from the 2nd Battalion 502 US Army Parachute Regiment stationed at Hungerford, the first parachute troops to arrive in this country some weeks before. Lieut Timothy was attached to them as liaison officer for the Brigade as a whole.

It is also of interest to recall that during September, when preparations for North Africa were under way, the Battalion was told to stand by to take part with the 1st Parachute Battalion in a raid to occupy the Island of Ushant, the object being to destroy or capture all occupying Germans and to gain as much information as possible. This operation was finally cancelled owing to the fact that the Royal Navy could not guarantee to evacuate troops taking part at the end of two days; this was due to the proximity of Ushant to Brest, the large German naval base.

On 29th October 1942, the Battalion entrained for Greenock. Morale was very high but a last minute blow was delivered when the Commanding Officer Lt Col Gofton Salmond was found to be unfit for foreign service on medical grounds, and had to disembark while the boat was still in port. Major JD Frost MC, who had previously become Second-in-Command, due to Major Pine-Coffin taking over command of the 3rd Battalion, assumed command of the Battalion. Major PR Teichman left A Company to become Second-in-Command.

At approximately 2130 hours on 1st November, 1942, the boat sailed and shortly afterwards sealed orders for operations in North Africa were handed to the Battalion.

John Timothy .... *reports for experimental jumping*

AT BULFORD in the early summer of 1942 I was told to take a section of my Platoon from A company and report to Ringway for some experimental jumping. The section included Sgt Dowey, Cpl Le Maitre and Bill Fishwick. On arrival I was told that the First Battalion were to take part in a raid but there were insufficient Whitley aircraft to lift the whole battalion and we were to evolve a drill to drop sticks of eight from Wellingtons. Only singles had been dropped up to this time.

A grounded Wellington was available and we started practising immediately. Next morning accompanied by a Lysander, since the jumping was experimental and was to be photographed, we took off for the first jump. It was without weapons and containers and I was to jump number eight, last man, to see what happened during the jump.

It was a very quick stick and I was caught around the ankle by the number seven's static line. Instinctively I grabbed it and when I felt the grip on my ankle ease, I let go. My 'chute opened and all was well but because of the momentary delay I was heading for the lake. The 'chute caught the top of a tree bordering the lake and the air from the canopy was spilt. The 'chute was dragged off the tree and I was left lying flat on my back on the ground, very relieved. I remember I tried to light a cigarette but could not get the flame from my lighter to meet my cigarette.

The lads who were not jumping arrived in a pick-up truck and off we went to the WVS van for tea.

Back at Ringway I had my damaged hand treated and was shown the photographs of the episode, these showed I had finished up at the tail caught by my ankle.

We were jumping again next day and for the next fortnight trying out various drills with weapons and containers. Then back to Bulford where after a few weeks I was given the Signal platoon from the Fourth Battalion and told to jump in sticks of ten from Wellingtons which we did and all went well. However when the raid did take place, I imagine it was the Dieppe raid, parachute troops were not used and this must have been a great disappointment for the First Battalion.

Gower Davies . . . . *enjoys his hardship amidship*

I WAS one of the surprised men who embarked on the troopship at Greenock in autumn 1942 for North Africa. In the Parachute Regiment and not flying out! The ship was so crowded that the only place I could find to sleep was in an air conditioning plant. During the second day out I was put on latrine door duty by the CSM, my platoon Sergeant ordered me to get on parade. In vain did I tell him of my previous order and next day found me on Company Orders and serving seven days in the cells. Did I worry? Meals in comfort, a bed to sleep in, none of the chaos below, even escorted walks around the deck watching the boys doing their PT. One of the best weeks I had spent in the Army.

Dave Brooks . . . . *first reinforcements for North Africa*

IN DECEMBER 1942, 200 rookie Para's left Hardwick bound for North Africa. Rookie Para's maybe, but trained soldiers nevertheless, drawn from a number of Infantry Regiments, among them East Surreys, Kings Royal Rifles, Devons, Dorsets, Norfolks, and my own Royal West Kents. We were under the command of Lt Colonel Gofton Salmond. By train to the Clyde, transferred by tender to SS Strathallan a P & O ex-passenger liner built in 1938, probably quite luxurious, but a different kettle of fish when carrying 5000 troops. Soon we slipped down the Clyde to take up station in what was a very large convoy. We were to take a wide sweep around Ireland in order to avoid U boats.

For some days an uneventful voyage, almost monotonous. Then we met very heavy seas, must have been Biscay, many of us became seasick. When you stood on deck you were able to see the ships nearest you doing all sorts of crazy things. It was something of a relief to enter the Mediterranean and quite a novelty to see towns full of lights on both Moroccan and Spanish shores. The weather was vastly different to that which we had left in Glasgow, we started to enjoy the voyage.

A few days later, at around 01.00 hours there was a terrific roaring crash, the poor Strathallan seemed to be shivering and shaking for what seemed like minutes. We realised we had been torpedoed, pitch darkness of course, but emergency lights were quickly taken from their glass cases. I don't remember any panic, in fact I am sure the transition from living deck to boat stations was very orderly by all units who were aboard. Nevertheless I was very happy to see the sky when we emerged on to our boat deck very high on the ship.

By the time we got to our boat station, all the lifeboats were away, only those on one side could be used, as by now Strathallan was listing badly, and in any case I don't think there were enough lifeboats for 5000 people. There was a certain amount of confusion on deck. This was quickly sorted out by the Captain, he was certainly Anglo Saxon. It was 'get those **!!** lifeboats away from my ship, get those people out of the water, who **!!** ordered them in anyway, and the rest of you shut your **!!** row, you are making enough noise to wake Davy Jones.'

My first realisation on our boat station was that we were completely alone, the rest of the convoy had gone. Next thought then was, what do I do if I have to go in the 'drink'? I didn't think much of those kapok Mae Wests, nor of the sea itself, though it looked calm enough. I espied wooden dining chairs in one adjacent saloon. I thought, one of those would do, then I saw a large life belt hanging on the rail, and thought that's better, so I commandeered it, and agreed to share it with the man next to me. There were others who saw the funny side of this, I wasn't allowed to forget the incident for months, me, I think they were just jealous, and would have liked the life belt themselves.

Nothing much happened during the rest of the darkness hours, the silence was eerie, broken only once in a while by the Captain talking.

When dawn came, we were joined by an ocean going tug, and a couple of Destroyers, they got lines aboard which broke very easily. An RAF flying boat passed low, one of the crew was trying to give us comfort by giving the V sign, someone should have told him that the V sign required the palm to be outwards, not inwards. All the lifeboats had disappeared, in the morning we heard that one of these with Army Nurses had been overturned by panic-stricken Lascars, causing loss of life.

Only five or six Lascars were still aboard in the morning, and I remember one was very good, he did his best to raise some food by taking small detachments from each boat station down to the galley to carry the food back. More Destroyers were arriving, and started to take people off, starting with lower boat stations. Around 2 pm it was the Para detachments turn, more or less the last off. We boarded a Destroyer which we later found was called 'Pathfinder'. For an hour or so 'Pathfinder' circled the stricken Strathallan, which had by now a terrific list, and the ropes from the empty davits looked grotesque. Then another Destroyer appeared to take on the policing duty, and off we went bound for Oran which was in American hands. We arrived just after darkness and were lined up on the quay. 'Pathfinder' slipped away into the night to three rousing cheers from our detachment. I remember thinking, 'Blow that for a life'.

Very soon we were put aboard SS Duchess of Bedford, a real old tub this one. Soon we were off on the final leg to Algiers, then to a tented camp at Maison Carree where we spent Christmas, no turkey or plum duff though. Then by train up through Algeria to join the 2nd Bn in Tunisia, although the journey was only 400 miles or so, it would take days, making frequent stops to gather wood to fire the boiler. Eventually we arrived at Beja, and in a school met members of the original Bn, you could tell by their looks what they were thinking, something like 'Gawd, look what they've sent us'. We told them of our ordeal and said 'aren't we entitled to "survivors" leave?' Do you know, they completely ignored us and talked only of a place called Depienne. However as you will know it doesn't take Paras long to get friendly, my reinforcement was accepted long before Corkwood, when once again we were savagely depleted. Many of us were to meet the Nurses of the Strathallen at the General Hospital on top of the hill at Algiers.

We hadn't seen the last of 'Pathfinder' either, when we got home from Italy and went on leave, quite a number of us lived 'south' when we got to Kings Cross, we made a beeline for the nearest pub (no buffet cars on those wartime trains). In this pub were a group of sailors, whose hatband just said 'HMS Destroyer', we got into conversation, and you've guessed it, they were sailors from 'Pathfinder' sent home like us for the Second Front. So we had a couple more 'jars' than was intended. Did 'Pathfinder' survive the war? If so, I wonder where that crew is now and where are the nurses? Wouldn't it be nice to find out? I don't suppose they got survivors leave either. Did Strathallan finally sink? One would think she must, the fire that was raging!

CHAPTER FOUR

Depienne – haphazard adventure

TWO WEEKS after arriving at Algiers in November 1942 the Battalion were ready and waiting on the airfield at Maison Blanche for a snap operation wherever the First Army Commander, General Anderson considered necessary.

The operation at Depienne suffered from a lack of Intelligence information and from inadequate arrangements for a link-up with our ground forces. The men were too lightly armed and comparatively immobile.

The Battalion carried out its orders to the letter and its presence in the area must have had a considerable effect on German operations elsewhere but the cost to the Battalion in loss of men was very high.

The following personal report on the Depienne/Oudna operation is reproduced with the permission of **Lieut Colonel JD Frost, MC** Commanding Officer 2nd Bn The Parachute Regiment.

29 November 1942

EMPLANING. The Bn emplaned at Maison Blanche aerodrome in 44 C47 aircraft. There was considerable confusion over the emplaning and loading of the containers owing to the markings of the aircraft, the order in which the aircraft formed up being different from that which it was expected they would form up and heavy rain turning the aerodrome into thick mud.

THE MISSION. The Bn was briefed as follows:– It was to drop near Pont Du Fahs, destroy enemy aircraft, stores and petrol there; then proceed to Depienne where another landing ground was to be attacked; then on to Oudna and finally strike North West to St Cyprien where contact was to be made with armoured elements of 1st Army.

On the morning of 29/11/42 information was received that the enemy was not using Pont Du Fahs therefore the mission was altered to a drop at Depienne, an attack on the landing ground at Oudna and a link up with the 1st Army at St Cyprien.

THE FLIGHT. The flight was uneventful, the leading aircraft took off at 1130hrs but owing to various delays the whole force was not airborne until gone 1230 hrs. Long range Hurricanes, Lightnings and Spitfires from Le Kef were escort. The aircraft flew high to clear the mountains

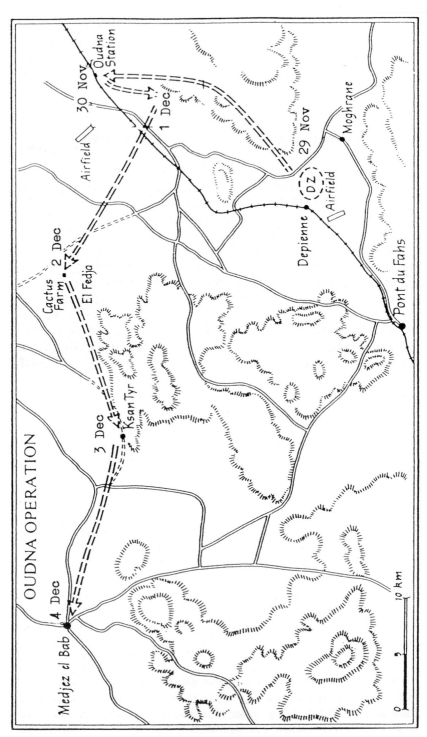

OUDNA OPERATION

Oudna Station

30 Nov

1 Dec

29 Nov

Moghrane

Airfield

DZ
Airfield

Depienne

Cactus
Farm · 2 Dec

El Fedja

Pont du Fahs

3 Dec

Ksan Tyr

OUDNA OPERATION

Medjez el Bab

4 Dec

10 km

5

0

Two days before the operation at Oudna the aerodrome at Maison Blanche was bombed. The Battalions weapon containers were destroyed. Photo: IWM.

and the temperature dropped to zero. No great discomfort was felt however though some men in the rear aircraft were sick. Approximately 30 miles from Depienne the aircraft came down to 600 feet and approached the dropping zone at this level.

THE DROP. First aircraft dropped its section at 1450 hrs, the pilot of the leading aircraft chose the dropping zone which was mostly plough. A large water course crossed the middle which considerably delayed some sections in reaching their containers. A number of sticks were dropped some distance from the main body. A total area over which the men and containers were dropped being 1½ miles by ½ mile. A number of containers failed to come off and some container chutes failed to open. There were some casualties on landing including one dead.

ACTION ON LANDING. Bn HQ was immediately established in some ruins North of Depienne, 'A' Coy was ordered to hold the area North of the dropping zone to block the road leading North and to prevent any local inhabitants from leaving and to commandeer all transport. 'B' Coy were ordered to occupy Depienne to commandeer all transport. 'C' Coy were ordered to take up positions South of the dropping zone, to block the road running East and salvage chutes and containers from the dropping zone. Major Teichman the Bn second i/c was sent into the village to arrange for storage of chutes with the Gendarmes also to arrange for transport, there was not motor transport available but a number of mule carts were impressed.

The injured were driven to Depienne by a local French official and were placed in the school house there, the local French were very friendly and helpful, I was informed that the Germans had been in occupation until three days before but had withdrawn to the North, that there were many Italian civilians in the neighbourhood and that there were German detachments in the area Djebel Oust.

At approximately 1600 hrs three armoured cars from Yeomanry appeared on the road running North from Depienne. The commander informed me that he was patrolling North as far as Cheylus where a German road block was suspected. He returned at 1700 hrs with information that there was a road block East of Djebel Oust and that he could not go as far as Cheylus, he said he would report us and would arrange to evacuate the injured from Depienne as soon as possible.

Lieut Charteris was sent forward with a small patrol to recce routes forward. Orders were given at 2200 hrs. The Bn was to be formed up by the road by midnight in the following order:– C Coy, Adv Bn HQ, B Coy, rear Bn HQ, mortars, signals, A Coy. Lieut Buchanan was to remain at Depienne to complete arrangements for salvage, evacuate the injured and collect a section of his platoon which was thought to have dropped some distance to the South. He was then to move North by the hills to contact the Bn South of Oudna.

30 November 1942

The Bn moved off as ordered at 0015 hrs. A certain amount of mortar equipment and ammunition was loaded on mule carts also wireless sets and RE stores. In spite of this, considerable fatigue was felt by the RE and Mortar personnel and incidentally the mules. Our route was the road for one mile, then by tracks across the hills into the Djebel St Dou Jadjessa. The track was fairly well defined but very steep and rough in parts so that progress was slow. No local inhabitants were encountered but the barking of dogs showed the presence of native dwellings not far from our route. After covering approximately 12 miles the Bn was halted, pickets were put out and at 0430 hrs the men were allowed to sleep. It was bitterly cold so that very little real rest could be had, the Bn 'stood to' at 0600 hrs. At approximately 0700 hrs 2 German aircarft flew over but we were not observed.

At 0715 hrs orders were given:– 'B' Coy were to act as advanced guard to the Bn, they were to move in bounds and halt in area Prise de L'Eau 'A' Coy were to picket the hills between the axis of advance and the main Oudna-Depienne road, Bn HQ and 'C' Coy were to follow 'B' Coy.

Communications were maintained by WS 18s and the move was carried out without incident. Again it was apparent that the men were far too heavily loaded, and the Mortar Platoon was unable to keep up with Bn HQ.

By 1100 hrs the Bn was established in position at Prise de L'Eau, 'A' Coy forward on the left, 'B' Coy disposed centrally round the well, Bn HQ immediately East of the road and 'C' Coy on the left with positions facing the rear.

There were a number of Arabs in the area but it was not possible to stop all movement of them, all mules, donkeys and horses were commandeered. Local Arabs informed us that the landing ground at Oudna was not being used by the Axis and that all the enemy troops were withdrawing to Tunis. The landing ground could be plainly seen from our positions and one crashed aircraft was observed on the centre, otherwise there was no activity of any kind apart from the sound of bombing or artillery fire well to the North. The men were given permission to brew tea, fill water bottles and wash. By this time it was fairly hot, 'A' Coy reported an enemy patrol consisting of armoured cars and lorries moving South along the road Oudna-Depienne.

At 1230 hrs the following orders were given:– 'A' Coy were to move forward by the most direct route towards Oudna with the object of making a complete recce of and with the object of occupying the landing ground. 'B' Coy were to move around to the right of Henchir Oudna, a dominating feature. 'C' Coy were to move along either side of the main ridge of the Djebel St Bou Hadjeba with Bn HQ and Mortar Platoon. At 1315 hrs 'A' Coy moved off and by 1330 hrs the whole Bn was on the move.

At 1430 hrs the sound of mortar and machine gun fire was heard to the North and a message was received from 'A' Coy that they were being fired upon from a low ridge near St Bon Sakouma; they had suffered a few casualties and requested assistance on their left. I ordered 'C' Coy forward on the left and 'B' Coy to close in behind as reserve and pushed on myself with a skeleton HQ, I also sent a message to the Mortar Platoon to follow as fast as they possibly could. By the time I was in a position to read the battle, 'A' Coy had moved forward again, the Coy was very skilfully handled by Major Ashford and by 1530 hrs the enemy had withdrawn to the North of the landing ground and 'A' Coy were in position on the ridge at St Bon Sakouma, while a platoon under Lieut Rendell had occupied Oudna railway station. By 1600 hrs 'C' Coy were well on their way forward and at 1615 hrs had occupied the farm Tete Amont De Siphon.

It was now possible to confirm beyond all doubt that the enemy were not using the landing ground, there were four native tents on the open ground South of the railway, which it was thought might contain stores, they were found however to be hayricks. At 1630 hrs 5 German heavy tanks appeared on the West of the landing ground and began to shell and

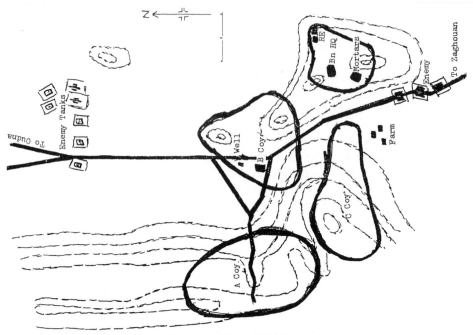

Sketch map No 1: PRISE BE L'EAU

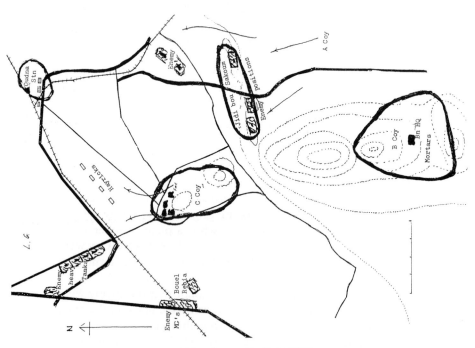

Sketch map No 2: OUDNA

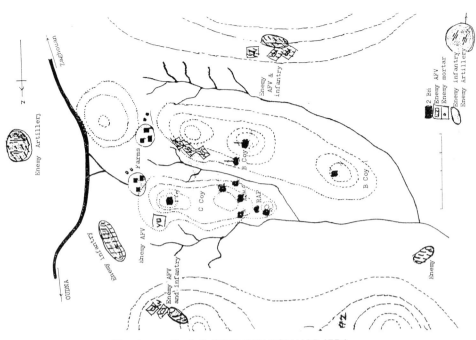

Sketch map No 3: DJEBEL SIDI BOU HADJEBA

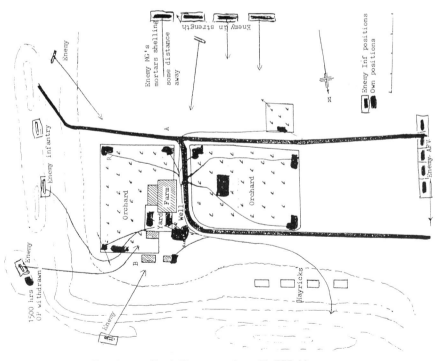

Sketch map No 4: The retreat from EL FEDJA

65

machine gun 'C' Coys position. Lieut Morrison was killed, Gammon bombs were thrown at one tank but it was not possible to estimate damage. The tanks made no attempt to approach our position, but were able to dominate the situation.

At 1630 hrs Messerschmitt fighters (ME 109s) came over the area, they made several low flights over our forward positions and then began several low-flying machine gun attacks, although no casualties were caused they paralysed movement. Owing to the vital importance of conserving ammunition I had given orders that the enemy aircraft were not to be fired at, our camouflage smocks and nets made it almost impossible to observe us and most of their attacks were made at unoccupied ground.

At 1700 hrs a flight of 6 Stukas passed overhead but dropped no bombs. Now as the whole object of the mission had been to destroy aircraft etc on Oudna and there were no aircraft to destroy, I made plans for moving westward to link up with 1st Army. I had been informed that an armoured thrust was to be made on Tunis but from our positions no sign of any battle or large scale movement could be seen and I decided to withdraw during darkness to our positions at Prise de L'Eau. Our positions near Oudna were very insecure, the enemy had had time to make a thorough recce of our probable dispositions and by this time I knew the enemy had considerable armoured forces in the area.

'C' Coy were withdrawn to the hills behind 'B' Coy at dusk and a platoon from 'B' Coy was sent forward to conform with the area held by 'A' Coy. At about 1900 hrs elements of 'C' Coy withdrawing became engaged with the enemy. Two of the hayricks had been set alight by fire from the tanks and there were sounds which indicated that the enemy were blowing up a dump of ammunition in the area. I considered sending 'B' Coy forward to obtain more exact information and destroy any enemy in the area but by now it became imperative to re-organise and rest 'A' and 'C' Coys. At 2100 hrs I ordered a withdrawal to the same positions as we held in the morning astride the road Prise de L'Eau. By 2200 hrs the withdrawal was completed. Again the night was bitterly cold and it was not possible to get much sleep.

1 December 1942

During the morning I received a wireless message informing me that the armoured thrust on Tunis had been postponed, I appreciated that this made my position untenable and in fact precarious, I knew the enemy had considerable armoured forces on the plains, that he had a considerable number of lorried infantry, that all the roads in the area were frequently patrolled by armoured cars, that Zaghoun in my rear was occupied, that I was only 15 miles from Tunis and 30-40 miles from the nearest points which I knew to be held by our own troops, i.e. Medjez El Bab and Tebourba.

For the moment my own position was fairly secure, we were in positions for all round defence, we had water and I was confident that we could hold out against anything but a full scale attack from a force of all arms. I decided therefore, to remain where I was until noon, then to move into the hills and secure positions from which I could move across the plains at night. An ambush was arranged in the bottle-neck South of Prise de L'Eau and all ranks were ordered not to fire at any enemy vehicles coming up the road until this bottle-neck was reached.

At approximately 1000 hrs a force consisting of 2 tanks, 2 armoured cars and 2 lorries drawing guns was seen approaching from the North. They halted about 1200 yards from our positions and one armoured car came forward alone, unfortunately this car surprised a small party filling water bottles at the well, an Italian Officer leaning out of the turret was shot and Gammon bomb was thrown but missed and the car was able to escape and rejoin his force, this then deployed and began shelling our positions from 1200 yards. The mortars were brought into action and the enemy withdrew leaving a number of bodies behind (believed 6). They halted after moving approximately a mile and appeared to be reorganising. It is thought that they suffered a number of casualties as a result of our mortar fire, several bombs were seen to fall among them.

At approximately 1100 hrs a force consisting of 2 armoured cars and one tank appeared on the road from the South, the leading AFV displayed 2 Yellow triangles which deceived the NCO in charge of the anti-tank rifle crew covering the road. The NCO went forward waving his own Yellow triangle and was taken prisoner, he was made to walk in front of the AFV which went up to the remainder of the crew and captured them. The NCO was then sent to Bn HQ with a demand from the Germans to surrender as the position was surrounded, a party was sent around the hill to the rear to cut them off but before they could be reached the enemy opened fire and made off. During the time the enemy were halted they were in a position, a deep depression, which could not be reached by any of our anti-tank weapons, except that which was captured, the enemy then began desultory shelling of our positions from long range.

At 1200 hrs the Bn started moving to new positions in the hills. 'B' Coy picketing to the right and 'C' Coy to the left with 'A' Coy as rearguard. All wounded were sent to a farm near Prise de L'eau under Lieut Mac-Givan RAMC. By 1430 hrs the Bn was in new positions in the hills called Djebel St Bon Hadjeba (*See sketch Map No3*): There was a spring in the Bn area and good observation could be had of the plain. Considerable enemy activity was noted, columns of AFVs and light artillery were moving North to South.

At 1500 hrs enemy lorried infantry were seen moving up to attack in half tracked vehicles, tanks were also seen and our positions were shelled and mortared. 'B' Coy were ordered to try to push forward onto the hill overlooking the houses but were unable to do so, at the same time enemy were seen approaching on all sides, no further manoeuvre was attempted and it became a matter of holding on until dark. The enemy put their maximum effort against 'C' Coy who beat off all infantry attacks, but they suffered heavy casualties from mortars which were behind the farm houses. The tank at Y was knocked out by Gammon bombs and anti-tank rifle fire but those at W could not be silenced. A section of 'B' Coy knocked out one at X and immobilised the other two, but could not get near enough to destroy them. At 1700 hrs Messerschmitt fighters appeared and flew low over our positions, later they were seen diving and opening fire on enemy locations, not once did they fire at any of our positions. Towards dusk the attack tailed off, the shelling ceased and the enemy appeared to withdraw.

I decided to split up into Coy groups and RV in the morning at Massicault. In my original instructions I was told to make for St Cyprien in order to link up with the armoured thrust, this I knew had been postponed and probably had not taken place. On the way to Massicault we would pass the Djebel El Mengoub which offered distinct possibilities as a place to lie up in should Massicault be in enemy hands. Lieut Playford was ordered to remain with his platoon to collect the wounded and take them to the farm at Prise de L'Eau where they could be attended to, he was then to move South toward Depienne and attempt to meet the recce patrol operating in that area. The order for withdrawal was given by myself on a hunting horn. I estimate the dead and wounded at this stage to be 150 killed and wounded from the time the Bn dropped.

The withdrawal by 'B' Coy proceeded and I then followed with Bn HQ, we allowed 'B' Coy to get well ahead. The route to the plains was very steep and difficult in the dark, I led the Bn HQ group with Lieut Charteris, we checked as soon as we reached the foothills and found all HQ present, we marched on a bearing of 312 degrees. The going was in the main difficult, large fields of plough had to be crossed and all ranks were feeling exhausted. We had had no real rest for 48 hours and had been moving over mountainous country all that time, also very heavy loads had to be carried. The rough ground was responsbile for a number of cases of sore feet and as there had been no time to attend to these, in quite a few cases septicaemia had set in. There were two deep river beds which had to be crossed and the river Miliane. Water bottles were filled from the river, the water was brackish and only just drinkable.

2 December 1942

A halt was called at 0100 hrs and we slept until 0230 hrs, at this halt it was noticed that Major Teichman the second i.c. and Capt Short, the Adjt, were missing. The March continued, at 0300 hrs rain fell, no local inhabitants were encountered, on one occasion a shot was fired from some distance away. By 0600 hrs we were North East of, and about a mile from the Djebel El Mengoub and I decided to halt until daylight, then to look for water, rest and information. At 0730 hrs Lieut Charteris went with a small party to recce a farm approximately half mile to the North, he returned at 0800 hrs and reported that the farm was inhabited by friendly Arabs, that plenty of shelter and water was available. He had obtained information that Massicault was occupied by the enemy but that Furna was occupied by Allied forces, Bn HQ then moved to the farm. A picket was placed on the hill behind, overlooking the farm and the surrounding country, the men cooked breakfast and washed.

At 0930 hrs an Arab brought information that another party of British were in a farm half mile to the East, contact was made and at approximately 1000 hrs Major Ashford arrived, he reported that his Coy had arrived safely in the area, that the owners of the farm in which his Coy were billeted were French who had warned him that the area was frequently patrolled by German armoured cars and that both farms were visited by enemy patrols. I then decided to concentrate at the Bn HQ farm (which will be called El Fedja), 'A' Coy were sent for and I made plans for defence, I decided that the enemy would not be able to launch a strong attack until fairly late in the day, and that provided we could hold out until dark we would then be able to move about the country again.

At about 1130 hrs I saw a German motorcyle combination on a ridge about one and a half miles away which appeared to be making a reconnaissance of El Fedja. 'Stand to' positions were ordered. Lieut Charteris and two men were sent to Furna to contact Allied forces alleged to be there, he was to return as soon as possible and not later than dark. At 1200 hrs 'A' Coy arrived and were placed in position (*See Sketch Map No 4*), at 1330 hrs a column of armoured cars was seen moving slowly to the South about 2 miles away. At 1400 hrs enemy infantry were observed setting up machine guns and mortars on and behind a ridge to the North. By this time there was very little ammunition left and orders were given that no enemy would be engaged at more than 50yds, otherwise there was to be no movement or noise in the farm area, this silence on our part seemed to mystify the enemy.

At approximately 1500 hrs they opened fire with machine guns and mortars, the mortar fire was concentrated on the orchard near the farm but only one casualty was caused, the farm buildings were not hit. Towards dusk the machine gun fire became more intense, most of it was very high and it appeared that some machine guns were firing at each other, so much so that at one time we thought Allied units were on the hills to the South and some of the more imaginative men fancied they heard words being shouted in English. Very careful observation was kept on the road running East past the hayricks as I intended to move out by this route in the dark. An enemy machine gun was located in this area at 1600 hrs but it moved after firing a number of bursts at the farm. Toward dusk the enemy became very bold and a party with two Officers approached within 5 yards of the cactus hedge surrounding the orchard at 'A', they were killed with grenades and Sten fire. I gave orders that when I blew my hunting horn everybody was to leave his position, run past Bn HQ and out to the South East passing near the hayricks and so out into Djebel El Mengoub where they would rally. We had not sufficient ammunition left to fight another battle and I estimated that the enemy were approximately 4 to 1 stronger in numbers. Lieut Charteris had not returned so I presumed that we were still a long way from other British Forces.

At about 1800 hrs the enemy attacked, their main effort coming in at B. This was beaten back and a number of Germans killed or wounded, similarly a party of enemy approached near A and the whole party were killed or wounded with grenades and Sten fire. At 1615 hrs the signal for withdrawal was given and the Bn moved out according to plan. The enemy made no further attack, it was however difficult to collect everyone in the dark, all had been told to make for Medjez El Bab. Bn HQ and 'A' Coy mustered approximately 100 when a halt was called in the hills; the remainder had been seen moving further to the South with Capt Vernon and the REs. At first I intended to strike North West to join the main Tunis – Medjez Rd, but when we reached a secondary road at Bou Khail I decided to move toward Medjez along it; we stopped to fill water bottles at a well along the route, at midnight a halt was called for one hour.

3 December 1942

The March continued. At approximately 0300 hrs some inhabitants of a farm were roused for information and they confirmed my suspicion that enemy armoured units were in the area. Almost immediately after leaving this position we joined forces with Capt Vernon's party who had arrived on the same road by a different route. By this time 0400 hrs all ranks were feeling extreme fatigue and we decided to lay up until dawn at the next farm. This happened to be at a road and track junction, the inhabitants were French, very friendly and helpful. By 0500 hrs the men were all under cover, sentries were posted and rest was obtained, at 0600 hrs 'Stand To' was ordered and some tea was made.

The French warned me that an Arab known to be pro-German had left to inform the enemy of our whereabouts. I decided to move back toward the high ground near Ksar Tyr which was thought to be held by British units. During the move an Arab who appeared to be taking undue interest in our movements was fired at. When the high ground near Ksar Tyr was reached Medjez and the main road could be seen and I decided to move across open ground in open formation. There were sounds of a battle coming from the direction of Tebourba. There were a number of orchards between us and Sidi Medien where I decided to join the main road, an Arab informed us that Ksar Tyr and Sidi Medien contained small numbers of enemy but that Medjez El Bab was strongly held by the Allies. We halted in the last orchard St Medien to eat a meal, at 1200 hrs an unidentified armoured car was observed leaving St Medien and later another, I learned that the enemy had just vacated St Medien (i.e. 2 armoured cars).

Shortly after reaching the main road an American armoured patrol was observed approaching across country from the North, they joined us on the road and gave me, the walking wounded and a small party a lift into Medjez El Bab. We arrived at about 1600 hrs, the wounded were taken to a dressing station and billets and rations were arranged for the Bn. At 1700 hrs I met the CRE 78 Div who took me to Div HQ at Oued Zaaga, there I reported to General Eveleigh, Capt Moore who was Liaison Officer to 1st Army was there and arrangements were made for an armoured patrol to search the country over which we had been moving on the following morning, the patrol was to leave Medjez at 0700 hrs; I then returned to Medjez.

4 December 1942

At 0500 hrs an Officer arrived at my HQ and informed me that a heavy bombing attack was expected at first light, followed by German Parachute Troops. The Bn was roused and positions were taken up outside and to the West of the Town. The attack did not materialise. At 0800 hrs the Bn was lifted in TCVs to Sloughia, the day was spent in resting and washing. At 1400 hrs Major Ross and a small party arrived. A defence plan was co-ordinated with the French at Sloughia and the Bn was moved into Arab houses for the night, the French were very helpful and friendly, the night passed without incident.

5 December 1942.

At 0800 hrs the CRA 78 Div arrived with the following instructions:– It was proposed to use the landing ground at Medjez for fighter aircraft, this landing ground being in front of the FDLs was to be held as strongly as possible against all forms of enemy attack, I was to organise and co-ordinate a plan for defence. 150 men of the Hampshire Regiment came under command at 2100 hrs, 80 men of a Field Battery came under command at 2300 hrs. The Bn was divided into two sections, 'A' under Major Ashford called Ashforce, the remainder under Major Ross called Rossforce, 1 Officer and 75 men of the Hampshires being attached to each, the men from the Field Battery being kept as force reserve.

At 1400 hrs CSM Sharp and 19 men arrived having been separated from the battalion since the action at Oudna. Defence force HQ was set up in the Gendarmerie, Capt Moore was appointed Adjt.

6 December 1942.

The night passed uneventfully, at 0830 hrs a staff officer arrived from Div HQ with fresh instructions, the RAF would now use the landing ground and we were to move to an area near Medjez and be prepared to:–
1. Assist in the defence of Medjez.
2. Be prepared to counter-attack in the event of enemy penetration at Sloughia or the bridge at Dar El Gassi.
3. Be prepared to thicken up any weakness in the French defences.

I decided to move to the area near Medjez railway station as the most likely threat would come from Tebourba, I alloted areas to Rossforce and the Hampshire Regiment who were by now organised under their own officers. I organised Ashforce into a mobile column standing by at ten minutes notice, I managed to borrow three lorries from an AA Battery as transport and I moved a section consisting of 4 x 37mm American anti-tank guns into the same area. The American FA Bn were contacted and agreed to provide some light tanks should the column be required to operate.

At 1400 hrs I made a recce with Major Ashford, Capt Mountfort and the American Anti-tank gun Comm towards Tebourba, we went as far as 11 Inf Bde HQ, I met the Brigadier and told him of our role and plans. A tank battle was taking place on the other side of the river about 2 miles away, we watched this for some time, then as it seemed to be progressing satisfactorily, returned to the railway station.

At 1700 hrs I visited Div HQ and told them what I was doing, I was informed that I was now under the French Commander at Medjez, I returned to Medjez and visited French HQ, while there I learned that the Corps Commander had ordered mines to be laid at all approaches to the town, Capt Vernon RE was in charge. The mines were laid during the night by parties from the Bn, the Hampshire Regiment and local Artillery formations.

7 December 1942

The day passed without incident, rained heavily.

8 December 1942

I visited Div HQ in order to obtain some news of future moves and to try to speed up various administrative matters, in particular the supply of blankets or warmer clothing, I was informed that we would probably be moved back to Souk El Arba during the night, I returned but was later informed that the move was cancelled.

11 December 1942

Attended a conference at French HQ. The Commander of 1st Guards Brigade was present and arranged to take over my positions during the day. In early afternoon the enemy attacked Medjez with tanks and infantry, a few shells and mortar bombs fell near our positions but no damage was done, later in the afternoon the enemy appeared to withdraw. By 1700 hrs the Coldstream Guards had taken over positions and the Bn was concentrated in the sheds near the station.

At 1930 hrs 7 TCVs arrived to lift the Bn and at 2010 hrs the Bn was on the move to Souk El Khemis. The move was without incident and we arrived in the billeting area at approximately 0700 hrs 12/12/42.

End of Report

Alan Johnstone .... *becomes a cavalryman*

LIEUT BRAYLEY joined 'A' Coy in Bulford and was promptly called 'Slapsie' by the cockneys who were in a majority in the company. My adventure with him took place during the retreat from Oudna, and started in the small hours of 3rd December 1942 when the remnant of the Battalion under Col Frost had halted at a friendly French farm. I was settling my section in a stable when an Arab came in and removed some harness hanging on the wall. As I moved to alert the sentry posted in the yard, the stocky figure of Lieut Brayley came down the steps from the house munching a large sandwich, and catching sight of me, stopped chewing and called 'can you ride Sgt Johnstone?' My equestrian experience was limited to sixpenny rides at the seaside, I murmured something about being able, if had to, and the ebullient Lieutenant replied with his usual gusto, 'right – get your sten – we're going to look for the rest of this Army – must get some armoured support for these boys!' I was taking things as they came now, and nipping in for my helmet and sten was soon back and hoisting myself without too much difficulty into the saddle of the upstanding white arab steed which Brayley indicated to me. He, though heavier than I, had mounted a smaller more spirited brown pony which he urged off down the road at a canter. When I attempted to follow at a similar pace by kicking my mount in the flanks with my heels in the approved fashion, I succeeded in producing only a full and very bouncy trot, which I found so disturbing that I soon slowed down to a stately walk, much to the irritation of the gallant Lieutenant, though I think I was proved right when at a later stage he had to dismount and lead his exhausted pony down and up the steep sides of a wadi.

However, it was still dark when my equestrian inadequacy became apparent and the Lieutenant knocked up an aged Arab, and waving his .45 automatic and shouting, forced him to harness a mule into a springless two wheeled cart. We climbed into the rear, hanging on to the reins of the horses over the tail-board and at a funeral pace creaking and bumping we were driven into the dawn. It was quite light when the ancient stopped in a village to chat to locals. Someone rushed up shouting news of soldiers, probably Germans and we were taken to a corner round which we peeped to see a line of figures straggling the hillside above the village. It was undoubtedly the Battalion, but we kept our counsel, remounted our horses, and turning our backs on the 'Germans' made off across country in the divergent direction.

I am always reminded of Don Quixote and Sancho Panza when I think of our ride. There was a medieval look about us, with helmets slung at saddle bow, the jerkin look of our belted smocks and my sten slung over my back like a cross-bow. We were quite vague as to where we would find 1st Army, and we therefore stopped and questioned anyone we encountered about the whereabouts of the Allemands and the Anglais, I in halting French and Brayley in English with the odd French word in loud fierce tones emphasised by menacing waves of his ugly .45 automatic. All were comically anxious to please, one camp of nomads rushing out with peace offerings of grubby pancakes, but information was vague and scanty. About mid-day however we had a very useful and pleasant encounter with a French farmer and his pretty daughter. They said that they thought our troops were in Goubellat recently and that German cars patrolled the dirt track which ran close by the farm. The girl brought us wine, bread and hard-boiled eggs which we consumed in the saddle. She looked at us compassionately as we wolfed it down, and I like to think that her concern that we should not linger near the patrolled road was prompted only by concern for our safety.

After two large glasses of wine we resumed our ride in exuberant mood which was not entirely dampened by our coming upon the riddled burnt out wreck of a light recce car. There was no trace of the occupants, but the Lieutenant salvaged the driver's log-book. At about four in the afternoon, after a long stretch over arid ridges, we came to a metalled road and saw in the distance white buildings which we took to be Goubellat. We were just approaching the road when a column of dark menacing tanks came trundling along it. There was no escape if they were not ours. The Lieutenant reined his horse into the middle of the road waving his yellow recognition silk. The lead tank stopped and the owner of the bereted head that poked out of the turret enquired in public school tones that rang musically in my ears as never before, the nature of our business and identity. 'Lieut Brayley 2nd Parachute Battalion' said the Lieutenant smartly. 'Oh, we've been wondering about you!' said the recce officer chattily as though we had made a late appearance at a picnic. Thereupon followed an exchange of information and the column resumed its patrol.

In the centre of Goubellat, Brayley collared a motor-cycle DR to ferry him to the recce unit HQ about four kms down the road. Shortly after this a DR came from the HQ direction and told me to get up behind him. At the Tank HQ, the Lieutenant and I fed and washed and I had a flesh wound on my back dressed. Then around 1700 hours, each behind a

DR, we sallied out to look for the Battalion. We cruised out into the blue, but saw no sign by the time it was getting dusk and our DR's were becoming uneasy. Then we encountered a Yank column of 'half tracks' and dismissing the relieved DR's, clambered aboard the lead vehicle intending to go with them for the night and go out next day for the Battalion. We were bowling along at a good rate through gathering darkness when a flare shot up ahead and the column jerked to a halt. There was a tense silence, followed by excited whispers but no decision in the lead vehicle. Lieut Brayley was consulted for his opinion and after a moment's pause said in a hoarse whisper, 'well, I'll tell you what – my sergeant and I will do a recce. Johnstone, we'll do a pincer's. You take the ditch to the right of that telegraph pole and cover me as I go along the left. Then we'll find out what's up along there.' 'Right Sir' I whispered in true British fashion but inwardly damning this prestige stuff.

I hopped down from the half-track, thankful for the crepe soled boots we then wore, and crawled up the ditch. There was a low whistle from the other side and when the Lieutenant was sure I was covering he hailed down the road. A reply came back which we both thought was French, so he whistled the Marseillaise which came back. He then ordered them to come out unarmed, and under the menace of my nervously trained Sten and the MG on the bristling half-tracks, a diminutive French Poilu came sauntering jauntily down the road. The source of all the alarm was just a French road block and as we passed through, they told us the Battalion had preceded us and soon we were riding gaily alongside.

The change of locomotion seemed to have rested me and I felt fine, but the boys were a sorry sight as they trailed wearily along in single file. They were mostly too tired and hungry to show enthusiasm for the mere fact of respite for the moment, from the menace of the German armour. Soon however it was bliss to stretch out on the tiled floor of the covered market secure in the knowledge that we were no longer alone and unsupported. Nevertheless, our relief was momentary, for in the small hours the Colonel himself came round urging us to our feet, and we trailed out at dawn to line a road outside the town to repel an expected 'large scale atttack'.

Dennis Rendell . . . . *recollects his disastrous Oudna experience*

I THINK we must have been following Bn HQ planes, I remember being briefed to jump when the CO jumped. After a very long take-off run, we were grossly overloaded, we eventually staggered into the air and formed up in some kind of order. After a flight of nearly three hours, by now very low indeed, I saw the CO jump, so I jumped followed by my No. 1 platoon. I landed softly, and was at once aware of silence with no small-arms fire or shell-fire – we had landed unopposed, and as this was my first operation I was heartened by the ease of the whole thing.

'A' Coy formed up, and moved to a defensive position roughly north of the dropping zone. I do not think we had any casualties, although I heard someone had bought it with a Roman candle. After a few hours a Humber light armoured car of the Derbyshire Yeomanry drove up and went through us, returning later to report a road block ahead.

We moved off towards a place called Oudna, with 'A' Coy bringing up the rear of the Battalion. By morning we were in position at a place called Prise de L'Eau, a well. On the way we had collected a somewhat motley selection of mules, horses and carts in order to carry ammunition and stores. This extraordinary group of men and animals was described by LCpl Berryman, an old Middlesex Regiment regular, as 'looking like a fucking travelling circus rather than a Parachute Battalion,' and he wasn't far wrong!

That afternoon Dicky Ashford gave out his orders, which boiled down to having a look at Oudna airfield and if possible occupying it. Anyway, we moved off with 2 Platoon on the left under Slapsey Brayley, No. 1 Platoon, mine, on the right with Company HQ slightly to the rear and 3 Platoon in reserve at the rear. I ordered 1 Section on the right, 2 Section on the left with Platoon HQ in the centre and 3 Section in reserve at the rear – all to keep well spread out in a kind of box formation and to head in the direction of Oudna station, plainly visible with white buildings. I recall the Company 2i.c. Captain Keith Mountford, saying at Ashford's order group that "the British Army could not a fight a war without a red-roofed house – without that they couldn't indicate any target, but here was Oudna station complete with a red-roofed reference point'! After about fifteen minutes the sound of machine-gun fire, very fast and certainly not our Brens, was heard and we all instinctively fell to the ground in the prone position. I was desperately trying to remember the crack/thump of bullets taught to me at my Small Arms School Bisley course, but I simply couldn't and as a result had no idea where the fire was coming from or if it was directly pointed at us. After a few minutes I thought it reasonably safe to continue, so shouted the order to move on, and this we did. No. 2 Section, however, was too far left, and I had some difficulty in getting them back on line. There was still a good deal of noise, chiefly small-arms fire with the occasional crump of a mortar bomb or shell. On the way 2 Section assaulted a small Arab dwelling which they thought might shelter the enemy machine gun – it didn't.

We were still making reasonable progress towards the station, but I had lost sight and control of No. 1 Section to the right. Sergeant Forsyth, my Platoon Sergeant, was making sure No. 3 Section remained with us. As Platoon HQ approached this tiny station I was looking beyond for any aircarft posted on the strip – there were none. The station seemed unoccupied, so Sergeant Forsyth and my batman, Private Fletcher, and myself took possession. I then realized that none of the Sections had shown up, but then 2 Section turned up on the left and

I called them over. I was delighted to have this additional strength, and set about preparing defensive positions around the station buildings. Later some men of No. 3 Section arrived.

I was rather pleased with the little operation, despite the fact that we were a section and a half down. I think all of us had been very scared, but at least we had got to the objective. As far as I knew, we hadn't killed any enemy or even seen them! We had certainly fired our weapons, but all at rather doubtful targets. I went out on to what was laughingly called an airstrip; there were no aircraft on it, but a few abandoned 50-gallon oil drums, which suggested some previous aircraft activity. Strangely, there were tyre tracks, but these I assumed were made by vehicles and not taxi-ing aircarft. We were out of touch with Company HQ and there was no sign of 2 or 3 Platoons. Incidentally, the stationmaster was found in one of the buildings, and he told me that enemy armour was in the vicinity. He was a French-speaking Arab who I sent packing which on reflection wasn't a very clever thing to do.

While we were preparing possible tank ambush sites we heard the sinister sound of engines and there, to the left across the airstrip, were three or four tanks and an armoured car about half a mile away. The armoured car approached us, running parallel to the railway. Our only anti-tank weapon was the Gammon Bomb, and that was only good at very close range. I ordered everyone to take maximum cover, and at the same time was trying to think what I must do if the bloody thing stopped close to us. Luckily it didn't, and drove by about fifty yards in front of us. If the occupants saw us they didn't react, but I suspect they did not even see us. It was huge, with eight wheels and festooned with wireless masts. I think it was a command car, and it drove merrily on towards Tunis.

At dusk we saw large fires to the left, I wrongly assumed it might be Slapsey Brayley with 2 Platoon or even 'C' Coy, who had been on our left when we started out. When it was fully dark we moved towards the fires, only to be fired on by something much bigger than small arms; someone said they saw a tank, and that may well be so – anyway it set off a firework display that both helped and hindered our ignominious withdrawal back towards the station. By now it was pitch-black, and we bumped into a previously unseen French Police Post. Very scaring, but they were helpful and offered us shelter for the night. This I refused, because I had in mind the need to get close to the protection of the hills in order to return to our previous battalion position at Prise de L'Eau. I had previously taken a back bearing from the station to where I thought we had come from, so I knew that if we went on that bearing we would end up somewhere near our original position. So off we set, but it soon became obvious to me that the men were done up, and that rest was essential for all of us. In addition I did not wish to bump into any other posts, be they French, German or our own FDL's; we had had enough for one night. So we largered up in the scrub where we were. It was devilish cold, and I doubt if any of us got much rest – our cotton jumping smocks giving little or no warmth.

We set off before dawn and made for the shelter of the hills, and at first light could clearly see our old Prise de L'Eau position with various small figures moving round. These I prayed would be our own men, and ordered my chaps to display prominently our yellow identification silks. Much to my relief the first recognisable chap was the tall elegant figure of 'Popoff', alias Lieut Peter Naoumoff of Bruneval fame and of 'B' Coy. 'And where have you bloody heroes been?' he said, closely followed by more pertinent comments from his men. Without the glimmer of a smile, Private Fletcher replied: 'Tunis'. I think each one of us was very chuffed and secretly a little proud to have this ribald welcome.

Back within the heart of our own Battalion and Company we felt safe and secure, and after a shave and clean-up felt 100 per cent better. Various other men of 2 and 3 Sections rejoined, so we were again about twenty-five strong. I was sent for by the CO and reported the result of our occupation of the station and airfield. I was rash enough to say that if we had wheels we could have reached Tunis. The CO was complimentary and made no mention of absence. Back at 'A' Coy, Dicky Ashford said we should have done it on foot, but Keith Mountford reminisced on the joys and advantages of having Battalion transport and what we could do with a few trucks right now.

We extended the 'A' Coy positions to the left of the Prise de L'Eau well, with 1 Platoon furthest right. Enemy armour and tanks moved towards the well, and attempted to come round behind us. We could clearly hear the revving of tank motors as they ascended the hill – a most frightening sound – and from my forward slope position the first thing I saw was the swinging radio mast, then the turret and finally the whole vehicle painted a sand yellow colour with a large black cross on the turret. 'If it come closer we'll have a go with the Gammons,' I said, but thankfully it turned off to the right along the line of the hill. We could hear its mate coming up the hill after it, so Fletcher and I jumped up and ran up and over the brow of the hill. To run on these scrub-covered hills was difficult enough, but when also high parachute boots and those awful gaiters were included it was very nearly impossible. Somehow we did it, and lay down and waited, but no tank appeared; it must have followed the other one, as if to make the final act of this battle, some ME-109s attacked the enemy instead of us. I very much doubt if the pilots even saw us, because our parachute smocks made excellent camouflage. Prior to the aircraft attack, Fletcher was very badly wounded by shell-fire. We carried him down to Doc Gordon's RAP. I think he died later that night.

We moved out when darkness came, the signal being a call by the CO on his hunting-horn. I was told we would make for Medjez El Bab, where 1st Army troops were said to be. This proved to be a most difficult march over appallingly tough hill country, and later on flat sandy plough land. 1 Platoon was leading, with both the OC and myself using compasses. Sergeant Forsyth was being a tower of strength by encouraging the exhausted men to make even greater efforts.

Just about dawn we came to a farm run by French settlers, where we watered from the farm well. Then what was left of the Coy was put in a large straw-filled barn where we slept. We were informed by the French owners that a German motor-cycle combination was coming up the farm road. Dicky Ashford ordered the men to hide under the straw, while he and I and some NCOs with Stens cocked waited. We had no intention of allowing these three Germans to leave the farm alive should they approach the barn. Strangely, they did not dismount from their machine, and spoke at length to the French family. The anxious and nervous tension was only defused when they simply started up and left, apparently satisfied that all was well. I can clearly remember these three German soldiers, and I believe the one on the pillion seat to have been Hans Teske, a man many of us now know well. I have reason to believe that he actually saw some black boots sticking out of the straw, but that he somehow forgot to mention this to his colleague! If this is so, he was just as frightened as those of us looking at him. We then heard that the CO and the rest of the Battalion were at another farm nearby, and we set off to join them; this farm was named El Fedja.

We, that is number 1 Platoon, were given the task of defending the northern part of the farm perimeter, which consisted of a big cactus hedge interspersed with stone walls enclosing an olive orchard. By this time I was greatly concerned about the shortage of ammunition; despite economy we had wasted a large number of rounds by firing at too great a range. I asked my second i.c., Keith Mountford, if he could arrange some re-supply, but he said we were all in the same boat.

I was quietly having a shit just behind the hedge a short distance from my Platoon HQ, and idly looking at the ridge about three hundred yards away, when I noticed a couple of dots moving long the skyline. Someone was looking at me, or more likely the Battalion position. I quickly finished my toilet and rejoined my Platoon HQ, only to find Keith, who said we would pull out as soon as it was dark. I quickly explained what I had seen, and together we studied the ridge through our glasses; by now there were several dots, easily identified as helmets – but who were they? Keith said hopefully 'maybe they are Yanks'. They were Germans all right, and soon the mortars started, followed by MGs. Before Keith left to return to Coy HQ he once again made us smile, and so helped to lessen the tension and fear. 'You know, Dennis,' he said, 'you are probably unique – you must be one of the very few British officers to be caught with his trousers down in the face of the enemy!' and left. Shortly after this we killed half a dozen Germans within fifty yards of our perimeter, but even then I had a job to stop the men firing. A little later we scuppered a more determined attack in the same way, but this time the effect was more deadly and the control much tighter. By now the light was beginning to fade, and various farm buildings were on fire; most of them had straw roofs. By dark the fires gave off a ghostly light which, combined with the smoke, made accurate shooting virtually impossible, and this was very worrying because we could hear Germans very close. Keith again arrived, to tell me we were moving out when it became dark, and that the signal to move would again be made by the CO sounding the 'gone away' on his horn. we were to withdraw through the farm and move out south-eastwards. I walked along the cactus hedge with Keith towards Coy HQ. We heard German voices on the other side; pistols were useless, and in case it was nearly dark, so after a frenzied debate decided to use our Mills grenades. In the approved fashion we hurled two grenades each over the fence in the direction of the voices. They burst with satsifying crumps, and this was followed by cries of pain. Keith and I got up from our prone positions. 'Good-evening to you, Mr Rendell,' he said, and disappeared. I returned to Platoon HQ and briefed the NCOs on the plan.

Soon after dark, mortar and machine gun fire increased, but the machine guns appeared to be firing on fixed lines over the farm and the mortar bombs seemed to be doing little damage. We heard the CO's horn, and as I slowly crawled from Platoon HQ I heard the whine of mortar bombs falling very close. My sole recollection is of a ghastly smell of sulphur just like school chemistry experiments. At some time I felt someone pulling my belt, and it was light. A German soldier in what appeared to be a pair of overalls was trying to remove my pistol from its holster, and I tried to help him – I couldn't; my hands were too cold and I was shivering. My right leg was wet, and my large pocket para trousers were torn. The man pulled me to my feet, and I was dumped gently but firmly into a motor cycle sidecar and taken to what I thought was a RAP. There was no noise, and no firing. I was eventually joined by some members of B Company and some Sappers. 'For you the war is over,' they said, and I was a prisoner of war, at any rate for a time – but then, that's another story.

This was written for Gen John Frost, my old CO and the date I completed it, 4 December 1990 was most significant. Because at that time 45 years ago 2 Parachute Bn was fighting for it's life.

Dusty Miller and Frank Welsh . . . . *help Cpl Dennis on a mule*

ON MONDAY at about 1600 hrs I was separated from the rest of the Coy and attached myself to the Anti-Tank Section. We went forward with the main attack on the aerodrome and came under heavy shell fire and machine gun fire from the aerodrome. About 1700 hrs German aircraft straffed us on the edge of the hill between the farm, that 8 Platoon 'C' Coy had been told to occupy, and the aerodrome.

Lieut Charteris ordered us to get back by sections into the hills, but in the withdrawal Pte Welsh and myself were separated from the rest of the section. At this point we overtook Cpl Dennis of 'A' Coy on a mule, his leg had been broken by shrapnel. Darkness was descending, so we decided to head for the water hole and we met Pte Keyes of 'C' Coy and Pte Stevens of 'A' Coy. As the shelling was still going on we decided to get Cpl Dennis to some place further back where we could make him comfortable and try to contact the rest of the battalion.

We utilised two pistol rods as splints and bound up Cpl Dennis's leg as best we could with shell dressing. We then headed for the dropping zone to try and contact Lieut Buchanan. We arrived at a gully about five miles from the dropping zone at dawn on Tuesday. We rested here as Cpl Dennis was in great pain, and had something to eat. We decided to have a recce of the ground and in the distance we saw planes searching the hills.

Keyes and Stevens suggested that they try and get water and find out any information they could about the ground between us and the dropping zone, while Pte Welsh and myself looked after Cpl Dennis. They took with them three of the four water bottles and headed towards a farm between us and the dropping zone. They didn't return, we were left with one bottle half full of water. About four hours after this we contacted an Arab who told us that the German tanks were a kilometre away with many English prisoners.

We decided to wait until darkness and head for the foothills and where we could get medical attention for Cpl Dennis. We made our way down to the road at dusk and hid in a hedge alongside the road, when we saw approaching from the direction of Zaghouan three motor cycles and an armoured car. The armoured car stopped about 300 yards away from us and the motor cycles came on very slowly. Pte Welsh threw the Gammon bombs and I fired my Sten as hard as I could, the first motor cycle was blown up and others evidently thinking our party was stronger than it really was withdrew in the direction of the town.

We held a hurried consultation and as it was open country we waited until darkness. About a quarter of an hour later, two shells whistled over our heads, so we decided to make a break for it and got Cpl Dennis onto the mule's back and travelled as fast as we could in a south-westerly direction towards the foothills. We had no water and did not want to risk going near the farm we passed during the night. At one point during the night we tried to relieve our thirst by licking split cactus leaves but this was not very satisfying.

Wednesday at 0400 hrs we stopped to rest until daybreak in a river bed, the mule was very tired and Cpl Dennis was in much pain. As dawn broke we saw that there was a small amount of water in the river bed. I tasted it and it was very salty, however, we made some tea thinking this might take away the bad taste. At daylight we saw a farm further up and to the right of the river bed. We had to have water and risked going up to it, there was a possibility of it being occupied by the enemy. Some Arabs made us understand that the farm was owned by a Frenchman and that no Boche or Italians were in the vicinity, so we went and saw the farmer who gave us eggs, water, bread, butter and wine, for which we offered to pay him, but he refused.

At about 1500 hrs on Wednesday afternoon we set off for Pont Du Fahs with the Arab who took us about five or six kilometres on the way and then pointed out the best route, and after giving him 150 francs we proceeded on our way arriving at Pont Du Fahs at dusk.

The Gendarmerie was the first place that we came to and after we had satisfied the Gendarme that we were English soldiers he took Pte Welsh and myself in to have food, wine and cigarettes while he sent his son with the mule and Cpl Dennis to the doctor. The Gendarme took us into the air raid shelter to sleep on some straw which he gave us. We rested here for about an hour, he returned with two French soldiers who took us with them on their motor cycle combination to the bridge west of Pont Du Fahs which they were guarding. They gave us a blanket and a ground sheet to rest on and asked us if we heard any firing to help them as they suspected German tanks were in the vicinity.

We went to the hospital and had our blisters dressed and to see if Cpl Dennis was all right. He was quite comfortable and we found several others were there including Magee of the 'I' Section and Coomber. The French troops offered to take us back to the nearest British troops by motor cycle that night, however, in the afternoon CSM Sharp came along and I went with him and the Recce people in their armoured car to arrange transport for the rest, we ran into German tanks on the way.

Corporal McConney . . . . *kills his guard and escapes*

I WAS attached to the 2nd Parachute Bn. with six men for operational signal purposes on the 29th November 1942. At approximately 1500 hrs I made my descent. I had several twists in my rigging lines and hit the earth spinning. I was conscious of pain in my right arm but was able to free myself and find the signals container. The MO gave me an injection of morphine in my right hand and told me to lie down for a few minutes until he was able to attend to me. Later on he put me under chloroform and put my shoulder in place.

I do not recollect anything further until I found myself, with other patients, at the school-room, Depienne. I then learned from the MO that the Bn had left for the objective at 2300 hrs. At approximately 0700 hrs, 30th November 1942, Mr Buchanan came to the school-room and with the aid of a French doctor, evacuated the sick to the hospital at Pont Du Fahs. That left Mr Buchanan, his batman and myself at the school-room.

We started to make a meal and by the time we had cooked the food we heard the sound of tanks and armoured vehicles on the road leading north. In between each AFV were a number of motor-cycle combinations. The three of us lay down in a ditch facing the road. The crews of the tanks etc were Italians. Shots came from the direction of Mr Buchanan and his batman so I too opened fire with my sten. The range was approximately 50 yards and I got off five magazines with good effect on the motor cyclists. Mr Buchanan gave a cry and rolled over on his back and the batman lay face down with arms outstretched. By this time the tanks had traversed their guns round and were ramming the building with fire. Seeing it was useless to continue firing, I crawled to the lavatory and put my sten and three mags on top of the wall to avoid detection and hid behind the half-closed door. About 30 Italians entered the yard and were very excited when they saw that a meal had been in progress.

A heap of parachutes in one corner of the yard aroused suspicion and several shots were directed on to them; then they lifted them up to see if anyone was hiding underneath, they began a systematic search of the out-houses. A few shots were fired and luckily none touched me. Three of them then walked in and were greatly alarmed at finding me. I was taken and put on top of an armoured vehicle. After three or four miles they stopped at a small wood and I was assisted off. One Italian was left with me and the vehicle went back. I at once set about a plan of escape. They had failed to detect my fighting knife which was concealed in the pocket, and my right arm was in a sling.

To the sentry I must have appeared a very poor spectacle, for he did not seem to worry a great deal about me. I think he thought there was chance of attack by the Bn. As dusk approached he seemed to get more nervous and whenever he turned his back I loosened the knife. At last I got it out and put it in my left hand trouser pocket. When he turned his back I whipped out the knife and struck at his back under the left shoulder. He gave a cry and fell on his face. I must have lost my head for I struck again and again at the inert form. I decided then to go back to the school and try and collect my arms if they were still there. I found my sten and mags still on top of the wall but all the equipment in the school-room had gone except two small tins of cheese.

I listened outside the door of the house and could only hear the voices of the schoolmaster and his wife. They had been very good to us so I knocked on the door and asked them if they knew where the English soldiers were. They said they were at Pont Du Fahs and gave me bread and water and told me to go, as the Italians might return. I went and lay down in the ditch and started to eat and drink. I had nearly finished when I heard the tanks etc entering the village. They came into the school and seemed to use it as an HQ. I thought it was time to get out and crawled along the ditch. Several times I was only a few feet from some of them. All the tanks etc were at the cross roads and I estimated them at about 20 to 30 Mk IVs and some 20 armoured cars (flat topped).

At last I got clear of the village and made off in the direction of Pont Du Fahs with the aid of a compass (part of my escape kit). After walking for a few miles I felt very tired so went to sleep in some hay. Next morning, 1st December, I set off again. I stopped at a French farm and they gave me sausage and eggs and then told me that Pont Du Fahs was in the hands of the enemy. This was rather a setback. I had heard that 1st Para Bn was somewhere near Medjez El Bab, so I changed my course for there.

The going was very hard over the mountains and the sun was very hot. On the morning of the 2nd, I made contact with the 56th Recce regt 'C' Sqdrn. They took me to Regimental HQ and questioned me as to the disposition and strength of the enemy. They told me that they had transport going to Medjez the next day and that I would have to make my own way after that.

Jimmy Sharp MM . . . . *wins a bar to his Military Medal*

ON MONDAY night after being separated from the Company I marched to the well where the Bn had formed up for the attack. There I contacted some more of 'C' Coy under Sgt Gibbons. As there was no one who knew what was happening we decided to wait in the hills till morning. About 0200 hrs Tuesday we heard troops moving south in the hills, but as we did not know whether they were British or Germans we decided to move parallel with them. This we did till we struck a road at 0300 hrs and found a red beret we presumed that the troops moving on our right were Germans, so I swung off south east and got in the hills. About 0400 hrs we turned south again and kept pushing on till 0500 hrs when we rested in some scrub. At daylight we moved into a valley and made tea. At this point two shots were fired at us and thinking that they must have been snipers or Arabs working with the Germans we pushed on again.

At about 1100 hrs (Tuesday) we contacted Arabs and when I questioned them they reported Germans practically all around. At about 1100 hrs a battle started about 3 miles north-west of us, we tried to make out what was happening but could see nothing as most of the fire appeared to be heavy stuff we thought it must be a tank battle. At 1200 hrs we lay up in a gully and contacted Arabs who got us water and bread. All afternoon German fighter aircraft kept circling the hills and machine-gunning somewhere north of us.

We rested near the farm for a few hours and from there headed across the fields going north west. We lay in the cactus until about 0600 hrs about 5km north west of Moghrane.

I placed a sentry with binoculars to watch the main road and during the day we saw a few vehicles passing along the main road. At about 1100 hrs a tank and an armoured car came from Zaghouan and went into Moghrane, they then went into the fields for the remainder of the day and it appeared as if they were covering the road. During the day an Arab came in and said British and American tanks were in Moghrane and Depienne. I had a talk with Sgt Gibbons and we decided to chance sending a message by the Arab to the tanks. We asked in the message for the person receiving it to send a message in reply but when the Arab came back and said he had delivered the message but did not bring a reply we got suspicious.

He said he was going to take us into the village of Moghrane to the tanks, he took us part of the way and then left us. At this point dogs were barking behind a ridge and presuming that the Arab had tricked us and that a German ambush was obviously laid for us if we headed for Moghrane I headed off North West and then swung West, crossed the main Zaghouan-Tunis road and passing between Moghrane and Depienne.

At about 0330 hrs (Thursday) we lay up at a French farm. In the morning at daylight the farmer informed us that the Germans were in Depienne and had captured the Paratroops there. He advised us to make for Pont du Fahs. We set off at daylight south west parallel to the road Depienne-Pont du Fahs. At about 0730 hrs we saw a motor cycle patrol come along the Moghrane-Pont du Fahs and I think that they must have been French.

We crossed the road and headed up until we contacted an Arab who gave us water, wine and food. He then guided us to Pont du Fahs where we contacted a French patrol and found some more of our men. I set off from there with two armoured cars (5 men and myself) to report to the nearest harbour of the armoured cars and to try and arrange transport for the remainder of the men in Pont du Fahs. We bumped into some German tanks and had to run for it so what happened to the two armoured cars and the remainder of the paratroops in Pont du Fahs I don't know. The last report we heard was that they were fighting and they may have got out by the south or west road.

The men with me were:– Sgts. Gibbons, Kennedy, McGuire, Webster, Coates, Bennett, and Privates Bennett, Bond, Erby, Fleming, Buchanan, Wilson, Wright, Flitcroft, Harkins, Baxter, Venters, Cooper, Griffiths, Steel, Maysmith, Batten. On Wednesday night Ptes. Maysmith and Batten dropped out and we did not know until morning that they were missing.

Les Shurmer .... *writes a letter home*

WE SAILED into Algiers Harbour on Thursday 12th November 1942. We weren't thrilled much by the place, the squalor and the smells were new to us and we hadn't learned to despise the Arabs as we do now. We were stationed about 9 miles from Algiers in an Arab school in a small town. There was lots of work to do. We emplaned at midday Sunday 29th November. Our job was to land on the airfield of Depienne (which is 25 miles due south of Tunis) capture it, march to the airfield at

Oudna (8 miles south of Tunis) capture that, and then meet some British tanks and attack Tunis. We had rations for 4 days and we thought we'd be coming back after that, but instead we stopped up the front for 5 months.

The flight from Algiers to Depienne took us about three hours. It was picturesque flying over all these mountains, and it was also pretty cold. I was attached to 'C' Coy. 'C' Coy were all Scots and were the lads that made the raid on Bruneval early last year, so they considered themselves good. The piper had even brought his bagpipes with him. Four of his mates were carrying a pipe each and he had the bag. He was going to play it as we went into Tunis but alas, we did not get there.

We jumped at about 3 o'clock and once on the ground I fixed my sten together and doubled for the wireless set which came down in a container. I had to cross a path across the field down which were running some Arabs. When I met up with them they asked, all smiles, 'Anglais parachutists?' I answered 'Oui'. So there was vigorous handshaking all round, and I thought to myself, 'This is a jolly fine war.' Midnight came and we moved off to find Jerry.

We marched till 5 o'clock over the roughest of country and very steep hills covering about eight miles, and then rested for an hour till daybreak. It was impossible to sleep because of the cold. Obviously we had no blankets, as a matter of fact we had no battledress blouse, only a shirt, pullover and camouflage canvas jackets. When daybreak came we started marching again, over the same type of country. So hard was the going that even the mules we had got from the Arabs bent at the knees and couldn't keep it up. Soon we were able to see Tunis and the coast, so that, though tired we were still in high spirits. It was decided that we would attack the airfield at 1 o'clock in the afternoon. Jerry had prepared a warm reception committee for us. Besides the ordinary defences, they turned out three tanks against us, which was the first time I saw men die, and the first I had bullets whistle about me. The shells they lobbed took a certain toll. We had no weapons to tackle the tanks, except bombs which we carried to throw at them. We gradually pushed on and captured our objective the railway station on the other side of the airfield. The tanks had to fall back or they would have been knocked out with our bombs. It was then decided that as Jerry obviously wasn't using the airfield we'd pull back to the valley and wait for the 1st Army to catch us up. Jerry hadn't finished with us, for as we pulled out, four MEs came over, up went two white signal lights in our direction from Jerry's positions and down came the MEs blazing away with their guns.

I was with Trevor Evans and we dug down for about twelve inches. Breakfast was a tin of cheese, half a bar of chocolate, six biscuits, six boiled sweets and tea. Trouble was, Jerry interrupted it. Tea was just on the boil when up bowled three tanks and started shelling us. Our mortars got onto them after a bit and they sheered off. Then three others turned up from the the other direction, and we thought at first they were Yankee for they flew our recognition signals. One of our sergeants went forward to them and they turned out to be Jerries. They sent him back with an ultimatum to surrender. Our obvious reply was to open up on them, so they just sheered off and started shelling us.

We moved off round the hill for about three miles. Our water bottles were filled from a very dirty trickle of water oozing out of the hillside. We carried sterilizing tablets, but to take a swig from the bottle meant getting a mouthful of dirt. I tried drinking it through a handkerchief, but the dirt clogged the handkerchief after a teaspoon of water came through. The only thing to do was drink the water and spit out the dirt.

We marched and marched till we came to a river. What a glorious sight! We had been gasping for water and I had imagined I could see rivers in the moonlight all night. I filled my bottle and swigged it down. I couldn't taste it at first because I was so dry, but then I realised it was salty and had a horrible taste. Still, I refilled my bottle, put in sterilizing tablets, filled my tin hat and poured it over my head. I felt fitter then. Still we kept marching, or rather stumbling along over rocks and dried up wadis.

At every halt we just dropped in our tracks and I poured a mouthful of salty water down my throat. Many a lad had to fall out on that march. Once we had a heavy shower of rain which was very refreshing for I sucked the water out of my jacket and that wasn't salty. Towards dawn we rested in some scrub while somewhere was found for us to harbour for the day. When daylight came we repaired to a farm about half a mile away. There was a well there with glorious water in it. Twice my mess tin was filled and emptied down my throat, and I felt better then. While we were washing, an ME flew over and spotted us, and before long we spotted a Jerry motor-cyle combination watching us from the distance. Then some armoured cars and lorried infantry began to move up to attack us. All the Arabs cleared out and we took up defensive positions, we were in rather a tight spot. Two Spitfires (the first we had seen) flew over, but the Spitfires never came back. Early in the afternoon the attack came in from all directions. Machine guns opened up from the surrounding hills and they started mortaring. We just lay 'doggo' for we had very little ammunition left, and the idea was to wait till they came in close. Jerry was puzzled by the quiet, and kept his distance, but sent a section to find out what we were up to. The officer poked his head over the wall – was grabbed and dispatched (to hell), and half a dozen grenades went over the wall, which settled that section. His mortar fire was intensified, and that is how I 'hurt my arm'. One bomb dropped about three yards from me, and a piece of shrapnel went through my arm. The MO put a couple of stitches in it and a dressing on and as the arm went stiff and wasn't much use, I was left to cover a hole in the farmhouse wall.

I later found out that a piece of shrapnel had gone through my sten gun, and it was useless. Soon after it began to get dark and so the CO said when he blew his horn, we would all stream past the farmhouse door, through the cactus and over the hill, tackling anything in our way. By this time the thatch of the farm was well alight from the tracer that Jerry fired into it. So the horn was blown and out we came. As luck would have it, Jerry had left open the side we came out, for there was no-one there and we sat on the top of the hill watching him firing away at the empty farm which was blazing away.

We left him to it and trekked away over the hills. We walked all that night except for an hour before dawn. Then we started again at 6 o'clock on Thursday morning, because we heard that British troops held a nearby village. We kept walking, dodging any place where Jerry might be, and late in the afternoon met up with some Yank armoured cars. You should have heard the cheer that went up from us when they turned out to be Yanks. We were then six miles from Medjez-el-Bab, which was the first town held by Allied troops. We arrived there late in the evening hardly able to put one foot in front of the other.

It was reckoned that we had walked over 100 miles since we had jumped out of that 'plane on Sunday afternoon. 550 jumped, 140 of us crawled into Medjez el-Bab, another 80 turned up in small parties of from 12 to 20 men during the next week. . . . love from Les.
(There were not many wives who received such descriptive letters).

Jack Parker . . . . *flies in a Junkers 52*

DURING THE third day of our retreat from Oudna we were engaged by a Messerschmitt taking repeated runs at us, a German DR was riding at a fast speed on our right flank, we blazed away at him but missed. On the following day I was wounded and had to be left behind. The Germans mopped us up and I was carried away on a rush mat by four of their men to a lorry and to two dreary years as a POW. Thirty years later at our reunion we welcomed a party of German ex-paratroopers and one of them asked me if I was wounded and taken POW at Oudna. I said, 'yes' and he told me he had recognised me at once. He was one of the men who had helped to carry me off the battlefield on the rush mat, he was also the DR we had tried to kill the previous day. It was none other than Hans Teake, I am pleased we did not kill him.

As a prisoner I flew from Tunis to Trapani, Sicily in a Junkers 52 with three other wounded men. We were tied to planks with ropes and shoved along the floor of the plane. Not exactly a comfortable trip and very cold for the door was open all the way. The German crew were very jittery because of the RAF Malta patrol who they said buzzed them sometimes. Fortunately the RAF respected the Red Cross markings on the fuselage.

Sticky Wood . . . . *bad news travels fast with Lord Haw-Haw*

ON THE aerodrome at Sicily when the prisoners from Depienne arrived in the JU52, Arthur Williamson met an acquaintance that he had known in Aberdeen, but now in German army uniform. This man had regularly appeared during Arthur's lunch break, pre-war in Aberdeen. He now boasted of having photographed the city and the coastline and sent the photos back to Germany. He then went on to promise that he would get Lord 'Haw-Haw' to broadcast all names and addresses on the German radio almost immediately, if they wished, and so save their parents a long period of anxiety. A couple of nights later a neighbour reported to Sticky's mother that her son was a prisoner.

John Frost . . . . *Surgeon and Padre to be exhibited*

WE HEARD later that McGavin, our surgeon, and MacDonald, the padre, who had stayed with the wounded and had been taken prisoner, were considered persons of great interest by both the Germans and the Italians. It was intended that they should be exhibited in Rome and Berlin and they were flown to Rome from Tunis in a transport aircraft, which was full of blankets and also carried a certain amount of petrol. The padre had been wounded in both arms and so was helpless and uncomfortable, yet this intrepid pair determined to continue to make their contribution to the war effort. When the aircraft landed in Rome, the sentries got out to inquire where they were to take their prisoners, and McGavin then poured petrol over the blankets and set light to them. When the mixture was well and truly ablaze they both jumped out and the whole aircraft soon disappeared in flames. Great rage ensued which our pair did not assuage as they found it necessary to roar with laughter, and frantic Italians took them off to shoot them out of hand. They were saved in the nick of time by a German Air Force Officer and, after some very unpleasant days, they were carted off to Germany, but not before McGavin had broken both his legs when jumping off a train and the Padre had enjoyed a short spell of freedom by escaping through a lavatory window.

TUNIS AIRFIELD, December 1942, our wounded and prisoners from the aftermath of Depienne are waiting to be flown to Italian prison camps. Photo shows the German Junkers 52 bomber.   Photo: Hans Teske.

90

CHAPTER FIVE

Tunisia – five months bitter fighting

T HE WAR diary for January, February, March and April 1943 tells
of constant contact with the enemy. Two hundred and fifty reinforcements from England were posted to the Battalion to help make up
the loss of men in December.

They were now to be used as an Infantry Battalion in 78 Division
owing to the lack of first class infantry to replace them in the front line.
The other two Battalions of the Parachute Brigade were to return by rail
to Algiers for operations in another area.

An abridged copy of document WO 175 526 held at the PRO, Kew

WAR DIARY of the 2nd Battalion THE PARACHUTE REGIMENT
Commanding Officer Lieutenant Colonel JD Frost, MC

date . . . JANUARY 1943 . . . Summary of events . . . .

---

1 Captain Moore rejoined the Bn.
6 Two Arabs remanded at 'A' Coy HQ and handed over to Field
  Security (FS) personnel at Ksar Myyouar for interrogation; they
  were detained. Patrols report contact with the enemy.
8 Major Rothery joined the Bn and took command of 'B' Coy. The Bn
  is ordered to move and reconnaissance parties are sent out to view
  the proposed positions.
11 Detachments from 'B' and 'C' Coys moved to relieve detachments
  from 'A' Coy.
14 Lieut Crawley rejoined the Bn having been in hospital since the
  operation; Capt Wardle joined the Bn as 2ic 'C' Coy; Capt Turnbull
  joined 'A' Coy; Lieut Hoyer-Millar to 'C' Coy; Lieut Timothy
  rejoined the Bn from 503rd (American) Parachute Bn where he had
  acted as LO; 198 OR's joined the Bn as reinforcements, these had
  come from England.
15 Lieut-Col Frost and Major Ross received the DSO, Major Ashford and Lieut Brayley received the MC, Pte's Welsh and Miller
  received the MM. They were decorated at Souk-El-Khemis by
  Lieut Gen Anderson CB MC, GOC 1st Army.

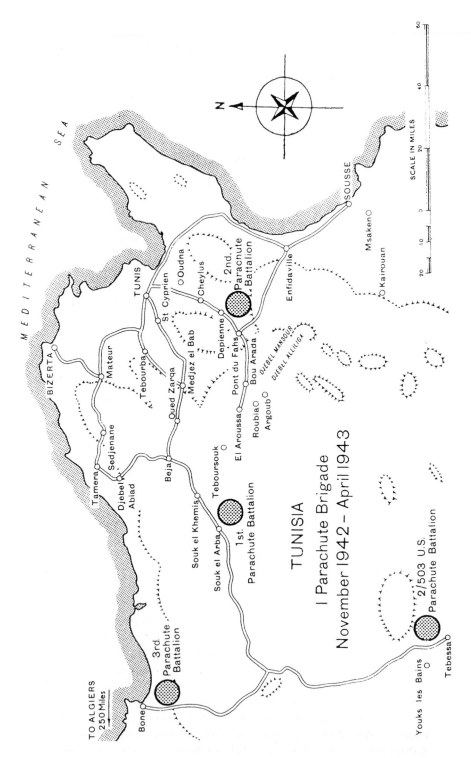

TUNISIA
I Parachute Brigade
November 1942 – April 1943

MEDITERRANEAN SEA

SOUSSE

Msaken

Kairouan

Enfidaville

2nd. Parachute Battalion

Oudna

Cheylus

St Cyprien

TUNIS

Depienne

Pont du Fahs

Bou Arada

DJEBEL MANSOUR

DJEBEL ALLILIGA

Medjez el Bab

Roubia

Argoub

El Aroussa

Oued Zarqa

Tebourba

Mateur

BIZERTA

Teboursouk

Beja

Djebel Abiad

Sedjenane

Tamera

Souk el Khemis

Souk el Arba

1st. Parachute Battalion

2/503 U.S. Parachute Battalion

Youks les Bains

Tebessa

3rd. Parachute Battalion

TO ALGIERS
250 Miles

Bone

N

SCALE IN MILES

92

16 Coys moved into battle positions. Bn HQ and HQ Coy moved into farmhouses 500 yards apart. Bivouacs were issued to 'A' 'B' and 'C' Coys as shelter in their battle positions.

17 One platoon under Lieut Brayley was sent to SI NSIR on attachment to 1st Bn E Surrey Regt for patrolling.

18 Bn Commenced to lay mines and wire in Coy positions: One platoon under Lieut I Alexander moved to Ameur-Ben-Rhils in preparation for patrols to the north-east of that area.

19 Bn continued to lay anti-tank mines and wire in Coy areas.

20 Lieut Brayley returned with his platoon from a patrol carried out in co-operation with a platoon 1 East Surrey Regt. Contact has been made with the enemy: our troops had spotted an enemy column consisting of one small car, five motorcycle combinations and four trucks heavily laden with troops; one of the trucks was thought to be towing an anti-tank gun: in the ensuing conflict our troops knocked out one P34 killing the crew and four others. The East Surreys killed six enemy making a total of twelve. Our losses were – Paras three missing; E Surreys four wounded and one missing.

19 Bn continued to lay anti-tank mines and wire in Coy areas.

22 Lieut Brayley returned with his platoon from a patrol during which contact was again made with the enemy; an attack was put in against a small party of the enemy at our OP Pnt: two were definitely killed and copies of 'Afrika Post' left in the position. Our losses were nil: Lieut Alexander carried out a patrol with his platoon but no contact was made. This platoon was then withdrawn from Ameur-Ben-Rhils as the enemy had moved light tanks and a gun into the area during the morning.

23 During the day two 25pdr btys in support of Bn registered their SOS and DF targets: there was considerable air activity over our positions during the day.

24 Lieut Brayley's platoon withdrawn from SI NSIR and replaced by Lieut Crawley from 'B' Coy.

27 'B' Coy sent out a strong patrol, two platoons, to investigate supposed enemy positions in area (Djebel-Si-Meftah) the patrol was led by Lieut Crawley and arrangements were made to meet the Coy Commander (Major Rothery) at a rendezvous at 1500 hrs.

28 'B' Coy patrol reported in having made no contact with the enemy and without connecting up with the Coy Commander. Report received that three British Parachutists had made contact with a French patrol. These are thought to be Major Rothery, his batman and CSM. Major Rothery reported to Bn HQ, he had had many and varied adventures on a mule and with the French patrol.

30 'B' Coy patrol to Beida Valley to investigate the circumstances of a number of Arabs whose activities had aroused suspicion during a previous patrol. An Arab farm was searched and a length of webbing

Beja, Tunisia. Captain Stark (Essex Regt), Lieut Brayley (Welch Regt) and Major Ashford (East Surrey Regt) who was killed in action several days later. Photo: IWM.

with two buckles, thought to be off a British parachute were discovered, also a few rounds of Italian ammunition. Two Arabs were removed for interrogation by the FSP but the Bn left the area before the results of the interrogation were known.

31 'A' Coy moved to Djebel Diaffa and reconnaissance was carried out with the view to also moving the entire Bn into that area.

date ... FEBRUARY 1943 ... summary of events ... ...

1 The Bn was warned for move to area Dj Diaffa, 'A' Coy were already in position.
2 The move to Dj Diaffa was cancelled: Bn handed over to the 4th Yorks and Lancs Regt (46 div) and moved to positions west of Medjez-El-Bab still under command of 11 Inf Bde.
3 Orders received to be prepared to move to ROBBA under command 36 Inf Bde. Bn embussed and started to move off: an 'A' Coy platoon position on Dj Diaffa was attacked by an enemy patrol as the Coy was preparing to move off: enemy casualties unknown. Own casualties 1 killed 1 missing.
4 'O' groups moved forward to reconnoitre positions for the Bn area X rds. Reconnaissance was carried out in Bren carriers one hit a

94

mine and blew up killing Major R Ashford and Capt Moore, Sgt Fisher 'A' Coy and driver were injured. Major Lane assumed command of 'A' Coy.

5 Enemy shelled Bn positions, Sgt McGuire 'C' Coy killed and 1 OR wounded. Supply route from B echelon to the Bn had been mined by the French, it was necessary to bring supplies across country by mule train. One mule was killed and the muleteer seriously injured as result of the mule stepping on a mine. Bn moved to thickly wooded country south of Dj Bargou. 'A' Coy moved to positions outside Pont Du Fahs rd due north of X rds.

6 'A' Coy lightly shelled.

7 6th Royal West Kents relieved this Bn. The Bn marched to embussing point arriving 2300 hrs.

8 Bn embussed and moved via Siliana and Gafour into positions previously occupied by the French. As a result of this move the Bn came under command of 1st Para Bde for the first time since early January.

9 Normal activities. Day spent settling in to new positions.

10 Three NCO's from 'A' Coy attached to a patrol of the Chasseurs D'Afrique.

11 Patrol brought back 19 Italian prisoners (111/92 Inf regiment). Three Italians from above regiment surrendered to 'B' Coy.

15 'B' Coy shelled, nil casualties. Bn commenced to mine and wire Coy positions.

16 A patrol with RE's attached set out to lay booby traps.

17 Booby traps laid by above patrol in area of El Ksar farm.

18 Patrols during night did not make contact with the enemy. Patrols sent out from 'B' and 'C' Coy positions.

19 'B' Coy patrol made contact with an enemy outpost containing a machine gun in farm area. The patrol attacked killing three of the enemy believed to be Italians. 'C' Coy patrol contacted enemy positions on the southern slopes of Dj Alliliga. The enemy appeared to be well dug in on the crest. An attempt was made to assault the positions but the approach was through densely wooded country and in pushing through this our patrol was forced to give away its dispositions. The enemy opened fire with a light machine gun and automatic weapons and threw stick grenades wounding two of the patrol. Total casualties amounted to:– enemy, three definitely killed. Wounded unknown. Own troops:- two wounded.

20 Reconnaissance patrols sent out.

22 Two squadrons of 4th Spahis carried out (as an exercise) a counter attack on 'B' Coy positions.

23 A strong patrol including 3in. mortar sent from 'B' Coy to assault known enemy machine gun positions near farm and to harass other enemy positions east and south-east of this area. Support from French 75mm was also arranged.

24 The patrol went into action. Unfortunately the machine gun position had been altered and assault party came under machine gun fire from the right flank and they found the previous position unoccupied. The other enemy position was severely mortar bombed causing, it is thought, a number of casualties. Own casualties nil.

25 'A' Coy sent out patrol to assault enemy machine gun positions and take prisoners.

26 As a result of this patrol 'A' Coy brought in 7 Italian prisoners, 1 Officer, 1 Sergt and five other ranks. The machine gun was not captured. Enemy casualties unknown apart from the seven prisoners. Own casualties nil. 'B' and 'C' Coys report enemy advancing but situation well in hand. Initial attack launched against 'B' and 'C' Coys. Coys replying with mortar and light machine guns; 'B' Coy forced to withdraw from forward ops and most easterly platoon positions. One Coy of enemy (Germans) moved round the left flank of 'C' Coy Djebel Salah and El Gaalil they were immediately engaged by 25 pdrs and forced to seek cover in a gully. At the same time an enemy force estimated at 2 platoons were engaged by 'C' Coys mortars and successfully pinned down. Enemy occupied farm despite determined mortaring by 'B' Coy. Artillery support demanded. Enemy variously estimated at 2 platoons and a Coy engaged by 25 pdrs, further advance stopped. Enemy started to shell the farmhouse where 'B' Coy had established their HQ prior to taking cover in the wadi to the south. Two squadrons of Spahis from reserve were ordered into position on our extreme left flank to counter the threat of enemy attempt to outflank 'C' Coy. All enemy thrusts successfully countered and enemy appears to be withdrawing into covered positions. Possibly to re-group. Our supporting Artillery continued to put down harassing fire and shelled possible forming up points. A strong patrol was organised to search the area immediately in front of our positions to bring in prisoners and secure enemy equipment.

27 Patrol returned having located an enemy (Italian) bivouac area and captured 50 after a spirited engagement lasting about one hour. Enemy retired to their own positions on high ground. The broken nature of the country made pursuit increasingly difficult. Prisoners were all from the 92nd Inf Regiment and a quantity of their equipment was secured. Two Germans were taken during the night by 'B' Coy, these were from the 11th Coy of the 756 Jager Regiment. Reconnaissance patrols were arranged for night of 27/28th.

28 Patrols report that enemy have retired to positions held by them prior to attack on the 26th. Our casualties during the battle amounted to 1 killed and 2 wounded. Of the enemy 52 were captured. POWs stated they had suffered severe casualties.

2 One German soldier from XI/756 Regiment gave himself up to 'C' Coy.

3 Warning order received for move North. Strong patrol sent out by 'A' Coy to attack enemy mortar positions.

4 Bn started to hand over to American combat team. HQ and the CP lightly shelled – no casualties. The American transport was utilised to move the Bn to Bou Arada where the RASC lifted us to an olive grove on the Gafour-Teboursouk Rd then on via another grove south of Thibar where a halt was made.

5 Bn reached Chemical Corner debussed and immediately prepared to assault suspected enemy positions on Dj Lebi.

6 Bn began moving up by Coys to the foot of the Djebel. Bn HQ set up at Hennchir Negachia. 'A' and 'B' Coys have reached summit of the Djebel without meeting enemy resistance and 'C' Coy were held in reserve. Order received from HQ 46 Div to clear enemy positions on the Kef Ouiba. The Bn moved along the high ground but found no trace of the enemy. Order received from 46 Div to clear the Dj Kermote. This feature was found to be held and a preliminary reconnaissance was carried out by 2 sections of 'C' Coy. Light failing and artillery support not forthcoming as promised. Ordered by 46 Div to call off the assault and proceed to Sidi Mohammed Belkassim to rejoin 1 Para Bde. Bn less one platoon of 'C' Coy withdrawn to Chemical Corner. The 'C' Coy platoon remained on in position throughout the night.

7 Bn moves to Sidi Mohammed Belkassim and sets up Bn HQ with Coys holding positions South of the road. (Dj Abiod-Mateur).

8 Enemy reported to be advancing on our positions. Enemy reported attacking our 'Coys' and the 1st Bn on our left. The attack was pressed home throughout the hours of daylight and it appeared in the morning as if 'A' Coy was surrounded as the enemy was infiltrating round the left flank. 'A' Coy of 3rd Bn came into reserve and two platoons put in a successful counter attack which cleared the enemy from their positions around the left platoon of 'A' Coy. In the evening the enemy still held machine gun positions in a gully on the low ground in front of our own Coy localities and a further counter attack was not completely successful in dislodging them though 2 enemy machine guns were knocked out. The support given by 70th Field Regiment Royal Artillery was of the greatest assistance in breaking up enemy concentrations and blunting the edge of the attack. Capt Radcliffe was killed early in the battle and Lieut Willcock slightly wounded. Seven ORs were killed and 35 wounded. Enemy casualties not known but thought to be considerably higher than ours. This was confirmed by prisoners subsequently captured.

9   A comparatively quiet day spent digging in and strengthening positions. Some shelling and mortaring of our positions resulting in one killed and 9 ORs wounded.

10 Throughout the morning our positions were subject to a heavy concentration of shells and mortar bombs. A further attack appeared imminent, enemy concentrations reported, they developed rapidly into an attack directed mainly against our left front and the 1st Bn on our left. Again determined efforts were made to infiltrate through our positions. Little progress was made and the main attacks were strongly repulsed. Our casualties were one officer Major Rothery, six ORs killed and 26 ORs wounded; it was difficult to estimate enemy casualties but they were fairly certain to have been heavier than our own.

11 On this day the enemy did not attack in strength nor with the determination of the previous day but light attacks made a little progress and the enemy infiltrating tactics brought him some success. A counter attack was made in front of our positions by a Coy from 3rd Para Bn. This was supported by two Churchill Tanks from North Irish Horse but was not completely successful partly because the soft ground did not allow the tanks full scope. Darkness found enemy machine gun positions still in the low ground and scrub in front of 'C' Coy and it was decided to attack these at first light with a Bty of 3in. mortar fire. 600 bombs were carried to the mortars for this purpose and all preparations made to start at first light. During the days fighting nine ORs were wounded.

12 Local patrols during the night established that the enemy had withdrawn from his FDL. This removes the need for smoking him out with a concentration of 3in. mortars. The Corps Commander visited the sector during the morning and later in the day a Coy of DLI came under command and were positioned to cover our right flank. Light and spasmodic artillery exchanges during the day resulted in wounding one OR.

13 Quiet day, 'C' Coy positions mortared in the evening. Capt Rutherfoord and one OR wounded.

14 'B' and 'C' Coys report heavy mortar and machine gun fire on their positions. 'B' Coy report one OR wounded. 'C' Coy report Lieut Alexander and two ORs wounded. Firing died down. OPs unable to locate origin of machine gun fire. Mortar fire believed coming from Djebel Bel Harch. 2 CFA (French) reports light enemy forces moving toward their positions Dj El Azib. Enemy forces occupied Dj El Azib. 2 CFA supported by 2/5 Leics counter-attacked and re-occupied Dj El Azib.

15 Sharp mortar concentration on 'A' Coy localities. Casualties 2 killed 6 wounded. Fire believed coming from Djebel Bel Harch. Enemy artillery shelled the batteries in valley below Bn positions. Several

shells landed in the BHQ area. One OR was wounded and Col Frost was hit in the leg.

16   Air reconnaissance reported 15-20 TCVs moving along rd Cap Ser-rat-Sedjenane believed to be either replacements or reinforcements.

17   During the morning the enemy put in an attack against the CFA holding ground north of the rd Dj Abiod-Sedjenane and forced them to give ground. No attacks took place against the Bn but dive-bombing and artillery attacks were made against gun positions in the Bde area. During the afternoon the 2/5 Foresters positions were penetrated by enemy attacks from Dj Bel Harch and the French having fallen back, enemy began to infiltrate southwards in the area held by 2/5 Leics. By evening the situation had deteriorated and the enemy were reported to be astride the rd about one mile north of Tamera which was still held by a Coy of DLI and later reported to be in Tamera itself. Leics, Foresters and DLI were withdrawn as far as possible during the night. This left the Bns left flank and rear dangerously open and one Coy of 1st para Bn were given the task of guarding this exposed flank.

18   Orders received from Bde that the Bn was to hold onto its present positions until new dispositions had been taken up on the high ground around Djebel Aboid. The Bn was then to withdraw to new positions on the Pimples, the signal for withdrawal was to be the code word 'Pimples' followed by a time at which to be clear of location. 1st Para Bn with No1 Cmdo were to operate offensively against the enemy during the day west of the rd. Code word "Pimple 09.00" received. Bn commenced thinning out with orders to RV at the Viaduct. 7 platoon of 'C' Coy with the protective section supported the rear-guard while the final withdrawal was covered by 3 Churchill tanks of NIH. All stores possible to evacuate were got away and such ammo as had to be abandoned was buried. Before leaving the Sappers blew the road and booby-trapped the area as effectively as time would allow. From here on the story of the withdrawal can best be told in narrative form. After assembling at the Viaduct it was decided that the best route back would be along the river to the river junction and thence onto the Pimples. Any movement along the rd was extremely hazardous since it came under enemy observation for the greater part and the Bridge was under heavy shell fire. Nevertheless the transport was taken back along this route by the Adjt and through without loss. Meanwhile the Bn moving in the order 'B' 'A' 'BHQ' and 'C' Coy commenced its movement down the river. No sooner had the withdrawal started than heavy shell fire was directed onto the river. It became apparent that the enemy intended to follow the withdrawal with fire. Utilising cover afforded by the river banks the Bn was able to work its way back under this fire with only slight losses. The going was very hard

and it was necessary at times to wade chest high in the water to avoid exposure. The Bn again came under heavy fire and some casualties were suffered. At about 1500 hrs the stream junction was reached and the withdrawal continued down the railway line to Nefza Station without interference. The Bn HQ contacted 'B' and 'C' Coys taking up positions on the forward hill with 'A' Coy holding the rear Pimples with Bn HQ on the wooded Pimple. Casualties during withdrawal were two killed, 11 wounded and 5 missing. It is interesting to note that 25 per cent of the enemy shells failed to explode. Had this not been the case casualties may have been considerably higher.

19   The day passed quietly with no enemy activity other than intermittent shelling of the Rd Nefza south – Djebel Aboid. Orders received that the Bn was to hand over its positions and return to the Mine for rest. The Bn handed over to 2/5 Leics and moved by march route along railway from Nefza south to where TCVs were parked. Heavy stores were evacuated by carrier.

20   Bn arrived in rest area. Billets were found for 'A' 'B' and 'C' Coys in the Mine itself whilst HQ Coy and Bn HQ were situated in houses nearby. An officers mess was set up. This being the first time all officers had messed together since the Bn left Beja in January.

21   Church parade was held in the Mine after which the commanding officer addressed the Bn congratulating them on their work during the last three weeks. He also said that he had received word that within a few days the Bn would be required to take part in a general attack, after which it was hoped that the whole Bde would be relieved by the 9th US Division.

22   Bn was taken by MT to the Tabarka area where the day was spent swimming and sunbathing.

23   Such elements of the Bn as had not been able to go swimming yesterday were taken to Tabarka. Sick parade was very large with many men suffering from bad feet due to the fact that they had not been able to remove their boots for weeks.

24   Bn resting. Remarkable change was noticeable. All the men looking much rested and in excellent spirits. Orders received that the Bn would move from rest area on the night of 26/27th and lay up that night and next day prior to attacking on night of 27/28th.

25   Bn carried out route march toward Tabarka rd. Had a short bathe and marched back. Platoon schemes were introduced to lend variety on the return march.

26   Bn paraded ready to move out and meet TCVs.

27   Bn takes over area from 2/5th KOYLI. Coys in laying up area on hillside. Bn HQ in farmhouse and HQ Coy in an olive grove about 200 yards away. A recce by the Bn 'O' group was carried out from the high ground. They were to capture the high ground immediately west of and dominating the Viaduct. The final phase three was to be

100

the re-occupation of our old positions on the Sidi Mohammed El Kassim. Zero hour originally timed for 2200 hrs was later put back to 2300 hrs. Briefly an artillery concentration was to fall on the Bns objective from Z until $Z+20$, the last five minutes being intense. From $Z+30$ until $Z+45$ a further concentration would fall on the enemy's reserve positions. Coy objectives were 'A' Coy to move by road to track junction, cross the stream immediately south of the SL by the ford and crossing the SL at Z hour seize Pt 224.

'B' Coy to move round right of the Pimple cross the stream by the railway bridge and capture Pt 247. 'C' Coy to move up in reserve following the route taken by 'B' Coy but crossing the stream by the pontoon bridge about 300 yards west of the railway bridge, mop up and consolidate between 'A' and 'B' Coys. An advanced BHQ consisting of the Commanding Officer and protective section would move between 'B' and 'C' Coys laying a white tape along their route as a guide to 'C' Coy, rear BHQ and HQ Coy. Each man carried a full water bottle and 48hr ration pack while mortars and spare ammo were brought up by mule under command OC HQ Coy. All Coys advance and rear HQ were in contact via WS18s. The small Pimple at present occupied by the enemy was to be captured by 'A' Coy 3rd Para Bn not later than 2015 hrs. Once the Bns objective was taken 'B' Coy 3rd Para Bn would take over. CO goes forward to contact OC 3rd Para Bn and gain further info of the ground. Coy 'O' Gps see the ground.

2100 hrs Bn moved up to start line. Sporadic enemy mortar fire on Nefza station. Artillery concentration begins. 'B' Coy cross SL and begin moving forward without incident. BHQ and 'A' Coy cross SL. 'A' Coy under enemy machine gun fire. Rear BHQ and HQ Coy crossing stream, mules cause some delay. 'C' Coys cross SL.

28 'B' Coy encounters minefields and wire suffering 7 casualties including Lieut Dover, are forced to detour to the left. Advance BHQ reached area expecting to contact 'B' Coy who were in fact moving around the left opposition encountered and 6 prisoners taken. 'C' Coy contact advance BHQ are ordered to capture ridge. Enemy shelling Nefza station and area. 'A' Coy on the right overcome 2 enemy machine gun positions held up by a further 2 behind. 'C' Coy occupy ridge after overcoming enemy resistance. Take one POW, suffer casualties, one killed 5 wounded.

0300 hrs. Unsuccessful enemy counter attack on 'C' Coy positions. 'C' Coy suffer 2 casualties 'B' Coy attempting to swing in from left are heavily engaged and forced back. 'A' Coy silence 2 remaining enemy machine gun positions and push on. 'A' Coy consolidating on their objective. Elements of 'B' Coy making contact with BHQ after splitting into small Groups. Rear BHQ, HQ Coy and 'B' Coy 3rd Para Bn move onto ridge. Enemy shelling and mortar fire intermittent. SMA fire continues. 'B' Coy HQ makes personal contact with BHQ. Heavy enemy artillery fire on railway line.

0800 hrs. 'C' Coy ordered to push forward and commence Phase 2. Held up by heavy machine gun fire. 'C' Coy attempting to work round enemy machine gun positions. Enemy resistance very fierce, casualties being suffered. 'B' Coy sent to sweep round the left of the enemy machine gun positions. Enemy artillery fire still heavy and lifting back toward our positions. Enemy counter attack developing especially against the centre and right flank. Artillery support called for via FOO.

1030 hrs. Situation becoming critical. Bde informed. Reply received, 'Hang on at all costs, things are rosy everywhere else'. CO gives the order that if the situation makes it necessary the enemy will be charged with the bayonet on a signal from the hunting horn. Situation very serious, our own Artillery doing great work dropping rounds 100yds in front of our positions. Enemy progress being slowed down, fierce fire fight in progress.

1115 hrs. Shouts of 'Whoa Mohammed' from 'A' and 'C' Coys made us think they'd gone in with the bayonet, but it was an expression of satisfaction at seeing our shells land among the enemy. Situation easier though still serious. Enemy progress checked. Heavy firing continues. Firing had died down, enemy definitely held but impossible to locate him accurately in the wooded country. Small enemy patrol located moving toward left flank. One killed and one taken POW. Bn fighting strength 10 officers 165 ORs.

2330 hrs. Orders issued for continuation of Phase 2, A composite Coy under the command of Major Ross was formed from what remained of 'A', 'B', and 'C' Coys. This was known as '1' Coy. 'B' Coy 3rd Para Bn under command Major Dobie became '2' Coy, while 'A' Coy 3rd Para Bn became '3' Coy.

29 No '1' Coy left area to clear any enemy from Pt 247 and then swing around to occupy the high ground overlooking the Viaduct. No. '2' Coy left area to reinforce '1' Coy should it be necessary. No. '1' Coy occupy Pt 247 without opposition, captured 11 prisoners. Advance BHQ consisting of CO, Intelligence and Protective section left area. 3 German stragglers were collected in the woods and another wounded. No. '1' Coy occupy their objective taking a further two prisoners. Bn in position on high ground overlooking Viaduct. A patrol from '1' Coy under Capt Brayley set out to move up the South West slopes of Sidi Mohammed Belkassem to find out whether it was held by the enemy. Patrol reported Bn's final objective clear of enemy having taken 3 prisoners. Bn commenced moving forward crossing the river and doing the last bound onto its old positions by rd. Five Italian prisoners were taken over from

our friends the Ghoums en route. Bn on its final objective. A further 3 German prisoners were taken over from the 1st Bn. During the course of the battle the Bn took in all 58 German prisoners in addition to 3 handed over to us by other Bns. No count of casualties inflicted was possible but these must have been considerable. The Bns casualties were fortunately not as heavy as at first believed:- 2 officers, 14 OR's killed, 3 Officers and 60 ORs wounded. 2 ORs missing. During the action the Bn came into contact with elements of four different German units. The counter attack delivered against our positions on the morning of 28th was made by Parachute Engineer troops reinforced with ordinary infantry. The counter attack which was carried out with extreme determination was later said to have been led by Major Witzig in person.

30 4 POWs passed to the Bn by 1st Bn for interrogation and evacuation. Two FW190s attempting to bomb and machine gun the road running past BHQ area. Dropped one bomb, no casualties. Further bombing attack cratered road setting fire to carrier. Further low level air attacks caused no appreciable damage or casualties. Bn received orders to move.

31 Bn in new positions. Regrouping into two Coys was carried out. 'A' and 'C' Coys forming one company under Major Ross, 'B' Coy under Capt Timothy. One platoon of 'C' Coy was in a French house 'The Maison Forrestiere' the other platoon being under canvas. HQ Coy and BHQ were both billeted in vacant French houses.

date . . . APRIL 1943 . . . summary of events . . . .

2 Several small parties were sent out to the Dj Bel Harch area to search for abandoned enemy equipment. One 3 ton British truck, captured by the enemy and abandoned was found in repairable condition also one British 6pdr anti-tank gun, out of action.

3 Further search parties sent out and succeeded in recovering some German tentage and a number of small arms. One ME109 crossed the Bn area at about 500ft.

4 OC HQ Coy lectured the Bn on anti-malaria measures.

5 Orders received that the Bn would move into reserve positions behind the 1st and 3rd Para Bns north of Sedjenane and prepare these positions for part of the 9th US Infantry Division coming up to relieve the Bde.

8 Major General Freeman-Atwood GOC 46 Div and Brig Flavell visited the Bn.

9 2 ME 109s crossed Bn area at approximately 2000ft. One ME 109 crossed area flying West.

14 A single ME 109 machine gunned the village of Sedjenane wounding two soldiers. Colonel Brown, US Army commanding 138 RCT
   came to visit the unit. 2 ME 109s carry out a low level bombing
   attack on the Bn area at Dj Guerra without causing any damage.
   Further low level attack by FW 109s cause no further damage.

15 Coys handing over localities to Americans. Low level air attack on
   the Dj Guerra positions and on the road Sedjenane-Cap Serrat,
   one aircraft brought down by ack-ack fire in the Cap Serrat area. 2
   ME 109s carry out low level bombing attack directed on Sedjenane-
   Tamara rd. No casualties. Bn moves out of 'line' and into 5 Corps
   reserve area Beja.

16 Arrive Beja.

17 2 MEs flew low over Bn HQ and attempted unsuccessfully to bomb
   a truck on the road about three-quarters of a mile away. Immediately afterwards they were engaged by Spitfires.

18 C of E Church Parade. RC Mass in farmhouse.

19 Lt Gen Allfrey GOC 5 Corps under whose command the Bde had
   been for much of the time in Tunisia inspected the Bn, afterwards
   made a short address thanking the Bn for the work it had carried out
   and expressed hope that he might find it under his command again
   in the future.

20 Major Mountford OC HQ Coy and QM left by truck for Boufarik
   near Algiers where the Bn is to go after leaving the Beja area.

21 Bn parades and embus in TCVs for Souk El Khemis railway station.

22 Train arrived Ghardimeau on the Algerian-Tunisian border and
   with its arrival the Tunisian story comes to an end. It had started
   nearly five months ago when the Bn had dropped at Depienne and
   since that date, with the exception of six days rest at Tabarka in
   mid-March the Bn had never been out of the 'line'. It had fought in
   almost every theatre of the central and northern Tunisia fighting. It
   had suffered heavily on several occasions and on like occasions had
   dealt heavily with its opponents. It had fought as infantry with none
   of the amenities such as carriers, transport and anti-tank guns which
   an infantry brigade expects. On occasions it had attacked with success but more often it had carried out a singularly aggressive form of
   defence often against heavy odds in the Tunisian mountains and for
   its labours had earned, with the 1st and 3rd Bns the name of 'The
   Red Devils' among the Germans. It came out of the 'line' with a
   total strength of 14 officers and 346 ORs out of an establishment of
   24 officers and 588 ORs. Having already absorbed some 230 reinforcements in early January. *A total casualty percentage of 80 per
   cent of establishment.*

23 Train delayed by blocked line at Setif.

24 Train arrived Maison Carree and delayed there for three hours. Bn
   arrived at destination Boufarik.

25 HQ and 'C' Coys commence moving by march route to their billeting area at farm and 'A' and 'B' Coys moved by MT to the farm Les
Quatre Chemins. Bn HQ moved to Les Tourelies. All these farms
were large enough to provide accommodation for all ranks.

26 These last three days were devoted entirely to letting everyone get
the feel of civilisation again. Men were allowed into Boufarik and a
certain percentage into Algiers.

28 In the former they quickly struck up friendships with the inhabitants who at all times were extremely kind.

Arthur Letchford . . . . *tells of some worrying moments*

WE WERE to take up defensive positions on the south side of Bou
Arada, Dickie Spender our platoon officer was given the task of carrying
out reconnaissance patrols close to the enemy lines. He decided to set
up a listening post some distance into no mans land aiming to achieve
more information of enemy movements. Brother Phil and I were the first
detail of this mission which was to be carried out 2100 hrs that night.
Our platoon sergeant led the way.

After we had stealthily made a distance of several hundred yards, he
quietly indicated that we were now in an ideal spot for a listening post,
Phil and myself made a brief survey of this hollow partly taken up with
grass and scrub.

The three of us clambered into the hollow and agreed it would be a
good listening post. Our sergeant reiterated instructions to keep ears out
for sounds of vehicles i.e., tanks, trucks or anything on wheels and eyes
open for enemy patrols that were known to frequent this area, then he
wished us good luck, and said that he would return soon after dawn. He
then climbed back up and left Phil and me to settle down to begin our
vigil of listening and eyeing through darkness whilst our bodies wrestled
with the nights chilled air.

Our army issue watch was ticking its way towards 0200 hrs when Phil
nudged me abruptly and whispered 'we've got f--k--g company'. I
looked to the left of Phil's side and saw pairs of staring eyes that were
bright luminous green and brown. More eyes gathered around us as they
closed nearer to our hideout. We decided to confront them by way of
moving and waving arms, they then stood still and simply stared at us
just some yards away. Having scant knowledge of nature in North Africa
gave rise to some trepidation on our part, especially when all you see of
an unknown animal is its eyes.

However, after some thought, we settled for them being African jackals
or wild cats and at that point thought it time they parted from our company, so we carried out our own little bombardment of stones and off
they scattered taking those bloody piercing eyes with them.

Gratefully more time ticked on bringing it close to 0300 hrs. We continued our vigil and looked to the approaching dawn and thoughts of

some hot food and drink on returning back to the line. These thoughts were disrupted suddenly by slight shuffles of noise, Phil and I reacted and hugging our frames flat, on the incline of the hollow with alertness that was tense as were our nerves, we slowly brought our rifles to the fore uncocked the safety catches and waited, but not for long. Before we could say 'Waho Mohammed', the enemy patrol cautiously strode past within a few feet from the listening post, the dreaded thought loomed in my mind that if one of those sods were to lose a footing it would be perhaps the worst dilemma Phil and I could ever encounter, as any warrior would find it difficult to deal with and could only be aware of the outcome of any action we took.

Unhurriedly they passed by us and hopefully without incident, but suddenly there was a 'clonk, and a bleeding missile from out of nowhere landed on Phil's helmet, bounced off, then rolled to a stop some inches from my face.

The tail end of the patrol at this time were moving out of sight. I picked up the missile which turned out to be a Maconochie can, Phil eyed it then whispered, 'f--k--g cheek, throw it back at the b-----ds'. Not feeling the desire to respond to his request, I tossed the smelly can onto the clearing above us. Thankfully dawn was making its presence felt, darkness deserted us, white clouds appeared, faint sunlight filtered its ray through small trees and bush, enabling Phil and me to observe our habitat and surroundings. We looked into our hollow and noticed a number of tin cans at the bottom. Maybe our listening post was a food resource for the African wild cats, but certainly a rubbish pit for our counterparts.

The voice of our sergeant broke the silence as he called out, 'Letchfords', then asked us if there was anything to report. We were not really sure on how to give him a run-down of what had occurred, we started to give the details, he said 'never mind, give it when we get back'. He went on, 'in the meantime caution in getting back is paramount as I have been informed of a possible minefield hereabouts, so keep behind me lads'. We did.

Joe Heys . . . . *bullet through the helmet!*

I WAS in Lieut Brayley's platoon at the battle of Cork Wood. We had travelled all night to get there before dawn, we couldn't sleep in the trucks as the roads were full of holes. When we got out of the trucks I saw Scottish infantry troops at the roadside, they were waiting to return in our trucks. Lots of them were wounded and when they saw we were 'the Paras', they said 'good luck lads, give the Jerry's Hell'. We were told to be quiet and follow. Dawn was breaking while we were sorting out our new positions when our forward scouts reported a German patrol approaching our position, we knew from past experience a German scouting patrol was about 30 strong. An order was quietly

106

circulated for Lieut Brayley's platoon to come forward and we were told we were going to intercept them. When we were fairly close to them, we set an ambush we had used successfully in the past, this was to allow the enemy to come through out position and we would follow behind them to ensure they would not escape. So we allowed them to go forward, my mate Dicky Davies said to me, 'they are big lads', we found out later they were Panzer Grenadiers. A few minutes later we heard machine gun fire and rifle and sten guns firing. They had encountered the forward members of the Battalion.

We stayed where we were and checked their attacks. They lost a lot of men in these attacks. We then had Artillery and mortar bombs from them, I think the denseness of the woods took the brunt of the shells and mortar bombs and saved us a lot of casualties. Two or may be three days later my Sergeant crawled over to me and said, 'come with me and take over the Bren gun'. I followed him about 100 yards or so to where the gun was, the two man crew had been shot by a sniper who was out there somewhere. The Sergeant said, 'so keep your eyes open and watch out'. About half an hour later the sniper got me, the bullet hit my steel helmet, went through taking about three inches of my hair and scalp with it, the force of the bullet knocked me on my back and I was knocked out.

A few minutes later I came to and sat up, blood was running down my face and neck and my smock was also covered, I felt myself and could find no wound, only a bad headache. I looked out and saw about 25 or 30 Panzer Grenadiers running past my position about 40 yards away. I jumped back to the Bren gun and mowed them down. I kept an eye on them for about half an hour but no one got up. A few minutes later my Sergeant came crawling towards me with a medic, he said, 'we thought you'd had it, until we heard the Bren going and all those Germans falling.' I showed him my helmet with the bullet hole he said, 'that bloody sniper is still out there.' The medic cleaned me up and I felt OK except for a headache.

We had lost too many men for another to join me on the Bren, so I carried on with the Bren, and some more ammo was found to make up what I had used. We were told to hold our positions if at all possible. I remember the first cup of tea after that little episode was nectar! The Germans were determined to drive us out of the hills and woods, and continued with the bombardment of our position, followed by infantry attack. We were getting short of ammo and we were told to let the Germans come right up to our position before firing to make every bullet count. On one occasion I aimed at the nearest German about 30 yards away, I pressed the trigger, nothing happened, a dummy bullet I thought, reloaded, pressed the trigger, again nothing happened. By now the enemy was quite close to me, there was about five of them, my sten was too far away with my pack for me to get to it in time, quickly I took out two grenades and threw them. I believe our grenades had a five second detonators, they did the trick and they were all killed. I never thought my old rifle would let me down, it had a broken firing pin. I had had the same rifle since I joined 2 Para 12 months previously.

Two days later I was shot through my right shoulder and then through my left leg. When the fighting died down, two medics came and carried me on a stretcher. As we were making our way back to the first aid post, we were caught in a bombardment of artillery and mortar bombs, and I received several shrapnel wounds on my neck, arms and legs. That was my memory of Cork Wood.

Neville Robinson .... *with the I section*

I WAS in the I Section during the Cork Wood, Sedjenane, Tamara battles and by that time, we were down to about 3 members. We lost the only pre-Oudna member the first night when he went out to deliver maps to the rifle companies in the woods.

I had a 1:250,000 map and 1:50,000 map, and one of my jobs was going around the platoons showing the sections roughly what was going on along the front line.

Just before the withdrawal I was sent to 'C' Coy because they had a telephone link with the French XIX corps on our flank and I spoke French. Just before midnight the phone rang in the trench and I talked to the Frenchman who told me he was disconnecting because they were going to withdraw in ten minutes. I asked him why and he said he thought the Germans had turned the flank. I then woke the OC 'C' Coy, Major Ross and passed the information. We were all told to pack up and prepare to move out. We moved down the hill through the trees and came out on the Tamara road near a steel bridge. Major Ross told me to stay and check the company through into the wadi to the right of the road. The company moved past and the last section of the 3rd platoon said there were soldiers moving about 200 yards behind them and they thought they were Germans. As they disappeared down the wadi two figures appeared at the edge of the woods and I ducked behind a rock and covered them, they kept coming and turned out to be two sappers from the 1st Parachute Field Squadron RE who had been holding an infantry position up in the woods and who had become separated. They went on and as they got down the wadi, a shell or mortar bomb hit the iron girders of the bridge and splattered the area with splinters. My rock did a good job of protecting me. Silence then reigned and, after a while, I decided that no one else was coming and set off down the wadi.

After a mile or so I came around a bend where a shell had landed in the wadi and there was a badly wounded private. I stayed with him for a while and heard tank engines and tracks. I thought it was Germans but looked out and saw it was a Churchill tank from the North Irish Horse. The commander said he would radio for medical help but he was going forward.

I kept going and then looked up to the right and saw a German platoon digging in on the edge of the woods so progress got very slow after that. About sunset I saw two of our lads near a stone wall and joined them, we spent a weary night. I still had the two maps and was anxious to get going so we parted company at dawn and I made by way to a feature called the Pimple, where a rifle company was dug in. Because all movement was restricted during the day I had to wait until dark to get back to BHQ and report to the IO, Lieut Elliot who I heard was later killed doing experimental parachuting at Ringway. He told me he was about to report me KIA but gave me a large mess-tin full of stew which an 18 year old appetite really appreciated after 48 hours on a water-bottle and the tin of emergency chocolate stuff! We then started to get ready for that night attack, which re-took our old positions.

The booby traps; in those days the compo rations contained a circular can of 50 cigarettes, the 36 grenade fitted exactly, we removed the pin, fitted a trip wire and tied it to a tree. We left some by the Sedjenane station before we left and after we retook the hill I returned very carefully and saw where the splinters had marked the trees.

Bill Bloys . . . . *celebrates the New Year and goes to hospital*

IT WAS New Years Eve 1942, Lieut Alexander's platoon consisting of Sgt Johnstone and twelve men had been detailed to take over the road block between the pig farm and the old mine, from Lieut Brayley's platoon. It had been raining continuously for five days, the fox-holes had about six inches of water in them, we settled in, sorted out the compo and had a brew-up and then went on stand-to. There was a good ration of rum to be shared out after stand-to, those that did not drink got their heads down. We went to the weapon pit and had a drink. Lieut Alexander was a good story teller, Thirkettle told a good joke, Alexander brought out a bottle of whisky and then the line shooting started. Alexander said he could shoot down a Very light with a Sten-gun in three bursts. Up went a red, three bursts and down came the flare. Up went a green and Bill Thirkettle brought it down with two bursts. Up went a third and L/Cpl Johnson gave it a full mag, Sgt Johnstone came racing up and put a stop to the entertainment. There were flares going up all over the place and a platoon came to investigate thinking we were being attacked by tanks. (A red Very light is the signal for a tank attack). The next morning we had a visit from Colonel Frost, Major Ashford, RSM Tite, CSM Mac Forsyth and there was hell to pay for our New Years Eve celebration. We were packed off on a four day patrol around Green Hill or Longstop Hill. It was a long patrol, Fishwick wore out his boots and moaned all the way back, so ended another wet patrol. I'll not forget that New Years Eve. Lieut Alexander was severely wounded at Cork Wood and did not come back to the Bn.

Later in the campaign I was sitting wounded in the front of a 16 PFA truck being taken to a field ambulance station from Cork Wood when we were stopped by a patrol of German paras. They looked in the back at our five stretcher cases, gave me a cigarette, saluted and waved us on. Within two days we arrived at number 5 or 67 General Hospital which was full and were put in the POW Ward, Hardy, Bob Fermor, Johnson, two Para engineers and myself. One nurse remarked how red we were, what she did not know was that we had not washed for three weeks. As I was having my blanket bath the red soil of Africa was falling off me and the other nurse said 'you are the filthiest soldiers I have ever seen'.

A German soldier from the Hermann Goering Regiment helping in the ward with the meals, told the Sister in perfect English, that he had fought us from Green Hill to Pont du Fahs, we always had red hands and faces so they called us the Red Devils from Hell, nobody liked fighting us and their Allies also did not. We did not like it there and were moved out and away from our friend Captain Robb, medical Officer of the 1st Bn. I don't know why they thought we were so dirty, I had shared a bath with Jacko of 'A' Coy ten weeks previously!

Len Langley .... *eagle eyed, spots enemy*

OUR GUNNERS had been in action during the night but now in the early morning all was quiet at Cork Wood. A trench in front seemed to be empty so I went to investigate. I carefully moved out keeping watch all round when through the trees I noticed lines of German troops being inspected in the valley. I could not believe my eyes it seemed so unreal. When I reached the forward trench it contained a Royal Artillery Officer and NCO. I explained all I had seen through the gap and suggested he could direct his guns on them, the Officer climbed out of the trench and using his binoculars confirmed my story, the NCO passed instructions back to the gun site by telephone. The first solitary shell came over our heads and found its target, then all hell broke loose as all guns fired. Jerries were thrown about like rag dolls, I returned to my trench with John Harding who later that morning, during the shelling of our positions was badly wounded in a leg, which was eventually amputated. This activity was the beginning of the Cork Wood battle where we used the battle cry 'Waho Mohammed'. Jerry came at us singing 'Farren Gegan Engeland' or some such, but we won through. I am very proud to have served at Tamara fighting German Paras and Grenadiers, it seemed at times that we were fighting the whole German army and airforce.

Jack Beeston .... *mud stops his Sten gun firing*

WE WERE lost, Bixby and me, halfway up a hill with full kit surrounded by gun flashes and explosions, this was supposed to be a quiet area so we got our heads down until first light. We were awakened by shells dropping all around us, we climbed higher trying to find our platoon when we found Sgt Hayhow's platoon watching the enemy coming up the valley in columns towards us, firing. Jenkins and Whitman on the Bren opened up and they both suffered wounds in their legs. Sgt Hayhow told us to make for our own platoon higher up the hill, we did, often crawling in mud and under mortar and machine gun fire.

Still in the prone position I froze when I saw, not eight feet away, a German officer standing on tiptoe peering from out of a clump of cork trees looking for us, if he had looked down he would have looked me straight in the eye. I raised my Sten, pulled the trigger, the bolt slid forward and stopped! A piece of mud had jammed between the bolt and the round. Burton was at my side, I poked him and pointed. Burton raised his rifle and as he fired shouted 'Deutschland Swine'. The German ducked, looked at us and ran off down the hill followed by his troops. That evening I dug in with Ronnie Bixby and two mornings later during stand-to shelling he was killed.

The mention of Fitzpatrick stirs the memory. Early 1943 I was in the same section as Fitzpatrick down in Happy Valley and it was our turn to go on a fighting patrol and capture prisoners. Our objective was a very steep hill with barbed wire stretched out half way up, behind which were machine gun pits and trenches. Fitzy was told to send up flares from his 2in mortar. As he pulled the lever the mortar rose vertically with the flares bursting above our heads. All of us were in perfect daylight whilst the enemy was in total darkness.

We went up the hill in the light, over the wire, captured a few prisoners who were Italians without any loss. All Fitzpatrick would say in his Irish brogue was, 'I didn't join up to fight a war for the English I joined up 'cause the pay is good'.

Fred Stevens . . . . *Known only to God*

IN THE Spring of 1943 after the end of the campaign in North Africa, my mother was asked by the War Graves Commission for her preference of wording on my headstone, she was also offered condolences from the King and Queen on the loss of her son. At about the same time she received a blue card from me saying I was a POW in Italy. It took her six months to convince the authorities that I was still alive.

My story starts with the loss of my helmet at Maison Carree, it had my number, rank and name inside. I reported the loss to CSM Tite who gave me another, I said it had been seen with a junior NCO, the CSM told me to forget it. Then we dropped at Depienne with 'A' Coy and later when I was captured at the Farm House I was taken to the convoy where we met up with Lieut Buchanan who was in charge of the wounded. For the next day or so we were employed loading all the German and Italian dead from the battle area, our own dead were left where they had fallen, some had been stripped naked during the night by the local Arabs, all identification had been removed. One of our comrades was obviously under my name and if any of the men from 'A' Coy know who wore my helmet I should be pleased to hear from them, even after this long time. For I believe whoever was wearing my helmet was killed and is buried 'Known only to God'.

Colonel Otway . . . . *sums up the campaign*

FIRST PARACHUTE Brigade (First, Second and Third Battalions) had completed their three parachute operations and five months operations as infantry with the First Army in North Africa. In the course of the campaign, the brigade captured over 3,500 prisoners of war and must have caused over 5,000 additional enemy casualties. They had fought in every sector of the British front in Tunisia during the course of which they suffered 1,700 casualties. They had more battles than any other formation and in the Tamara valley, in the period 6th March to 14th April, did most of the fighting for 46 Division. In fact, it may be safely said that the brigade bore the brunt of the original operations of First Army.

It is not generally realised that during 1 Parachute Brigade's operations in North Africa they had to contend with frightful weather conditions in some of the grimmest and most forbidding country in the world. Add these factors to a tenacious, brave and well-trained enemy, and the distances involved, and some measure of the great tasks which the brigade accomplished can be realised.

In addition, they had another problem to face. This was the unfriendliness and general unpleasantness of the Tunisian Arabs, who not only looted wounded and dead, but also gave away information to the enemy on many occasions.

112

CHAPTER SIX

Into Europe via Sicily

**The parachute operation was short, sharp, successful
but costly. Colonel TBH Otway DSO gives his resumé.**

THE PLAN of 1 Parachute Brigade was that 1st Parachute Bn
was to capture the Ponte di Primosole itself, while 2nd and 3rd
Parachute Bn's held the approaches from the South and North respectively. It was expected that the leading troops advancing up the main
road, would make contact with 1 Parachute Brigade that morning. One
hundred and thirteen parachute aircraft and 16 gliders with their tugs
left the African mainland for Sicily. The first trouble to be met was
anti-aircraft fire from the Allied Naval Forces, 55 pilots reporting that
they had been fired on when approaching the coast of Sicily.

The final result was that only 39 parachute aircraft dropped their
troops on or within half a mile of their dropping zones, 48 more dropped
them over half-a-mile away and 17 returned to base with some troops
still on board. A further 12 were unable to reach or find their dropping
zones at all. A total of 11 parachute aircraft were shot down. Less than
20 per cent of 1 Parachute Brigade were dropped according to plan and
nearly 30 per cent, through no fault of their own, returned to base
without dropping. Twelve officers and 283 other ranks, out of a total of
1,856 all ranks who left North Africa, were available for the battle for
which they were intended. They only collected 147 out of the 428
parachute containers which started.

In the first phase about 170 all ranks of 2nd Parachute Bn collected at
the Bn rendezvous near their dropping zone by 2240 hrs on 13th July.
At 0215 hrs, having failed to find any more of their men as they were
expected to be in their positions holding the Southern approaches to the
bridge by 0400 hrs, the Bn moved off to its forming up position to attack
the enemy. Soon after 0330 hrs their leading platoon captured their first
objective, and by 0500 hrs the battalion held all the positions allotted to
them and the high ground about 1,300 yards South of the bridge was
firmly in their hands. Enemy opposition had been overcome without
much difficulty but the Bn had no heavy weapons and no wireless sets
for communication with other units.

At 0630 hrs on 14th July, German parachute troops, supported by

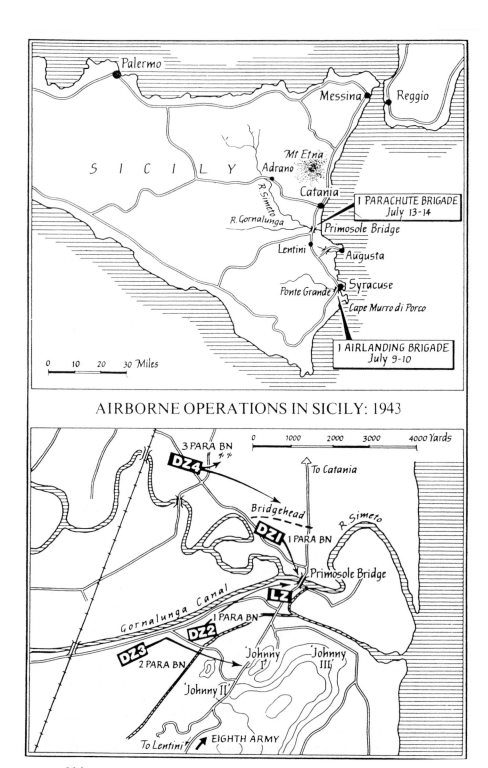

AIRBORNE OPERATIONS IN SICILY: 1943

machine guns and mortars, counter-attacked 2nd Parachute Bn from the West. At 0700 hrs the forward observation officer from 1st Air-Landing Light Regiment RA (Captain V Hodge) arrived and started to open communications with a British 6in. gun cruiser lying off shore in support. By 0900 hrs 2nd Parachute Bn were in difficulties as their light weapons could not reply to the longer range weapons of the enemy and it was very hard to dig cover in the rocky ground. By 1000 hrs, however, the cruiser had opened accurate fire and the enemy, closing in, were forced to withdraw. Light enemy howitzers found in 2Bn Parachute Battalion's position, were also now used against the Germans North of the bridge.

While the battle was being fought at the bridge, the enemy had kept up continuous pressure against 2nd Parachute Bn but without dislodging them. Fighting was hard but the Bn held its own, although it could not spare any reinforcements for the bridge even if they could have got there. They took over 100 Italian prisoners. The shelling by the cruiser in support was a very valuable aid and the forward observation officer was able to direct fire against the enemy attacking the bridge. At 1945 hrs on 14th July, the first tanks of 4 Armoured Brigade arrived in 2nd Parachute Bn's area and at 2350 hrs more tanks and the infantry arrived. One company of 9th Bn, Durham Light Infantry joined 2nd Parachute Bn in their position.

An abridged copy of document WO 169 10344 PRO Kew

WAR DIARY of the 2nd Bn THE PARACHUTE REGIMENT Commanding Officer Lieutenant Colonel JD Frost, DSO, MC.

13 July 1943 . . . . *Summary of Events* . . . .

2000 hrs   Block 10 takes off from Airfield at Sousse, North Africa. The route taken was from base airfields to Malta thence 10 miles East of Cap Passero on the South East tip of Sicily, thence Northward to a point 10 miles East of the North of the River Simeto, thence inland to dropping zones six miles South of Catania.

2215 hrs   It would be quite impossible to give in normal War Diary form the complete account of the action fought by the Bn during the early hours and throughout the day of 14th July. So many men were dropped miles from their objectives, resulting in small isolated engagements carried out for the most part with great initiative, that it would be impossible to put these many stories into a comprehensive whole. In the main they are stories of attempts to join up with the main body, carried out by small groups of men intent on inflicting as much damage and disorganisation to the enemy in the meantime as possible.

Accounts of these actions told, where possible, by the stick commanders concerned, or where they did not return, by other members of the stick who were more fortunate, are attached. The main account of the battle is as follows.

'A' Coy and two planes from Bn HQ were dropped between 2215 hrs and 2230 hrs with extreme accuracy on the correct dropping zone. Of the two 'S' Coy planes in this leading wave one was forced to return to base after being badly shot up by AA fire and was unable to make sufficient height to drop its stick, while the second stick dropped on the extreme West end of the dropping zone. The leading planes got in without much flak opposition, but those which came in later experienced fairly extensive AA fire. The whole block dropped slightly before scheduled time due to a favourable wind.

2245 hrs Bn HQ moved forward from their dropping area to the Bn CP at the road junction 913665 and on the way made contact with about 50 men from 'A' Coy under their Coy Commander. At this time the enemy were sending up a considerable number of flares and firing heavily at aircraft coming across the dropping zone in what seemed to be a variety of directions at once. Very few of these planes dropped their sticks and as was subsequently found out many missed the dropping zone and eventually dropped their loads well out to the North and North-West. Bn HQ and 'A' Coy remained where they were for some 30 minutes in the hope of collecting stragglers.

2315 hrs 'A' Coy and Bn HQ moved to the Bn CP arriving there at about midnight. The dropping zone area was burning in many places where incendiary bullets had set it alight but in spite of this the enemy failed completely to put any effective fire down, such as he did being spasmodic and extremely ineffective.

14 July 1943 . . . . *Summary of Events* . . . .

0015 hrs The party at the CP waited in the hope of collecting more men together and were in fact joined by two sticks from 'C' Coy and various bits and pieces from other sticks.

0100 hrs A check taken at this stage gave a total of 112 all ranks at the CP. During this stage there was no contact with Brigade HQ or with any other of the Bns due to the fact that our 22 set dropped on the dropping zone was out of action.

0200 hrs Since it appeared that no further men were likely to join up, the force moved towards the FOP at 936665 without encountering any resistance. The enemy were firing shrapnel bursts over the dropping zone and firing desultory machine gun fire without effect. The CO who had injured his leg on dropping was walking with great difficulty.

0215 hrs A proportion of the Brigade Defence platoon was encountered moving back towards the dropping zone in search of an 18R/T

116

Set. They gave the information that the Brigade Commander and the Brigade Major were some way on. The CO accordingly made contact with him and it was decided to attack 'Johnny I' with the force at our disposal.

0300 hrs Force crossed the Bridge at 936668 pausing to pull down telephone wires which ran up to the enemy position. On proceeding it was found that the pillbox at 935666 was unoccupied, pushing on again the force moved East along the road running from road junction 936665 and then turned South across country towards the North Eastern slopes of 'Johnny I'.

0315 hrs Meanwhile an engagement began to take place unknown to the CO or any of the main body which was to be the decisive feature of the night's work. Proportions of three sticks each under command of an Officer, two from 'A' Coy and one from 'B' Coy had dropped on the dropping zone and failed to contact the main body. One of the three sticks had been very actively engaged in dealing with both German and Italian positions on the Southern edge of the dropping zone. At about 0230 hrs they joined up after searching without success for the rest of the Bn. Being vague as to the situation they formed a composite force totalling 3 officers and 25 other ranks and decided to attack 'Johnny 1' by themselves. Although they had no definite confirmation of enemy positions on the feature, they had captured a DR on the track leading up to it and this led them to believe that the enemy were there. Accordingly at about 0315 hrs this force moved South up the track to a position North-East of 'Johnny I' at 936664 From this position a sweep was put in, one section moving round the North of the feature, one round the Eastern edge, while the third under the command OC Force moved up the North-East slope. The section moving round the North met no opposition but captured several Italians hiding in caves, they then pushed forward to the summit looking West into the valley. The other two sections met with slight light machine gun fire which was soon silenced and with the aid of a few grenades succeeded in extracting 40 Italian prisoners from the caves about half way up the hill. They again pushed further up, again silencing light machine gun fire, and the left hand section captured a further 80 prisoners.

0400 They again encountered light fire from the South-East corner of the feature but by the time they got there the enemy had disappeared. There was also some ineffective fire from 'Johnny II'. Thus finding themselves in possession of Johnny 1 and about 130 prisoners. Accordingly OC Force put out two sections in the olive groves at 632655 to cover the Southern approaches, and sent the remaining section back to the Bn FOP to pick up the prisoners who had been dropped off and to collect water. One Officer had already been sent back to try and contact the CO and tell him the situation.

Meanwhile to return to the main force. At about 0315 hrs the CO had sent 'A' Coy about 50 strong to occupy 'Johnny I' unaware of the operation described above. 'A' Coy reached the summit at 0400 hrs finding the crest, or so it seemed in the darkness, to be completely unoccupied, a little unaimed rifle fire was coming from 'Johnny II' and an occasional shot could be heard but nothing else.

0430 hrs By this time the main force consisting of Bn HQ and elements from 'S' and 'C' Coys had reached a position at the North-Eastern base of the feature. The CO was by this time in great pain owing to his damaged leg, he sent a part of Bn HQ and the remainder of the force onto the hill to contact 'A' Coy and to take up defensive positions. This force reached the summit just as dawn was breaking meeting no opposition, and some 15 minutes later contacted OC. 'A' Coy who had by this time discovered the real situation.

0500 hrs Accordingly a reconnaissance was made with a view to taking up defensive positions. Meanwhile the prisoner situation was becoming out of hand, prisoners appearing from all directions at once including naval and air force personnel. At the Northern summit of the hill (934659) was a farm house surrounded by huts which had been used as a barracks by the enemy. This farm has a 'large yard' surrounded by high rock on the West and huts on the East; this was used as a PW cage, and the house itself which overlooked the main bridge as an HQ and also an OP.

0530 hrs A perimeter defence was taken up with the troops at our disposal which now totalled about 140 men roughly half of them from 'A' Coy. To begin with the disposition took the form of a close perimeter on the high ground round the farm house which had already been wired and a few trenches dug by the Italians. Three positions dominated the plain to the North and the valley to the East and West. To the South there was a limited field of fire of about 200yds, through the olive groves outside the perimeter a platoon from 'A' Coy was pushed forward to the Southern end of the grove to watch the valley and the road to the South. Orders were given to dig in as fast as possible. One German recce plane flew very low over the positions.

0545 hrs Passive air defence was adopted. A few minutes later 4 Messerschmitts crossed the area without taking any action.

0600 hrs The position came under heavy machine gun fire from 'Johnny IV' and also from the area of a farm house some 200 yds to the South-East.

0630 hrs Positions still under fire which is now reinforced with mortar fire. Owing to the fact that none of the Bn heavy weapons – MMGs and 3in. mortars were available it was quite out of the question to take any counter action against this, since it was not within the range of our Brens and we were anxious to conserve all possible ammunition. All through the morning we were to feel the need of these weapons which had they been available would have saved us many casualties.

0700 hrs Enemy fire especially mortars becoming more accurate. Casualties beginning to occur amongst the forward Coy in the grove which never had a proper chance to dig in.

0730 hrs A patrol from 'C' Coy is sent out to try and knock out the German machine gun positions located about 200yds South-East. They were heavily engaged by the enemy long before reaching it and are shot up by three armoured cars suffering casualties.

0800 hrs Forward troops are withdrawn inside the perimeter. At this time it became apparent that we were under machine gun fire from three sides and the enemy were closing in on us, not in very great strength but with heavy fire power and considerable skill. A great deal of sniping had taken place on both sides. At about this time a German MG34 crew was shot up and the MG brought in along with two prisoners, one badly wounded. It was then that we learned definitely that we were opposed by troops of the 4th German Parachute Regiment who had dropped two days before on our dropping zone. Meanwhile the Naval FOO was trying desperately to get in touch with his ship but without success.

0830 hrs Situation becoming rather serious. We were suffering casualties fairly regularly and the enemy fire was increasing in accuracy. There was no doubt that the position could be held indefinitely and if the enemy chose to assault we could inflict heavy casualties. The main danger was that our force originally 140 strong would dwindle under prolonged fire and our ammunition was extremely limited. Four ME109s crossed the position and proceeded to machine gun our forces on the bridge.

0900 hrs Naval FOO makes contact with cruiser and brings down fire at about (932654). The morale effect of hearing those shells coming over was tremendous; the fire was lifted steadily back for pockets of enemy well concealed were engaging us with MG 34 and Schmeisser fire from a range of about 400 yards. Finally at about 0930 hrs three rounds of gun fire landed with 150 yards of our position, one shell landing about 30 yards from the POW cage, wounding some 2 or 3 prisoners and throwing the remainder into a state of hysteria for about five minutes.

1000 hrs Decrease in enemy fire. It appeared that the Naval shell fire had forced the enemy to withdraw from their nearest positions. A considerable amount of MG 34 fire was still being laid down on the positions, and snipers were active, one in particular firing accurately and with considerable zest.

1030 hrs Enemy machine gun positions on 'Johnny IV' shelled by naval fire. These targets were not however suitable for a shoot of this kind and were never silenced though they changed their position from time to time. Meanwhile artillery fire could be heard several miles away to the South and it was apparent that no relief could be expected from the 8th Army for several hours to come.

1100 hrs   One enemy howitzer abandoned and in working condition was found in the valley between 'Johnny I' and 'II' with plenty of ammunition. Several men of 'S' Coy with gun experience set to work to move the gun into a position from where it could be fired and to charge the ammunition. The fact that this gun was eventually used was due to the initiative of OC 'S' Coy to whom the idea was due and who took a large part in the preparation and in directing the fire. No sights could be found that day but 15 shells were eventually fired onto enemy positions in the areas of 'Johnny III' and 'IV'.

1200 hrs   Situation easier. Sniping and machine gun fire still continuing but a general lessening in tension was apparent.

1300 hrs   Little activity in the Bn sector. Enemy guns on the Catania plain started shooting shrapnel bursts onto 'Johnny II' which was unoccupied.

1500 hrs   Fire from Naval guns brought down on enemy battery position West of Catania which had commenced shelling the 1st and 3rd Bns on the bridge; their OP was set alight and a few minutes later all their Ammo blew up. The battery did not fire again. A further battery more to the West was also shelled and though it was never silenced it was forced to change positions regularly.

1600 hrs   Enemy troops and transport in the farm at 924660 was shelled. These had been observed during the afternoon but were just out of range of infantry weapons.

1700 hrs   Troops on the bridge seen to be strongly engaged by enemy artillery.

1800 hrs   CO is able to move up to Bn HQ bringing with him the news that the force on the bridge had been obliged to withdraw. About 15 men from 3rd Parachute Bn joined us on 'Johhny I'. Situation on 'Johhny I' fairly quiet.

1930 hrs   Sicilian farmer informs us that German armoured car is approaching from the South: as several high velocity shells had landed only a few minutes before this seemed fairly probable and a patrol was organised to deal with this. However before the patrol set out AFVs appeared in the olive grove. It was a Sherman tank, the leading elements of the 8th Army.

1945 hrs   The IO was sent back to contact the OC tank force and also the CO of the leading infantry – the DLI. When contacted they were originally intending to take up positions some two miles South of 'Johnny I' and had received orders that they were to attack the bridge at dawn the next morning with heavy artillery support. They agreed however to send one Coy forward to support us on the high ground.

2340 hrs   One Coy of DLI reinforce the Bn on the high ground.

0600   Two Bn's of DLI with artillery, machine gun and tank support make a determined effort to retake the bridge but without success. The bridge though slightly damaged by shell fire was still intact owing to the fact that Sappers of the 1st Parachute Squadron, RE had removed all charges prior to withdrawing.

1100 hrs   OC 'B' Coy with about 8 men rejoin the Bn after having made their way from the lower slopes of Mt Etna.

1130 hrs   A further 20 rounds were fired from the captured Italian howitzer at targets between the bridge and Catania. The enemy honoured this gesture by putting down CB fire in the valley where the gun was. After all ammo had been fired the gun was left to its fate.

1300 hrs   The afternoon passed without incident. Artillery exchanges took place most of the time. During the afternoon various stragglers joined the Bn.

2300 hrs   The Bn, DLI and a Coy of MMGs, move into position in the area preparatory to a night attack on the bridge.

2400 hrs   Very heavy artillery and machine gun barrage commences on enemy positions lasting until 0200 hrs.

0200 hrs   Bn DLI attack the bridge.

0300 hrs   Bridge once again in our hands.

0630 hrs   Bn Moves out of positions which had been handed over to the DLI during the night and move about three miles South down the Syracuse road.

1000 hrs   Tpt collects the Bn and transports it to Syracuse via Lentini and Augusta. Two trucks meet General Montgomery en route who stopped and congratulated them, offering packets of cigarettes all round. During the action the Bn lost two Officers – Lieut MG Dunkeld and Lieut JC Horner killed – and 14 other ranks killed. 33 ORs wounded, 9 Officers and 129 ORs missing. Of the missing many turned up over a matter of days and weeks including 4 of the 9 officers. The reason for this large number can be seen at a glance by reading the airtables and seeing where the majority of the Bn dropped.

A total of 460 Italian and 2 German prisoners passed through the Bn POW cage.

We now know there were 23 OR's killed on this operation as well as Lieut Horner and Lieut Dunkeld. Major Lane, Major Mountford, Major Ross, Lieut Tite and Lieut Pye were taken prisoner.

Lieut Col JD Frost DSO MC remained in command and Major JA Fitch became second in command.

121

Peter Barry .... *tells how he volunteered and arrived in Sicily*

During the Winter of 1942-43 I was a subaltern in the 1st Battalion The Royal Ulster Rifles, stationed on Salisbury Plain at Bulford Field Camp. The Battalion was part of the Brigade of airborne forces which were glider borne.

In February 1943 reinforcement volunteers were needed for the 1st Parachute Brigade in North Africa. John Horner, Dan Woods and myself, known as Peter Barry (aged 19), were drawn out of the hat to go. For two weeks, along with sixty other ranks, we did intensive physical training, doubling everywhere, lifting logs up and down, swinging on parallel bars until every muscle could strain no longer.

Next we proceeded to Ringway, the training centre for parachuting. We learnt to land on feet close together and roll over on the ground in a continuous movement. Fortunately although I am 6ft. 4in. tall my experience of rugby on the playing fields of Ampleforth had conditioned natural reflexes when falling. We also trained "Exit Drill" slipping through a deep circular hole with full equipment from a sitting position. One had to straighten into a vertical ramrod attention-like position pushing foward just sufficiently for the back parachute to be clear, but not too far to bang your head on the opposite side known as "Ringing the Bell".

We ascended over Tatham Park to the eerie sounds of a swaying balloon cage. As the cage tilted sideways I gripped the rail and wondered whether I was cut out for this experience. I began to realise there was only one way down to earth.

The Instructor took no notice until we were stationary then he ordered Action Stations No. 1. No. 1 swung both legs into the exit, sitting bolt upright. "Go" the Instructor shouted. Seven hundred feet below the birds eye view of the woods and fields of Tatham Park was uninviting. Action Stations No. 2 – "Go". Who was I to argue. I closed both eyes and was gone. I felt a pull as the chute opened and the world was before me. I reached upwards to grasp the harness straps. I bent my knees and for a few seconds enjoyed the swing. A loud speaker on the ground was shouting instructions. Then the ground looms nearer, your heels touch down and you roll over into reality and exhilaration.

We had a short course of four balloon and three Wellington aircraft parachute jumps. For some reason, probably the deafening roar of the engines, it was less of an ordeal jumping out of aircraft. Sitting on the floor and shuffling along to get to the exit was awkward but occupied ones mind.

We had a weeks embarkation leave with instructions to tell no one, then off we went down the Clyde, steaming along in a troopship out into the Atlantic.

It was an emotional farewell to Blighty with the Clyde banks lined by dockers and groups of folk cheering and waving us good luck. We waved back until we were out of sight. We joined a convoy escorted by The Royal Navy, sailing far out into the Atlantic. We had daily U-Boat drill and were very cramped being six in a small cabin. The food was very good and we passed the time playing cards. The voyage lasted about twelve days until we disembarked in Algiers. We poisoned ourselves with Algerian wine and burnt our feet on the sands bathing before we endured an eighteen hour slow train ride to the Mascara area, miles from anywhere.

We were interviewed in a tent by Brigadier Gerald Lathbury, commanding the 1st Parachute Brigade. He was a tall, elegant, clean faced, cultured man. He welcomed us and I was assigned to the 2nd Parachute Battalion. The Mascara area was a vast expanse of open uncultivated land. The ground was dry and a brownish red dust cloud followed our truck.

2nd Parachute Battalion was grouped in tents around a slight rise in the landscape. The Colonel's tent was isolated near the summit, and the Companies were spread out in a semicircle fifty yards down the slope. H.Q. – A-B-C- Companies, then the officers mess. We slept in sleeping bags on the ground in small tents for two. Each Company had one large tent for administration.

A water wagon came daily amid a dust cloud. The officers mess was a rectangular tent with trestle tables and plagued by a mass of flies. The hot sun shone every day and at night the stars could be used to set our compasses for guidance across the desert.

We were interviewed by Colonel John Frost. He was quiet spoken and reserved. He assigned me to H.Q. Company but I was not going to be separated from the men I had trained with from the R.U.R. who were infantry men. I asked for another interview. John Frost listened to me and my reasons which he obviously understood and liked. So I was placed in command of 9 Platoon C Company alongside those I had trained with.

Major John Ross was the Company Commander. He was hero worshipped by all for his personal coolness and bravery in the North African campaign. He looked young and understanding. I can still remember during a break from training waking up on the beach at Mostaganem after a blinder and John Ross was putting a piece of melon into my mouth.

Until July 1943 we trained daily. We rehearsed as a Battalion and then a Brigade drop by moonlight over ground, very similar to that planned for us in Sicily. We learnt to jump with our weapons strapped to one leg and lowered to the ground by a cord released before landing. American Dakota pilots flew us to our drop zone. It was much easier to walk out of the tail door than shuffling through a hole in the floor. After the night drops we captured our objectives and then had a long march back to the camp in the heat of the day. John Frost took the salute as we reached the camp and congratulated us. The operations went like clockwork and we were ready.

At the beginning of July 1943 we flew to the Sousse area near the air fields of Kairouan where we were concealed in olive groves. We suspended our tents from the olive trees and slept on the ground in camouflaged sleeping bags.

On the 8th July 1943 General Montgomery arrived to inspect the Battalion, which was formed in a square. Monty stood in the back of a jeep wearing a parachute badge in his beret, in shirt sleeve order and carrying a baton swish. "Come round" was the order. The whole Battalion broke ranks and stampeded to circle the great man. He was a Master of the Art of leadership. He enchanted everyone with a few brief words.

"My word (cheers) you look fit (cheers). You are a very fine Battalion. Shortly you are going into battle, I give you two words (pause) kill Italians (pause). Just two words (pause) kill Italians. I have the greatest confidence in you and your Commanders. Three cheers for Monty. The cheers resounded over the desert. The cavalcade drove off to the next Battalion for a similar performance.

Personally I had a great admiration for Monty, but I was a bit nonplussed about killing Ities. They are not a warlike nation, quite different to the Germans.

On the 12th July 1943 we set off to the airfield prepared to fly to Sicily. Our drop zone was south of the River Simeto, six miles south of Catania and close to the Primosole Bridge. Our Battalion objective was the high ground commanding the road bridge and the Catanian plain, on hills code named Johnny One, Two and Three. The first Battalion was to capture the Primosole bridge.

We arrived at our Dakota, got our chutes on and ready to go when word came the operation was off. However, the next day it was on again, this time we were airborne. As dusk came we flew low over the calm sea. The moonlight reflected on the water, which I could see through the open doorway, as being No. 1 in the stick I was almost opposite and facing the doorway. The pilot was neatly dressed and experienced in commercial flying. With our chutes on we were heavily laden and it was an effort to move.

I carried a Bren gun strapped to my right leg as I had the easiest exit. Each of us had a haversack with rations, ammunition, grenades, a water bottle and an entrenching tool. We flew over Malta and on for a long time when suddenly there was gunfire. The pilot veered sharply off course and revved up.

We could hear shot striking the fuselage. After a few minutes we were still flying and out of range. Later we heard that it was our Royal Navy taking defensive action against us. Most of the aircraft split up and lost course. Some flew back to Tunisia. Unaware we flew on. The navigator came and told me we were in sight of land. I ordered the stick to stand ready. I stood by the door as we crossed the coast line, very close to the ground. The red light came on. I recognised the panorama I had been briefed on. The whole area was alight with burning crop stacks and tracer being fired wildly in all directions.

As we crossed the road the aircraft lifted and on went the green light. My chute opened very close to the ground. I reached down to release the Bren gun but at that moment I struck the ground. The padding of the Bren gun broke my fall and I was thankfully unhurt. I signalled to my stick with my rubber torch.

Slowly one by one they appeared. We struck off towards the road and on the way met Malcolm Dunkeld. Together we went to the Battalion collecting point. It appeared that only twenty of us out of the Company had arrived. Going across the drop zone we had seen containers which were German. Later we heard that German Paratroopers had used the same drop zone, sent in to harden the Italian Resistance. Fortunately they had headed southwards and so were trapped between us and our ground forces.

Fresh plans were made and we were ordered to take the eastern side of the diamond shaped feature, known as Johhny One. As we advanced in the half light the Italians came streaming out wanting to surrender, amid much chatter and wavings. It was a short lived anticlimax. My section was put on the southern side of the eastern side of the diamond crest and we started to hack at the hillside to make cover. The ground was rock hard and we could only scrape a few inches from the surface. At this point some ominous groups of Germans appeared on the horizon south of our position. Then bursts of machine gun fire started to come our way from about 1,000 yards. Our position was very exposed and they were out of range. I reported this to Malcolm Dunkeld, who was on the reverse slope, and offered to take out a patrol along the lower slope to our east from where I could reach a point above an olive grove to shoot them up.

Malcolm referred to Head Quarters in a big square recess in the centre of the northern slope. Permission granted I was on my way with Henderson and Cochrane, two brave Irishmen armed with a Bren gun, rifle, and myself with a Sten gun. We quickly went down the slope across the valley, the bend in the valley concealing us from the machine gunners. We crossed a deep dry crevice-like wadi and came to the olive groves. I was looking for a way to reach higher ground when the Germans launched their attack on foot.

They were obviously trapped and needed to take Johnny One to escape. I ordered Henderson to fire on the infantry by the roadside. We then saw an armoured car. Henderson did good work but then bullets started to spurt all round us. I took over the Bren gun and told Henderson and Cochrane to get back to the wadi.

After they had left I saw a section of Germans in a group about 50 yards or less to my left. I emptied the Bren Gun at them. The whole group went down as one. Amid a rain of bullets from the armoured car I retreated back to the wadi. Henderson and Cochrane had gone on and I heard shouts as first one then the other was hit. I ran on zig-zagging at top speed. I was grazed in five different areas but bore a charmed life as I reached a rounded stone on the slope. I lay down and peered over. I felt a bullet pierce the front top of my helmet, being deflected it grazed my left cheek. I looked round and saw a small inlet cut in the face of the slope. I dived in and lay there looking at the sky. My face was bleeding and I was breathless. My boyhood days floated before me and I prayed to God. After about a minute there was a lull. All the firing stopped. I got up and ran across the valley to where I had started from. I was greeted by Sergeant Cowie. Malcolm Dunkeld and Sergeant Norris had been killed. We were withdrawn back into the central dug out to take up safer positions. The German attack had failed.

I reported the position of the German armoured car to Capt. Hodge who directed naval gunfire onto it. We stood by all day with a commanding view of the road and bridge. At 6pm the first Sherman tank arrived over our parapet firing a resounding shot, but fortunately they knew we were there. That night I led a patrol out round the eastern slope. Malcolm Dunkeld's face shone in the moonlight like an angel. Sergeant Norris appeared as if he had been in hand to hand combat.

The next day I found a German NCO lying dead within a few yards of the inlet I was in. His right arm was outstretched above his head and in his hand was a grenade. Who killed him I do not know, but whoever did saved my life. In going for me he was an obvious target. We watched the Durham Light Infantry advance to the River Simeto. We then had a long journey back to Syracuse, Tripoli and across the desert to Sousse.

Back at base the story unfurled. John Ross had been dropped in the Mount Etna region and was taken prisoner. John Horner was killed by one of our Spitfires. My Platoon Sergeant's stick had flown home after the encounter with the Royal Navy.

We swallowed our Mepacrine malarial tablets and prepared for the Italian campaign.

In retrospect operation "Fustain" had been well planned and practised. The encounter with The Royal Navy was the flaw that caused the chaos. The few from the second Battalion who arrived in the right place achieved their objective.

The small patrol that I led played a significant part in defeating the German counter assault. At the onset our surprise attack from the flank, though not our original intention, inflicted casualties. It also caused a diversion and confusion to the Germans by the necessity of dealing with the patrol As a providential survivor I would like to pay tribute to my comrades for the part they played.

Len Langley .... *repatriated in 1944, unfit for further service*

I WAS unaware my right foot had been hit by three bullets when dropping into Sicily, near Catania at approximately 2300 hrs, on the 13th July 1943 I soon found out when I landed that I had been hit. The following day I was taken prisoner by German paratroopers and moved by truck and then ship to the Italian Military Hospital in Lucca 202km North of Pisa.

When the Italians capitulated, the Germans took over and we were all moved by train to Lamsdorf Stalag 8B, later to be called 344E. Lieut Col Wilson operated twice on my leg and also arranged for me to go before the Repatriation Board. On 24th April 1944 I received my pass to return home.

I was moved to Stalag 4D where all repatriated troops were collected. I travelled by train and ferry to Gothenberg, Sweden, where we were given a fantastic welcome, together with plenty of fresh food, which unfortunately made most of us ill. It was a year or so before I could eat well again. By ship to Liverpool and then on to Richmond Park, Surrey, where I had served with the East Surreys. After showers, medical examination, clothing, passes and money, everything required for home leave, I was taken by car to meet my family. They were all at home, a telegram had informed them of my home coming.

Seaborne landings at Taranto, Italy

THE FIRST part of August 1943 was spent by companies in turn at a Divisional rest camp by the sea South of Tunis. On 6th September Company Commanders were briefed by the Commanding Officer to the effect that the Battalion was to undertake a seaborne operation in Italy in a week's time. 1st Brigade was to follow in after the 2nd and 4th Parachute Brigades respectively. Later in the day it was learned that the landing place was to be Taranto, the Italian naval base.

The next few days were occupied in preparation. On the evening of the 8th news of the Italian Armistice was heard over the wireless.

On 9th September, the Battalion embussed for Bizerta and after thirty-six hours' rest in a staging camp, embarked on the afternoon of the 11th in the *Royal Ulsterman*, sailing later that night.

During the voyage the Battalion's destination was announced to all ranks by the Commanding Officer and further briefing carried out. The actual role of the Battalion after landing would not be known until after arrival there.

At 1700 hrs on 13th September landings in assault craft carried by the *Royal Ulsterman* began. They were uneventful apart from a slow disappearance below water of an ancient barge laden with a good proportion of the Battalion's kit-bags!

Capt Dr RR Gordon RAMC,
Bn MO Africa
POW Arnhem

Capt Dr JW Logan
RAMC, Bn MO Arnhem
POW Arnhem.

Capt Rev B Egan
Chaplain
POW Arnhem

Barletta, Italy, November 1943. L to R standing: Sgt Le Maitre MMG pl, CSM J Bishop, Lt Dan Woods Mortar pl, died of wounds in Germany after Arnhem and his pl Sgt Jackman, Lt RH Levien Assault pl. Sitting: Lt J Monsell MMG pl and Sgt Leslie A-T pl.

128

By 0300 hrs on the 14th the Battalion had settled down in an area two miles North-West of Taranto harbour. The next five days were occupied in taking up and perfecting a very strong defensive position facing West in this area, in the event of a South-Easterly thrust by the enemy.

On 20th September orders were received to move twenty miles North to a village called Castellanetta, the Brigade taking over in this area from the 4th Brigade, 2nd Brigade being still farther forward in contact with the retreating enemy. One company was sent out to the Northwards to try and contact the Germans, but without success.

On the 22nd, it was learned that the Germans had evacuated Altamura, a town approximately twenty miles due North. Orders were received for the Battalion to move there at once. The remainder of the month was spent at Altamura, units of Eighth Army now passing through and carrying on the offensive. The Battalion now reverted to normal training.

At this time, Lieut. Buchanan and Sgt Laughland rejoined the Battalion having escaped from a prison camp. Both had been captured at Depienne.

The remainder of the month was spent in normal training including field firing, on 26th October the Battalion moved to Barletta, a port on the Adriatic coast. A few days later instructions were received for a dummy landing in infantry landing craft farther up the coast. All preparations were made, including practice embarkations and disembarkations, to give the impression that the operation would actually take place. At this stage Major AD Tatham Warter arrived from England and took over 'A' Company from Major Lonsdale, DSO MC.

Further practices including a Brigade landing exercise, took place in infantry landing craft but the operation was postponed.

John Timothy . . . . *hunts for our escaped prisoners*

AFTER THE Italian armistice of September 1943 many of the Allied POW's left their camps to escape into the country. Others stayed in their camps to await release by the advancing Allied troops. Unfortunately German troops entered quickly into these camps and took over. At all events there were many Allied POW's roaming the countryside and various schemes were tried to help these troops to our lines.

In the 2nd Bn, I was told to select eight OR's from volunteers selected by their Coy Commanders. Similar parties were being formed from the 1st and 3rd Bns. Parties were to operate in separate areas.

The tenth man in my stick was an American who had been born in the area we were to operate in. He had never parachuted before. Our job was to contact escaped POW's and send them back to a rendezvous which would be manned by the SAS.

We were briefed in Bari and I arranged we should have two RV's, the first on the dropping zone and the second in the event of trouble further away. We all had maps and escape money.

We took off from Bari aerodrome on 2nd October in an Albermarle, a new aircraft to us and were dropped at dusk but some 30 miles North of the planned dropping zone. I dropped number 10 in order to see the stick out but landed in trees and by the time I had got down the others had moved off as local Italians were gathering. From these Italians I gathered we were adrift and I spent the rest of the night looking for the stick, of course the RV did not apply since we had been dropped off course.

Next day I moved down to our operating area hoping to meet the others there but without luck.

For a fortnight I contacted farms and found prisoners of war hiding up and through them I found more soldiers. These I directed to beach RV's where they would be looked after by the SAS.

Morale among the POW's was not always high, some had been in the bag for some time. I remember meeting some who would not believe there was such a thing as a British paratrooper. It did not help matters when as a test I was asked when the Crystal Palace was burnt down and I answered, 'early in the war'.

I remember going to one place where I was told I had better be careful because a Captain Timothy doing the same job had been shot. I was fortunate for they were playing cribbage which I have played and was able to convince them it most unlikely a German could play cribbage.

Then I was lucky in meeting up with Sgt Smith a POW ex 2 Para. We joined forces and the fact that Sgt Smith was himself a POW was a great help in convincing others.

After a month we reached our beachhead RV (Porto Civitanova?) and found a party of about 500 assembled nearby and looked after by ten men of the SAS. That night we moved them forward to an area just behind the RV and at the pre arranged time signalled by torch out to sea. After a time contact was made with the navy and the boats were coming in but shooting broke out along the coast road behind us. Apparently some of the POW's had tried to break into a farmhouse and the farmer had opened up with a shotgun. This attracted German motor patrols and there was more firing. The SAS were only ten men and our POW's scattered.

We tried to find as many as we could but all we got back to Termoli were about 45 men. Two of the original party shortly rejoined the Battalion. Sgt Power used his map and escape money to get to the coast and hire a boat while Private Cook worked his way through the German lines to rejoin the Bn. He was awarded the Military Medal. Sgt Smith returned with me.

We know that Fred Martin was reported missing on 28 January 1944, how he died we do not know, he is named on the Cassino Memorial for those with No Known Grave. Bill Hall and Bob Leigh were subsequently taken prisoner. The fate of the others is unknown.

John Measures .... *with Freedom in sight*

Captain John Measures was captured at Depienne in December 1942 and in September 1943 when the Italian prison camp guards deserted, everyone in the camp moved out to look for the Allied Army that had invaded Italy.

When John died, his widow Ann showed me the story of his escape carefully typed on 120 pages of foolscap paper. I reproduce a very abridged version for your enjoyment. It is interesting to note that his original escape party included Pat Playford and Pat Callaghan both from the Second battalion.

INTRODUCTION: We made it a principle always to avoid villages or passes of any size, particularly those near traffic routes and in the plains or in valleys, to go out of our way to avoid the places known as communes because we knew that each contained a Fascist HQ and not to band together with other parties. A large group of travellers was obviously suspicious and also led to difficulties over finding a billet at night. We avoided popular routes or RV's which we knew were being used by other British or Allied fugitives. We resisted temptation to stop and rest in any particular spot for more than 48 hours, in case local gossip should give our presence away to the Fascists. We made a principle of passing for Italians as much as possible, and when necessary, Mac let me do the talking, since his Italian was not too good, and we nearly always succeeded in these efforts. For billets, we always tried to choose isolated farms, or those on the outskirts of villages. We always enquired whether there were any Germans of Fascists in the vicinity. Usually we preferred asking for help or information from the women folk, or old men. Children were sometimes most helpful.

We carried our washing kit, spare socks etc., and odd items of food in sacks over our backs. After the first twelve days, we marched by day, and wore civilian clothes, having found out the attitude of the civilian population towards us. Before this, we had marched by night, and lain up by day in the woods. We had one small button compass, which served us extraordinarily well.

The only item we really needed was a pair of boots apiece, leather and all clothing materials were so terribly short in the whole of Italy. The Italian people themselves, or rather those of the peasant class, amongst whom we moved, we found uniformly helpful and kind. Once or twice only did we meet with downright refusals of help, but we found their reliability especially in the matter of direction giving, left much to be desired. They were mostly uneducated, very simple minded and had a child-like faith in things, accepting circumstances as being the direct outcome of fate. They respect the English, hate the Boche, fear the Russians, and find the Yanks rather distasteful –

because of their bombing raids. Our main source of news was of course, the BBC and we more often than not found a place with a wireless set either on the premises or somewhere near. It was extremely pleasant to hear an English voice, and to listen to Big Ben occasionally. We usually slept like logs at night-time, apart from the rare occasions when we were visited by various animals and insects. We managed to keep fairly clean on the whole, in spite of having only two or three baths during the twelve weeks, and in spite of the almost total absence of hot water in any quantity. The Italian peasants never encouraged washing, anyway.

Finally, I should mention that at every house we stayed at for the night, we left a slip of paper addressed to the Allied Area Commander (when he should arrive), asking for the family concerned to be compensated for the help they had given us. We were invariably asked to leave our own names and addresses as well, and one cannot help wondering whether one will ever hear anything of or from these friendly households after the war. Their kindness, and the certain risk involved in assisting us, could only be appreciated fully by those, like ourselves, who were personally concerned; and by those who were eye-witnesses of the severity of the German reprisals taken against any Italian they caught or suspected of giving help to fugitive prisoners of war.

John's Diary starts on the **9th September 1943**. The Italians have capitulated and Camp 49 have opened the gates for the inmates to leave if they wish. At 1250 hrs a British bugler sounds the Fall in and the prisoners march out in column of threes, three companies of 150 each. They were marching to rejoin their Army units via the South of Italy. By 2000 hrs the companies had moved in different directions. Two days later they split into platoon strength and the following day came down to section numbers. John shared his tin of Spam and records that it was quite cold during the night. It is a fascinating story of hardship, determination and courage when twelve weeks later he writes with thoughts of freedom on the morrow.

25th November 1943 It continued to snow, hail and sleet during the night and a heavy thunderstorm, of all things, broke on us. Our breakfast consisted of a piece of bread each; lunch, the other half chicken and some bread. In the middle of the snowstorm we ran into a party of Italian refugees who told us that the Germans had finally evacuated, that they themselves had met a British patrol there last night. They said that the Germans were on our side of the river only and not on the other, and thought that if we could negotiate the river, which was in flood, we should be all right.

Numerous shell-holes, though, told us that our gunners had the range of it all right. There were two Boche gun positions tucked away at the side of it, where the woods began, but we passed these without let or hindrance, and made our way on towards the Sangro about 2½ miles away. We passed within feet of two Boche positions (how they didn't see or hear us, I shall never know) and crawled under a large railway viaduct which had sentries on the top. Just after this we lost the bed of the stream, and had to walk under the trees and suddenly stumbled over a notice board, which said 'Danger Mines'. We realised that for 100yds we had been walking over mines, luckily the snow and ice had been thick enough to support our weight, I nearly collapsed with fright! However, we went on, and half an hour later met our Waterloo, Mac was leading the way down the side of a wood and caught his foot in a trip-wire; ten yards to the left a mine went up and some bits of it hit him and knocked his left eye out, and made a great hole in his thigh. The other two dived into the wood for cover and did the same with another trip-wire. This time the effects were not so bad, but Ven was chopped about a little in the face, and Duggy had his right wrist injured and some bits in his back. I shouted to them all to lie down in case of fixed-line machine guns opening up on us, and eventually there we lay all night 2am onwards, in the pouring rain. Mac was very bad and I had to nurse him like a child. As soon as it was light, Duggy went towards the German lines and they sent us help. A stretcher for Mac who couldn't walk, and bandages for everyone else. They were extraordinarily good to us, gave us food and smokes and dried our clothes for us, then took us off to the MDS at Roccaraso, which was being evacuated by them that day. Various demolitions were in progress. Had more food and smokes there, and were told that when the accident happened we were only one kilometre off the Sangro, that we had got through their lines, that there were no more German troops ahead of us and that we were about 3 kilometres from our own lines. All the Germans said what bad luck it was and when they found out that we were all paratroops, made a great fuss of us. (They seemed to appreciate the efforts of all the British Officers and men to get through the lines, and said they hadn't any time for these Italians and others who got near the fighting lines, had one look, and then turned back). At Roccaraso we separated, and I left the others, being unwounded myself. They were to go to hospital at Rocca Pia and I left in a staff car for the same place a little before them, where I had a damn good meal of salmon sandwiches and steak and onions at some HQ. This place was also on the point of being evacuated. After a short stay there I was taken on to Introdacqua, where I spent most of the evening in a comfortable room, eating and drinking and smoking and chatting to one or two 'American' Jerries. Then at about 930pm I was driven over to the old Italian POW camp just outside Sulmona, where I found Major Tennant and Capt Clifford from Fontanellato. Thus ended our attempt to get back through our lines. Naturally I am disappointed, but am glad to have had s shot at it.

Dennis Rendell . . . . *with the Luftwaffe at a shooting booth*

AT THE time November 1943, together with other Allied escaped POWs I was running a small organisation to assist escaped and released Allied POWs living in the mountains, villages and towns of Sulmona in Central Italy. I was in touch with a larger outfit based in the Vatican City, Rome.

This little band in Sulmona had been told, amongst scenes of great excitement, that a travelling fair was to visit the town for a few days beginning 21st November. Apparently this was an annual visit combined with a market and a couple of Saints days. Our Italian helpers and friends assured us that it was a great occasion, a splendid party and that we would certainly enjoy it. It would be based on the town square and everyone for miles around would come to celebrate and take part in the dancing, eating and drinking, a rare treat in this period of wartime shortages and restrictions. We were urged to join in this bonanza and enjoy all the fun of the fair. Much to our surprise by noon on 22nd November several stalls and roundabouts, swings and even a dodgem rink had been assembled whilst parked in between were the showmen's caravans. It was quite astounding. Where had they come from? Where on earth did they get the fuel to move these fairground machines? How could this be done in wartime? Done it was and that evening from about 1600 hrs onwards we heard amplified music and noise coming from the square.

The music sounded gay and attractive and so I strolled that way. It was very cold and light snow was falling and I entered the square with maximum caution. I consoled myself by saying I was simply making a recce and remembered the time honoured truth that time spent in reconnaissance is seldom wasted. It certainly paid dividends that evening. It was great fun and I enjoyed the jostling and happy crowds, among them many German servicemen. I was attracted to a kind of rifle range. It seemed that if the customer hit a target about twenty yards away with the ·22 air rifle provided a flash light photograph was taken of him and anyone else who happened to be standing near him in the butts area. This stall also much fascinated various German troops and I was much impressed by their keenness to hand over their money and their rather poor efforts to set off the flash.

When I returned to my billet I was conscious of the lack of noise, it was now 1800 hrs and the show had closed down in order to be ready for the 1900 hrs curfew. It was not wise to be in the square area after curfew for from there were mounted the patrols of German troops and the dreaded and very Fascist Italian African Police, a hangover of Italy's once African empire. Those chaps were to be avoided at all costs. The silence was uncanny and so I called on one of our safe houses to let my comrades know the result of my recce.

Over a vino or two I explained the set up to them and as a result it was

134

Lieut Dennis Rendell an escaped POW at Sulmona, Italy, in November 1943 scores a 'Bull' at a travelling circus shooting range. Photo: Dennis Rendell.

decided that six of us would visit the fair next evening. Over more vino we discussed the sheer impossibility of this fun fair, the downright cheek of it. Here in Sulmona, less than 100 miles from the front line where great and bloody actions were continually taking place. Yet here was a full grown fair working about three hours from mid-afternoon until six pm. The whole thing was beyond belief! We later found out that the third day they quickly packed up and moved North at a sharpish pace. Very sensible!

The next day, 23 November 1943 Lieut Gilbert Smith 4RTR, Lieut Henri Pagonne, Free French Foreign Legion, Lieut El Dukate USAAC, Cpl Joe Polack and myself entered the square from different directions. We slowly gravitated to the photographic rifle range where as on the previous evening German Wehrmacht and Luftwaffe servicemen were trying their luck. They were singularly out of luck or incredibly bad shots, maybe both for the camera seldom flashed. Two Luftwaffe chaps made such a hash of it I could stand it no longer. I took off my mac and my hat, threw them to the ground and grabbed the rifle. Ramming a round up the breach I aimed and fired. A satisfying clang followed by a large flash announced success.

I think we were all more than a little shaken, both Germans and POWs but while waiting for the film to be processed Gil Smith sensibly whispered in my ear, 'Enough success for one night marksman, come on let's piss off while the going's good!' Having got the film, that's just what we did leaving Joe to tell the stall holder in his perfect Italian that the Germans would pay. We certainly had a good laugh at their expense on the way to our billets, and I confess to feeling somewhat smug. Safely home we celebrated but wondered if the showmen had been tipped off that we were escaped POWs and were deliberately making things difficult for their late feared and despised Allies. We will never know.

I have visited among fairs since, both on the continent and in USA but have never come across a similar stall. Many years later when stationed in Germany I had copies made of two photographs. A friend of mine, a Luftwaffe officer, arranged for copies of them to be sent to all Luftwaffe Old Comrades Association branches in Western Germany in the hope of tracing the two German airmen. Despite knowing the location and exact date and time we had no success. A great pity!

Maybe they did not survive the war or possibly they lived in Eastern Germany where no Old Comrades organisations of the Third Reich were allowed.

Jim Barnbrook . . . . *fair shares always pays*

WE ENTERED Altamura in darkness crossing a bridge that was mined, we searched the town and went to the outlying farms. I heard the screech of pigs and it meant the smell of lovely bacon sandwiches to me, so I found a sock and grabbed a large piglet. On return to town I cut it up into three parts, oh, I killed it first, gave pieces to the Sgts Mess and the Officers Mess, the rest to the Company. No questions were asked. Next morning CSM Dent said, 'You're on a charge for stealing a pig,' he marched me in front of the CO, standing by the desk was an old Italian farmer pointing a finger at me. I no spik Italian! This is a serious charge said the CO. In for a penny, in for a pound, I thought, 'well sir, they were lovely bacon sandwiches, sir, and the men did enjoy them, sir, and so did the Sergeants . . . and the Officers! That was my trump card. The CO's eyes bored through to the back of my head. He turned to the Adjutant and said, 'we will pay for it from the funds'. What funds I thought, he looked at me for what seemed hours, 'don't come in front of me again Sergeant.' As CSM Dent closed the door I heard the CO say to the adjutant, 'that was a tasty piece of bacon.' What a relief I thought, thank God he wasn't Jewish.

. . . . and most likely the last man to converse with the General

We were digging slit trenches on the outskirts of Taranto when Major General Hopkinson pulled up in a jeep and said 'stop digging, we are going to chase Jerry up to Foggia'. 'Thank God,' I said, 'the ground is solid concrete'. 'Do you know who I am,' said the General. I had not saluted him. 'Yes sir, but saluting you would have given Jerry a good target'. 'Good point Sergeant', and off he went. half an hour later he

136

returned stretched out in the back of the Jeep, dead. His passion for landing troops on the objective was just what we needed at Arnhem. If only a Rommel or Patton had been driving the troops up to Arnhem it would have been a different story.

Sticky Wood .... *tells of his escape and Jim Smith's death*

JIM WAS shot in cold blood by one of the PG66 Capua prison guards whilst attempting to escape. His death was the subject of a War Crimes trial resulting in the conviction of his killer.

On the 19th April 1943, while the rest of the compound was marched to collect the Red Cross parcels, Jim and a Commando POW Andy Walker, both dressed in American service uniforms, were marched out of the camp gates by Sticky Wood dressed in German army uniform, giving a very smart 'eyes right' as they passed the Camp Commandant at the exit.

They had planned the escape with the aid of an 8th Army Sergeant from the Tank Corps who had arranged for the 'cover up' at the next roll call. Unfortunately, all did not go well, for soon after leaving camp they walked into the middle of some German army manoeuvres and after being under observation for some distance they split up and hid themselves in a cornfield. It was here that Jim was shot, with his hands up.

After recapture Andy and Sticky were stripped and taken before the Commandant, their clothes were ripped up to inspect for hidden articles, and they paraded separately, starkers. Sticky was told he could be shot for wearing a German uniform, 'oh, but it isn't,' claimed he, 'it only looks like one, besides I was wearing my identity discs.' Sentence was thirty days solitary confinement. The Italians boarded up the single window to within two inches of the top. The padre passed 10 Players through the gap and shouted he should report sick next day. He did and rested for a few days but then some genuine cases needed his bed and he returned to the cell. Andy suffered badly from dysentery and was taken to hospital. After hostilities, Andy Walker went back to Italy and identified the murderer.

Fred Stevens .... *adds his recollection to the story*

FRED IS sure that the escape from the Italian POW Camp 66 by our men was set up by the Italian staff at the camp. There had been a previous abortive escape attempt and the staff were afraid of the Germans finding them lacking in soldierly duties.

Fred writes, 'Two hours after the escape I was told that Sticky Wood had been shot and his friend was in solitary behind the guard-room. On the second or third day after the incident, I was on a working party with a friend when a horse and cart drew up with what appeared to be two Red Cross tea chests end to end. The Catholic Padre came out of the church and told us he was taking our comrade to be buried. He said he would be conducting a short service and that everything would be done correctly. I asked if we could go with the body but was refused. As the cart moved off we both stood to attention and saluted. And all that time, since 1943, I had thought it was Sticky Wood being buried.'

Sticky Wood . . . . *missed his Red Cross parcel while in solitary*

FOR THE benefit of Sticky Wood who missed his weekly parcel when he marched out of the prison gate, I reproduce a Scottish parcel. Contents include: tea, sugar, condensed milk, butter, cheese, dried egg, spam, salmon, apple pudding, cocoa, jam, rolled oats, bacon, chocolate, casserole steak and cigarettes. Sticky wrote to say, 'I can never repay the Red Cross and their sponsors for supplying those necessities, God bless them! The Italians punctured all the tins when we collected them so that we could not hoard them for an escape. We had dried milk tins in the Canadian parcels that frequently ended up as pint sized drinking mugs.

Creative wizards transformed cans into effective heating machines, complete with bellows. Powered by a bent nail-handle through a system of multi-sized tin plate pulleys and string belts it delivered a constant supply of forced air to the firebox. The kettle for tea was dancing like magic in moments. While in Germany, one chap made an enormous grandfather clock out of tin plate, it was accurate too.

Red Cross parcels – always a necessity

138

Seven Months in the UK

ORDERS WERE received for the Bn's return to the United
Kingdom and on the 19th November 1943 the Battalion embarked
at Taranto on the *Ville d'Oran,* the first port of call being Algiers. After
approximately a week in a staging camp outside Algiers, the Bn once
more embarked, this time on the *Samaria,* arriving at Liverpool after an
uneventful voyage on 9th December.

Billets in the Grantham area were occupied by the Battalion and
shortly afterwards Christmas disembarkation leave was granted.

Events leading up to 17th September, 1944, may be summarised rather
briefly month by month as follows:–

January 1944. – Major DW Wallis joined the Bn as Second-in-Command. Lieut Colonel JD Frost, DSO, MC, remained in command with
Captain D McLean as Adjutant.

February 1944. – Company drops, from Albermarle aircraft, were
carried out at Stoney Cross, notable only for the use of a new type
kit-bag strapped to the leg, with a quick-release device to allow it to
hang below the man at the extent of a stout cord about twenty feet long,
this proved successful.

March 1944. – An inspection of the Brigade was carried out by Field
Marshall Montgomery in Belton Park, Grantham. Two days later HM
the King visited the Bn during a brigade exercise, the second of a series
carried out during this month.

April 1944. – A Brigade drop took place, followed by experimental
drops by the mortar and medium machine-gun platoons, carrying all
their weapons and ammunition in the new-type kit-bag. These experimental drops were completely successful and obviated the use of
containers for this purpose in future.

Towards the end of April, an Airborne Corps exercise took place with
the Division in an airborne role opposed by 6th Airborne Division in a
ground role. Once again the drop was very successful.

May 1944. – The only item of note was a Divisional non-dropping
exercise of approximately a week's duration. This took place on the
Yorkshire Moors and during the course of the exercise over 100 miles
were marched, culminating in a battalion field firing exercise supported
by artillery.

Dave Brooks . . . . *pays tribute to his Company Commander in England*

I FOUND a glaring difference in the use of Kings Regulations between my parent regiment the Royal West Kents and the Paras. The status quo in the RWK was 'Bull' and yet more 'Bull'. Never use your brain, do as you are told, or else. In consequence the ORs did not have a lot of faith in their officers.

All that changed in the Paras. I personally had no complaint about any of the officers I served under. They were all capable of doing everything that was asked of me, they sought opinions from ORs, and all were 'sharp end' leaders.

Major Douglas Crawley MC, had a very keen perception of how to interpret KRR's. On one occasion I and a mate were caught 'out of bounds' in Taranto, soon after we landed in Italy. He bypassed OCs orders and just told us to report to Father Egan in the early hours of the next day, which we spent in a rowing boat looking for the poor chaps who had perished on HMS Abdiel, we found a number, a dreadful day. On return to our camp outside Taranto, Doug just said, 'I trust you two have learned your lesson.'

Major Crawley was to show his common sense again at Colsterworth. 'B' Coy were welcomed by the whole village. The village Bobby was Bill Beech, a friend to us all. One morning in 1944 he turned up at early morning parade, spoke quietly to the Major, who then turned to the assembled Platoons and said, 'Fall out those who pinched the 30 mile an hour signs from near the Easton turn off.' No one moved, so we were all threatened with CB. Then out stepped Tom and Claude Gronert look-ing very sheepish. Doug turned to Bill and said 'have you to make a case of this?' 'God, no,' said Bill 'just get them back before my super finds out.' The Major then said to Tom and Claude, 'Go to your hut and put on full battle order, and bring the signs with you.' When they returned the Major said to the twins, 'I'll give you one hour to return the signs to their proper place and get back here, if you don't make it you will be in for 14 days.' They made it all right, but they knew all about it. The Easton turn off was a long two miles each way,

These two yarns show the worth of a very good Major, capable of maintaining discipline with an element of training, with no black marks on the record of those concerned. With the added plus that both solu-tions were not 'soft'. It would have been a very different story in the RWK. *(The Gronert twins were both killed at Arnhem).*

. . . . *an evening to remember – collecting gifts for the newly formed Airborne Forces Benevolent Fund*

I WAS instructed to select two men and to report to Lieut Grayburn at the Stoll Theatre in Kingsway, London in time for the matinee per-formance, on the last day of a popular revue. The other Coys sent the same number of men. We were to collect money for the newly

140

formed Airborne Forces Security Fund. The revue was called something like 'Red, White and Blue', and starred Flanagan and Allen, Florence Desmond and Monsewer Eddie Gray. At the end of the matinee we collected money in boxes in response to an appeal from the stage, and we did very well.

We were not to know what would happen in the last performance. The items from the stage bore no resemblance to the matinee. Bud, Chesney, Flo and Eddie spent the whole time amongst the audience. They had all had more than a 'couple'. It was a riot, and very, very funny. The chorus girls decided they wanted the Paras on stage, so we obliged despite our innate shyness. They quickly had our berets and blouses off and donned them themselves. Lieut Grayburn was also taking part in the fun and games. Little did that audience know that he was shortly to die a hero. Ernie Cole was also to lose his life at Arnhem, and for all I know others as well in that party. The time came to collect money. The boxes were useless so much was being given, so the berets were brought into play. Flanagan and Allen were extorting money, almost going into pockets, there was no escape. The Fund did well, and so did we, for we were all invited to the party at the bar that followed the last performance.

Normandy and we stand ready

June 1944. – All ranks were bitterly disappointed at not taking part in the invasion of Normandy on D Day 6th June.

Shortly after D Day two operations in France were planned and briefing began but both were first postponed and then cancelled. The only consolation was to be found in the tying up of several German divisions in the Pas-de-Calais area, who could not be moved to the battle in Normandy while the threat of 1st Airborne Division remained.

July 1944. – Normal training was undertaken, including field firing and four-day company marches.

August 1944. – The Bn was warned for another operation and on the 12th August, a seaborne administration party, under the Quartermaster and including almost all the battalion transport, left for a staging area in the South, from which they sailed three days later. On 15th August, the Bn moved south to a Transit camp at Down Ampney Aerodrome, preparatory to taking off for an operation South-West of Paris. After several postponements, this operation was finally cancelled and the Bn moved to the Grantham area.

On the 31st of August the Bn was warned to standby for operation LINNET. But the Allied forces were moving so quickly in Belgium that the operation was cancelled. On the 7th of September we were warned for operation COMET, the 1st, 2nd and 3rd Battalions were charged to capture the Bridge at Arnhem by coup de main. This was cancelled after a postponement and all were sent off on five days leave with orders to report back on Friday 15h September, without fail.

We did and were confined to Barracks. On Saturday 16th we were briefed for operation MARKET GARDEN and again we were to make for the Bridge at Arnhem but this time to drop in a ploughed field several miles away from the town. We packed our G1098, and as much ammunition as we could carry in our uniform pockets and pouches and waited for the morrow.

Sunday the 17th September was a beautiful day, 3 ton TCV's took us to Saltby aerodrome for 09.30hrs. The local WVS ladies were handing out delicious bacon sandwiches. At 1146 hrs American crewed Dakotas took off with 2Bn's 31 Officers and 478 OR's for Arnhem. England looked a lush green, the sky was a light blue, in the North Sea boats were going about their business, fighter planes were escorting us all the way and when we crossed the Dutch coast we experienced anti aircraft fire bursting around us. Nobody guessed what was in store!

CHAPTER EIGHT

Arnhem – the Battalion annihilated

Thirtyone Officers and 478 ORs take off – seventeen ORs are evacuated ten days later

THE FIRST British Airborne Division was given the task of seizing Arnhem and the 1st Parachute Brigade were to land on a dropping zone some seven miles north-west of Arnhem. The 2nd Battalion were to make it their business to take the bridges. There were three bridges, the first carried the railway and lay to the west of the town, the second was a pontoon bridge, which had possibly been dismantled, and the third in the centre of the town was the main road bridge.

Information about the enemy was very favourable. It was thought that there were 2,000 SS recruits in Arnhem itself and that the only other opposition would come from Luftwaffe ground staff who manned an aerodrome some ten miles to the north. There were, however, a large number of ack-ack guns defending the bridges.

The Battalion emplaned in Dakotas from Saltby aerodrome on Sunday morning 17th September, 1944. The American pilots had complete confidence in the successful outcome of their part of the operation. Weather conditions were perfect and large numbers of fighters escorted the huge armada of troop-carrying aircraft. At about 1400 hours, the Battalion began to drop according to plan and within forty-five minutes it was ready to move from the rendezvous.

Report written by **Major AD Tatham Warter** *in Holland after he had escaped from a POW hospital in Arnhem.*

The GOC 1 Airborne Division

Sir, This is an accurate account, as far as I can give it, of the battle at the bridge. I have written it in case no one else is able to give you the story.
I have the honour to be Sir,

Your obedient servant

AD Tatham Warter, Major

D-DAY The Bn was dropped accurately in first class conditions. There was no opposition on dropping zone. 'A' Coy captured six vehicles and 12 POW's at rendezvous. Moved off at approximately

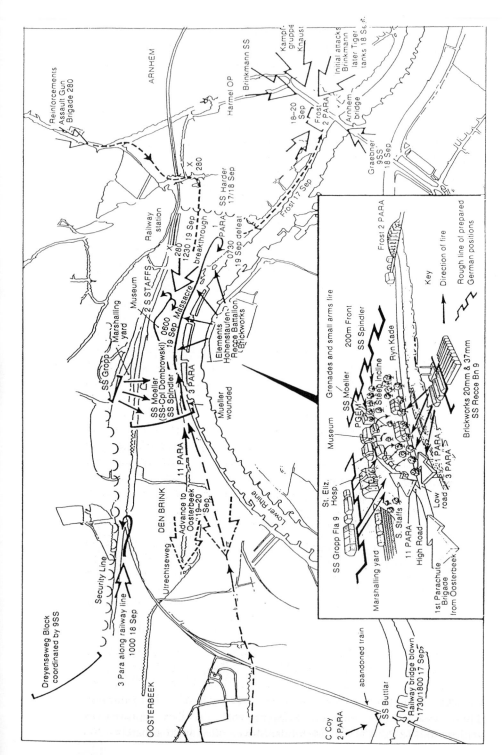

1530 hrs with 'A' Coy leading. After approximately two miles 'A' Coy held up by machine gun and mortar fire. A left flanking movement by one platoon drove enemy back and we were able to continue keeping slightly to South. It seemed we had struck the flank of the enemy positions as we could hear sounds of battle on 3Bn route. No further opposition until we reached railway, when a few snipers in station caused slight delay. Just East of railway an armoured car appeared and caused some delay and casualties. It pulled out before we could bring PIAT or 6 pdr to bear. This armoured car appeared two or three times, but 'A' Coy were able to get round through the back gardens. The railway bridge (Charing Cross) was blown as 'C' Coy were crossing.

'B' Coy were ordered onto Den Brink where they met considerable opposition and suffered casualties. At this stage wireless communications with 'B' and 'C' Coys broke down. Nothing more was ever heard of 'C' Coy. Meanwhile 'A' Coy pushed on south of Den Brink and entered town keeping close to the river. They encountered several small parties of enemy with light automatics, but these soon packed in when outflanked. Altogether some 30-40 POW's were taken by 'A' Coy during this advance. 'A' Coy reached bridge at approximately 2000 hrs and occupied buildings 8 and 10 and area A. Enemy traffic was crossing bridges at the time. At 2045 hrs, 'A' Coy put in an assault with one platoon South end of bridge. They were met by a light flak gun from South end of bridge and an armoured car on the bridge The pl suffered 8 casualties in the first 50 yards and the attempt was abandoned. The CO had now arrived and decided that the South end must be taken from the south. He sent a patrol under Major Murray (1st Para Sqn RE) to recce for barges and to contact 'B' Coy at Putney (pontoon bridge) with orders to cross and take South end of bridge. This patrol never made contact with 'B' Coy. Meanwhile Bn HQ and HQ Coy arrived and occupied houses 2, 3 and 5. Shortly afterwards Bde HQ and attached troops less Brigade and IO arrived.

Lieut Col Frost took command of the force which now consisted of 1 Para Bde Gp less 1 and 3 Bns, 'B' and 'C' Coys 2 Bn. Brigade HQ tps were disposed as follows: Approximately 45 men (RASC and Sgts) under Capt Briggs in houses 14, 15, 16, 17. Bde Def pl despatched to cross river and take South end. (Still no news of 'B' Coy). They failed to cross and later occupied 12 and 13. Remainder in 1, 2 and 4. All tps East of the bridge were placed under command OC 'A' Coy.

D + 1 Major Lewis, 3 Bn with the remnants of his Coy, (one pl and 12 men) arrived. Major Lewis and 12 men occupied house 17 and the pl was ordered to occupy 12. This pl was never seen again. At approximately 0500 hrs, 'B' Coy less 1 pl arrived and occupied 7. They had met strong resistance at Putney and suffered some casualties. At first light 'A' Coy evacuated area A. During the night some enemy ammunition and petrol trucks were set on fire in this area and a strong counter attack from South of bridge was driven back with casualties. 'A' Coy now held 8, 9 and 10.

Later a party of sappers under Capt O'Callaghan RE, A/L Coy were placed under command 'A' Coy. The bridge was kept under careful observation and the sappers reported that it was not prepared for demolition.

During the morning armoured cars attempted to cross bridge from South to North – 6pdrs accounted for six and PIAT for four – a total of 10 armoured cars and half tracks being destroyed. The Bn area was heavily mortared throughout the day and House 9 received a good deal of light flak from South of river. During the late afternoon and evening a strong attack supported by mortar fire and two Mk III tanks developed from the East along the river bank. Bde Def pl suffered heavy casualties from tanks in 12 and 13, and withdrew to join Capt Briggs in 14 and 15.

House 10 then bore the brunt of the attack and one pl of 'B' Coy was moved into 11. The attack was finally driven off. One tank was accounted for by PIAT and one by six pdr. Just before dark, Houses 17, 11, 9 and 1 were set on fire by enemy and subsequently burnt down. Bde HQ in 2 narrowly escaped fire. Throughout the day there had been rumours and great hopes of 1 and 3 Bns arriving, but by night it was accepted that they would not get there. Later, hopes were revived when we were told 2 S Staff followed by 11 Bn were on their way to join us.

Soon after dark Major Wallis who had been commanding 2 Bn was killed and Major Tatham Warter took over command, handing over 'A' Coy to Capt Franks. Area A was occupied during the night by 'B' Coy and another attempt from the South was driven back. The small Bn reserve of ammunition was distributed mostly to troops East of the

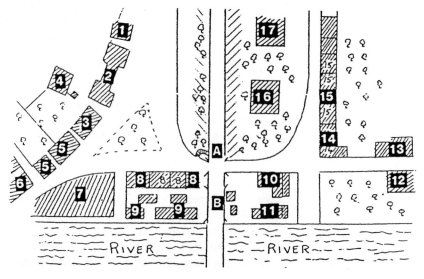

146

bridge. During the night it was decided to strengthen our positions East of the bridge. Orders were issued for 'A' Coy to move East of bridge and occupy ruins of 11 and area under bridge at B. 'B' Coy were to take over 8 and ruins of 9. This plan was put into effect early D + 2.

D + 2   The attack East of the bridge was resumed with heavy mortaring and attempted infiltrations throughout the morning. At midday three tanks got into position near the river and started to shell 10 at point blank range. The pl holding the house suffered casualties and had to evacuate into Area 'B'. Two PIAT were despatched and closed with the tanks and scored three hits. Two more tanks were observed, after obtaining three more bombs from 'B' Coy, the party returned to see the tanks pulling out. Meanwhile some enemy had occupied 10. The pl counter attacked and reoccupied the house. The pl commander was severely wounded and the pl suffered several casualties. An attempt was then made to resecure House 13. This resulted in heavy casualties and the attempt was abandoned. Shortly after this a heavy gun South of the river started to shell block 8. The top two stories of all these houses were demolished and 'B' Coy suffered some casualties.

Two armoured cars penetrated along river bank to 9, where one was accounted for by PIAT. The other withdrew. At about this time Capt Franks was wounded, but remained in command until dark: pressure continued throughout the evening. Block 8 and House 10 were now set on fire, forcing the remnants of 'A' Coy into area 'B' and the ruins of 11 and 'B' Coy into block 7. Just before dark a Tiger tank drove down the line of houses 1, 2,3, 5, and 6 firing two or three shells into each house. The two remaining six pdrs could not engage it, but its withdrawal was hastened by bombs. During this episode the CO was injured and severely affected by blast. Major Gough was placed in command of 2 Bn. He later handed over to Major Tate. Meanwhile Houses 16, 14 were set on fire, and Capt Briggs' position began to look sticky. The position as a whole was now greatly weakened. We had suffered heavy casualties – particularly in 'A' Coy. Ammunition was getting very short. We had lost the key position East of the bridge, House 10. The enemy were occupying all houses to the North and West of our positions. Although they did not attempt infiltrations from this direction, they were able to keep us under continuous automatic fire, to which we could not afford to reply. The numbers of wounded were reaching serious proportions – they were all kept in the extensive cellars of Bde HQ (2).

D + 3   During the morning pressure from the East continued. Capt Briggs party were finally burnt out and fell back on 'A' Coy. Between them they held area B and the ruins of 8 and 9 throughout the morning. They put in a series of small counter attacks at different times on enemy setting charges under the small arch. Finally tanks were brought up into area B and blasted them from every position they held. There were no PIAT bombs left. Previous to this most of block 7 had been destroyed and 'B' Coy had been withdrawn to 5 and 3. At about midday the remnants of 'A' Coy (approx 15) and Capt Briggs party (25) were withdrawn to the main position.

Earlier in the morning Col Frost and Major Crawley had been wounded. Major Gough took over active command of the force referring important matters to Col Frost. Capt Hoyer-Miller took over 'B' Coy. Major Tatham Warter now resumed command of 2 Bn. Houses 1-6 were now strongly held and alternative positions were prepared in the gardens. All the remaining houses in the sector had been burnt down. It was anticipated that the remaining houses would be fired and we intended holding the gardens until they had burnt out and were cool enough for us to return. We appreciated that the enemy would not be able to use the houses either and furthermore they would not be able to seriously damage us with tanks from any directions. During the afternoon four or five tanks crossed the bridge from North to South. The 6pdrs were unable to fire as they were now under direct small arms fire. Later in the afternoon the enemy brought an 88mm gun into position West of block 7 and started shelling 3, 5, 6.

We now received the news that 30 Corps were to attack the South side of river at 1700 hrs definitely. We were all full of confidence that, even if this should not develop, we would be able to hold on throughout the following day. The mortars engaged the 88mm gun with good effect, silencing it for quite long periods. Throughout the battle the mortars had done most valuable work engaging targets South and East of the Bridge. Just before dark the enemy started to set fire to 3, 5 and 6, and houses to the West, by firing phosphorous bombs into the already demolished roofs. They were soon burning fiercely. Just after dark Bde HQ in 2 caught fire. The wounded had to be moved into 4, but before this was completed this house was also on fire. There was nowhere else to move the wounded as all houses at the back of our position that were not burnt down were held by enemy. Col Frost then ordered all opposition from Bde HQ to cease and the wounded to be surrendered. This meant the Bde HQ party approximately 120, under Major Hibbert moving North to new positions. Strict orders were given to 2 Bn NOT to open fire on enemy.

The enemy took advantage of the situation to bring larger numbers into the area of 2 and 4. A German officer entered our garden and demanded assistance to remove all the wounded. Later he demanded our surrender. Several of his men followed him in and the situation became tricky as we were powerless to open fire on the enemy or counter attack until we had been certain that the wounded had been evacuated. To add to this confusion we were surrounded on three sides by burning houses and the enemy were throwing grenades into the gardens from the

148

List of 2 Bn men taken prisoner in the town

2 Bn A Coy
Pte Sullivan W
Pte Cox RTB
Pte Anderson A
Pte Brookes D
Pte Jones J
Pte Watkins JG
Cpl Priestley R
Pte Norton LM
L/c Miles TE
Pte Foster T
Pte Smith J
Pte Harding A
Sgt Kinsey SM
 Strength = 13

2 Bn B Coy
Pte Johnson L
Pte Goodwin J
Sgt Avis J
Pte Smith D
Pte Dellar N
Pte Barnett F
Pte Eyre W
Pte Kelly D
Pte Fitzpatrick J
Pte Hughes T

Cpl Chilton C
Pte Wainwright L
Pte Kingwell H
Pte Izzard C
Cpl Wood H
Pte Nichols H
Pte Ward A
Pte MacGilvray A
Pte Boost W
Pte Groucher A
 Strength = 20

MG Platoon
Pte Pullinger A
Pte Jenaknes J
Pte Gregory H
L/S Riddle E
Cpl Cook W
Pte Painter F
Cpl Campbell A
Pte Searle I
Pte Fishwick W
Pte Timms E
Pte Stevens W
Pte Wade R
Pte Mullins T
Pte McCline W

Pte Madgley J
Pte Ralphs W
Pte Smith A
Sgt Le Maites B
 Strength = 18

Mortar Platoon
Pte Flannery J
Pte Miller W
Pte Dawson J
Cpl Mason HP
Pte Forsythe C
Sgt Smith C
Pte Mason WF
Pte Murphin S
Pte Hutton M
Pte Crawley L
Pte Hayden S
Pte Letchford A
Sgt Jackman A
L/c Youngman R
Pte Pope R
 Strength = 15

2 Bn HQ Coy
Sgt Carter E
Sgt Cloves W

Cpl Mapp W
Cpl Tucker T
L/c Allen S
Pte Davies S
Pte Kelly M
Pte Hudson A
Pte Tait T
Pte Wren J
Pte Rolfe T
Pte Pettitt T
Pte Kent L
Pte Fitzsimmons G
Pte Lumsden A
Pte Ramsey S
Pte Langford S
Pte Lund G
Pte Hindmarsh H
Pte Hellier W
Pte Edwards T
L/c Paddon W
Pte Palmer SR
Pte McCracken G
Pte Gilder W
L/c Back H
L/c Travers T
CSM Bishop JE
 Strength = 28

---

area behind 4. It was clear that this position was no longer tenable, so after consulting Major Gough who had now joined 2 Bn, the CO ordered a move to our adjoining warehouse which was known not to be strongly held, 'A' Coy took the house with little opposition and the Bn, Sappers and Anti-tank gunners followed. The enemy soon had this building partially surrounded and it was clear that it was quite undefendable. The CO then decided to split the Bn into two more manageable parties, one under himself and the other under Major Tate. The two parties were to find separate areas for the night, and to reassemble at the original positions at 0515 hrs.

The CO's party set off, but before long came under MG fire at very close range. The party became divided, half eventually occupying a building some 200 yards from the original position. Soon after, a party of RASC from Bde HQ under Capt Gill joined us with the information that Bde HQ had been unable to find a defence position and had to split up into parties of 10 to make their way out of the town.

It was now clear that we were no longer a fighting force, and that as the area was very thoroughly surrounded, a similar fate must have befallen Major Tate's party – this proved to be the case. It was then decided to hide in the area in the hope that 30 Corps would arrive before we were discovered. A thorough search was made of the whole area the following morning and most of the Bn and Bde HQ were rounded up.

When the 2Bn left the garden position it consisted approximately of: CO: Major Tatham Warter, Adjt: Capt McLean, 'A' Coy: Capt Frank and 15 men, 'B' Coy: Capt Hoyer-Miller, Lieut Flavell and 35 men. HQ Coy: Major Tate, Capt Panter, Lieut Monsell, Lieut Tannenbaum and 60-70 men.

After the evacuation of wounded from Bde HQ there was no means of dealing with further casualties. 60-70 more wounded were brought in the following morning. It is not possible to give accurately the total casualties, but the MO's estimation of 2 Bns wounded was 210.

There has been no news of 'C' Coy.

End of report

John Wallace . . . . *successful escape attempt despite bullet wound*

AT 2300 hrs on Wednesday 20th September after Major Tatham Warter had refused to surrender, the Germans opened up a terrific barrage of shells, moaning minnies and mortars. We were instructed to break out in small parties and try to contact the other Brigade.

It was during this barrage that I received a wound in the calf of my leg. Pte Bacon stayed with me, we hid ourselves in a destroyed house by crawling into a hole in the debris. Two days later on 22 September we moved to a nearby house where we found a cellar containing a fair amount of food. Here we stayed until 28 October. Periodically Germans searched the house but not once did they search the cellar.

Within a week of being here we tried to get through the town. A number of roads were blocked off and Germans were living in houses either side of the blockades. We considered an attempt to cross the river, but we thought it would only be a matter of days before our troops would enter Arnhem. Organised looting by the Germans confirmed our opinion they were preparing to evacuate. Truck loads of furniture, pictures and clothing were being hauled out of the town.

On the 28th October we both went off in search of food, on leaving a house I saw Pte Bacon being escorted down the street by 3 or 4 Germans. I returned to the house, stayed for an hour and then decided to make a break.

I made for the bridge which had been bombed previously and discovered the broken iron girders were only a matter of inches below the water. I crawled across to the other side, this was around 1800-1830 hrs. I made my way across fields looking for a contact.

On hearing German voices I hid in a nearby haystack. There I stayed until 1800 hrs the next day. While following the river in a westerly direction I was challenged, I stopped and shouted 'Kamerad' thinking he was a German. I had run into a patrol of the 101 American Airborne

150

Easton Hall, Lincolnshire, June 1944. 'A' company on parade. They were the first men on the Arnhem bridge, sixteen were killed in action. Only one man, Sgt Wallace, 4th from left of the sitting Sgts and Officers, escaped without being captured. Sgt Meads acting CSM 5th from left was KIA. Of the five officers shown Lieut McDermont was KIA, Captain Timothy won a 2nd bar to his Military Cross after posting to the 1st Bn as a Company Commander. Major Tatham Warter won a DSO and Lieut Grayburn a posthumous Victoria Cross. Lieut Vlasto was wounded.

Division. I was taken back to platoon HQ, Company and Regt and then to 30 Corps. I was asked to give any information I had picked up. Finally I was sent back to Brussels and England.

Roger King .... *researches the Pigeon Post*

IN THE event that radio communications failed between the First Airborne Division and the Airborne Rear HQ, a number of homing pigeons were taken to Arnhem. It was intended that they be used to take urgent messages to their lofts in London, about 250 miles from Arnhem, where the message would be retransmitted.

Wally Rook the CO's signaller was in charge of four 2nd Battalion pigeons. Major Wallis, 2 ic of the Bn, released one at 0845 hrs on 18 September and it was found in England on the 26th.

A copy of the signal is kept in the divisional war diary at the Public Record Office and reads as follows:

```
2ND BN CAPTURED NORTH END MAIN BR AT 1720.
NOW HOLDING PERIMETER 300 YDS RADIUS FROM BRIDGE.
BDE HQ AND C COY 3RD BN WITHIN THIS PERIMETER.
C COY 2ND BN HOLDING BUILDINGS 42 ON TOWN PLAN.
1ST BN ABOUT 1 MILE WEST OF BR ADVANCING AGAINST
LIGHT OPPOSITION. 3RD BN POSN LESS C COY UNKNOWN.
2ND BN CAS ABOUT 60. ENEMY ARMD CARS TOTAL 20
CROSSED BR DURING LAST MM 1/2 HR 10 DESTROYED.
EXPECT TO CAPTURE SOUTH OF BR TONIGHT.
ADDITIONAL AMN ESPECIALLY A-TK REQUIRED.
END OF TEXT TOO 0845. SIGNED DW WALLIS, MAJOR
```

Two more pigeons were released on the morning of the 19th with messages from the Brigade Major, Tony Hibbert, and the last pigeon was released at about 1100 hrs on Wednesday. He said there was so much noise and unpleasantness flying about that we had great difficulty in getting it to leave us and it kept flying back to perch on the window-sill. However when the Germans put a 6in. shell through the roof, it took off and that's the last we saw of it.

One of these birds, called William of Orange, arrived at its loft in London within 5 hours of its release, having flown about 250 miles. The bird was awarded a Dicken Medal, the animals' VC, and died in 1960. Of the 82 pigeons taken by the division, a total of 14 eventually returned to their home lofts, although only three of them carried messages, at least two of which were from the bridge.

David Russell .... *Platoon commander 'C' Company makes his report*

I SHALL probably never know why 7 platoon became split up on the second day in Arnhem, as its platoon Commander the responsibility must rest with me. Most of D Day seemed too good to be true, the sunny calm misty weather as we drove out in 3-tonners to Saltby airfield, cheese and bacon sandwiches as we stood around waiting to emplane, the smooth flight, the backchat of Sgt Fleming and Pte Cockburn, Pte McKernon the irrepressible bren-gunner managed to be airsick. No fire on the ground, a beautiful still afternoon, a soft landing on the right dropping zone – fantastic!

Soon I had 32 out of 33 in 7 platoon at our RV, Pte Goozee alone being left as a dropping zone casualty. Moving off with the Battalion column, we first had a check outside Heveadorp, where 'A' Coy at the head of the long file of heavily laden men on the 8-mile march in to Arnhem had been fired on, I recall passing Battalion HQ, seeing for the last time till after the battle the CO talking to a wounded 'A' Coy man.

Through Heveadorp we came in sight of the railway bridge over the Rhine. It was the task of 9 Platoon under Lieut Peter Barry to capture this, covered by Lieut Ian Russell's 8 Platoon, with 7 Platoon in reserve. We were by this time surrounded by happy Dutch people, applauding our arrival, plying us with fruit and drinks, jeering at German POW's. Not conducive to conduct of warfare! After some firing we saw smoke go down and 9 Platoon's attack begin. Shortly after there was a vivid flash and heavy detonation as the bridge was blown, Peter Barry had been wounded in the arm and Pte Sadler killed. Sgt Knowles took over command of the Platoon. O Group; we were now to move to our secondary objective, the German HQ, a building just south of the railway station, order of March 8 pl. Coy HQ, 7 pl, 9 pl.

Shortly after our move off, a large party of Germans, who we at first thought to be POW's were seen debussing on the North side of the road; 8 pl opened up on them with PIAT and bren, with great effect; some surrendered and came over to us, I knew some German and found out from them that things were not going well for us, and that they were but the advance party of a strong armoured force in the town.

As we entered the town proper along a completely built-up road, 8 pl were fired on by machine guns from ahead, sustaining some killed and wounded. We were ordered into a large house on the left, 7 pl on the first floor 8 and 9 pls ground floor, Coy HQ and casualties in the cellar. Pte Anthony formerly 7 pl, now a rear link signaller, was one of the wounded, LCpl Loney and Pte Shipley, 8 pl. had been killed. We moved in, barricaded the windows with whatever was to hand, posted a sentry at each window, remainder to get their heads down. The three POW's still with the Company were to be kept in my pl HQ room, I remember we kept them in the frame of a double bed, two were quite badly wounded we did what we could for them, which wasn't much.

Sgt Campbell and I kept awake in turns, going the rounds all night. We were all uneasy with the lack of action and felt like sitting ducks; the night was pitch black, the sentries could see nothing, and we were kept under sporadic sniper fire. I have a memory of someone shot through the forehead.

At dawn we stood to and the POW's were taken down to the cellar. O Group; Company was to withdraw through the gardens of the houses till we could cross the road, go down to the riverside road and continue the advance into the town to take over from 'B' Coy who were joining 'A' Coy at the bridge, 7 pl leading. At about 0700 hrs we moved off, Sgt Fleming and 1 Section leading, then pl HQ, 2 and 3 Sections. The gardens were very tricky with high walls and many little yards; progress was desperately slow with enemy fire all round us: a woman signalled from a top window, I thought to us but now I think to the enemy.

We eventually had to crawl along through rosebeds, our equipment catching in everything until we reached the point where I decided to cross the road. Cannon fire had set the house we had just left ablaze and the road was covered by machine guns on fixed lines, 1 Section rose as one man and made a dash for it. I crawled on for a few more yards, gave the signal to go to Sgt Campbell, and got across the road, luckily unscathed. I soon found Sgt Fleming, LCpl Vernon and Ptes Vale, McKernon, Spicer and Cockburn, neither Sgt Campbell nor anyone else followed, I tried to contact him but saw no way of doing so. Forming the opinion (correctly, as it transpired) that the rest of the Company was pinned down, I decided that we would press on to the Bridge.

Descending the wooden slope to the river, we met up with a platoon of 3rd Bn under Lt Jimmy Cleminson trying to get to the Bridge and joined forces with them. The leading Company of 3rd Bn then hit heavy enemy opposition and we took up a defensive position under persistent small arms, cannon and mortar fire, their Company HQ in a warehouse 300 yards back on the riverside was mortared and Major APH Waddy was killed. The Bn then decided to withdraw to the woods at Den Brink until dusk. We went with Cleminson's platoon back up to the road, made a successful dash back across it though it was still under fire, slipped through the St. Elizabeth Hospital and into a residential area to the west of it. Here we had a cat-and-mouse game with a half-track, during which we unfortunately lost touch with McKernon and Cockburn, two of the best, who were acting as scouts.

Eventually we got into the Den Brink woods which were subject to considerable enemy searching fire and had a rest until evening. At about 2200 hrs we moved out, heading for the glow in the sky which marked the action round the bridge. High fences, rabbit wire topped with barbed, tiny gardens and vegetable plots made progress very slow, but

154

eventually, having lost touch with 3rd Bn, we fell in with 'A' Coy, 2 South Staffs, who were going to make another drive for the bridge, at 0400 hrs Tuesday morning, so got out heads down for an hour or two till then. At 0345 hrs we moved off with 'A' Coy HQ, 2 S Staffs, heading East along the road 'C' Coy had taken on Sunday evening. At about 0600 hrs the leading Company hit heavy opposition in the area of 'C' Coy's overnight position, and 'A' Coy and our detachment of 7 platoon took up positions in the Museum building on the South side of the main road. We were ordered to occupy the upstairs rooms and observe, but as no-one seemed interested in our reports we carried on our own battle with any enemy movement we saw. We passed a target to the S Staffs mortar officer who was in action close to the museum, and at a minimum range after a couple of sighting rounds he engaged a machine gun post with great success – certainly it never came into action. However, enemy tanks and assault guns were now in action on all sides, plus an 88 firing into the gardens around the museum from across the river. The basement was filling with wounded and all the buildings around us were on fire. A tank came up and opened fire on our building, the first two rounds bursting in the room we had just vacated. With little prospect of a successful break-out, I agreed with the South Staffs Company Commander that further resistance was pointless. After capture we eventually were taken to a large warehouse in Zutphen where we met up with Sgt Campbell and most of the rest of the platoon who were put in the bag after some fierce fighting on the Monday morning, missing still were Shuckburgh and Watts the PIAT team, McKernon, Cockburn, Butler and Gowenlock of 1 Section, Cpl Neilly and Ptes McKee, Marsden and Morris of Sgt Frew's 2 Section and Pte Flitcroft of Sgt Craig's 3 Section. Goozee had been left on the dropping zone and Ives 3 Section's bren gunner had been wounded. Apart from the one or two I met briefly when 2nd Bn reformed at Oakham, I had never seen any of my platoon again until I met David McLaughlin in 1990 at my first reunion. What a lot we could have achieved given the chance!

John Hey . . . . *War crimes; Allen and McCracken remembered*

IT WAS by accident that I discovered in the Public Record Office at Kew a file WO 309 186125 called 'Case K' (shooting of POWs at Zutphen, Holland). A War Crime Commission made investigations in 1945 and 1946. The evidence provided by Major Byng-Maddick 1 Para Bde, Major Murray and Capt. Livesey RE, Lt Morley MP Section, Capt Gell RASC, Capt D McLean and Lieut Tannenbaum 2nd Bn and Major Gough of the Recce Sqdn produces agreement on these facts.

In the afternoon of Saturday 23rd September about 25 prisoners were sent by lorry from Velp to an interrogation centre at Zutphen, about 30km North of Arnhem. When the lorry wound through the centre of Brummen village, 6km South of Zutphen, the Majors Hibbert and

Mumford suddenly jumped off and disappeared between the houses along the main road. The Germans in the lorry were a driver and co-driver, 1 or 2 Luftwaffe guards on the rear and an SS guard with a Schmeiser on the running board.

The SS guard fired at the two escapees but only punctured the right hand back wheel and killed the SS NCO Hatska. Eye-witnesses also reveal that at least 3 pistol shots were heard. The SS guard ran to the rear and emptied his Schmeiser into the back of the lorry, killing and wounding several men.

A truck full of young SS soldiers arrived at the scene from the opposite direction and intended to shoot the other prisoners. According to Major Gough this was avoided by a German staff officer, who – concerned at the delay in the arrival of the prisoners – had come by car from Zutphen. The situation was under control very quickly.

In the meantime a local doctor had made an attempt to take care of the wounded but was kicked away by the SS soldiers.

The War Crime File contains some conflicting information on the names of those killed and wounded, as well as when and where some of them died. From what I have gathered it seems justified to say that Capt Platt was killed outright and possibly Pte Allen, whilst Pte McCracken and Lt Mills died later in the evening at Zutphen. From there the dead and wounded were taken to Enschede, 53km Eastward on the Dutch-German border. The German Ortskommandant informed the bur-gomaster of Enschede that five dead were delivered to the local mor-tuary on 23 September and that these 'were shot when attempting to escape on the road from Enschede to Gronau (Germany). We now know this was a pertinent lie.

For my opinion it is clear that the German authorities at Zutphen had in fact nothing to do with the shooting and preferred to send dead and wounded out of their district. The cities Zutphen, Deventer, Apeldoorn and Lochem all had hospitals at the time and cemeteries.

The five dead were all buried in the Eastern General Cemetery of Enschede on 25th September 1944.

Grave 196 – Pte George Ernest McCracken 7017277, age 29, 2nd Bn Parachute Regt., of Stoke Newington, London.
Grave 197 – LCpl Sydney Allen 14302633, aged 20, 2nd Bn Parachute Regt., of Birkenhead.
Grave 198 – Capt Horace Anthony Platt 224694, aged 30, 1st Airldg. Squadron, Recce Corps RAC, of Woking, Surrey.
Grave 199 – Lieut Kenneth Stanley Mills 255204, The Glider Pilot Regt., age 21 of Bristol.
Grave 200 – an unknown Soldier.

On 27th September Lieut Trevor Victor Patrick McNabb 245232, Mentioned in Despatches, 1st Airldg. Squadron, Recce Corps, age 22, of Kensington, London died of his wounds in the Roman Catholic Hospital (in use as a war hospital) and buried in Grave 195.

The unkown casualty in Grave 200 proved to be the War Correspondent Major Anthony Cotterill.

The man (or men) responsible for the death of these six British soldiers was never found, anyhow the file does not mention it.

The six are not forgotten: every year at 20.00hrs on 4 May (in Holland Remembrance Day for the Dead of WWII) many civilians attend the ceremony in the cemetery and flower the graves, which are beautifully kept by the gardeners. They rest side by side with their comrades in arms of the RAF who were shot down and soldiers of the Guards Armoured Division who fell during the liberation of Enschede on 1 and 2 April 1945.

We, in Holland, will continue to remember them. They had no chance to grow old, 20 years, 21 years . . .

Vince Goodwin . . . . *covered all over in Sweet Violets*

HERE IS a short story that happened on the Bridge on Wednesday 20th at around 1100 hrs. Col Frost had volunteered myself and another chap, I think it was Cpl Chilton, to take a verbal message to the blokes at the other side of the bridge – and I must admit my 'bottle' was going as we made our way under the bridge. Machine gun fire was constant.

As we were coming back we ran into pretty heavy mortar-fire, so we ran into a damaged blacksmiths workshop – the obvious place to take refuge we thought was under the blacksmith's forge where the coke was. I suppose it was about 10ft long with an opening at each end, big enough for us to crawl into anyway. We moved about while we were in there and found after some minutes that we just had to get out because of the terrible smell coming from the coke. We thought we would brave the mortar bombs rather than stay under the forge. As we came out we found we were covered from head-to-toe in yuk! Apparently when the Smithy wanted to go, he just did it on a shovel and threw it into the coke under the forge.

We eventually reported to Major Crawley and I remember him telling us quite plainly to piss-off and get a bath! It hurt me and my mate at the time – to think we had dodged bullets and mortar-bombs to deliver a message, got covered in shit, and all he said was piss-off. Where could you get a bath round there anyway?

Harold Smith . . . . *with bullets through his knee*

I WAS a member of HQ Company Assault Platoon and caught four bullets through my left knee when the able bodied had to leave the cellar under HQ, to try to make contact with any of our troops. Six of us went up those step into a hell of a reception from the enemy, Sgt Nick Carter, Sgt Welsh, Tommy Pettit, myself and two others that I can't remember.

I didn't hear about any of these men again for I was taken prisoner as I lay wounded. At Stalag 11B in one of the so called hospital huts, I met Arthur Wrigley who was wounded in the spine and lay on the bedboards behind me. Arthur could not move from his waist down and had bed-sores and was in a terrible state, but always cheerful. Now this man really was a hero, and I admired him greatly. Arthur Wrigley died of his wounds in England in April 1947.

George Stubbs .... *every man for himself was the cry*

WE LEFT in tens, every man for himself, it was dark, the only light being from the fires in blazing buildings. We had not gone far through the ruins when we were trapped in a burnt out building, two soldiers climbed over a wall and they may have been killed or wounded – I don't know. Then a burst of Machine Gun fire, I recall sparks from a radiator nearby caused by ricochets which were literally inches away from my legs. In this burst two chaps were hit, one had the top of his left arm shattered, the other was hit in the abdomen. I gave them both shots of morphine and placed field dressings on their wounds. Then of course we had to surrender. Remov-ing my smock and with the help of others, I placed the Sgt on it and with one man on each corner we carried him to the German HQ which was only about 30 yards away from where we were trapped! I distinctly remember the Panzer SS man spread out behind an MG 42 and to our left was an 88mm blazing away at I don't know what.

I have often thought since about the wounded men. I was told later that one died of his wounds in the night but cannot confirm this. What hap-pened to the man with the shattered arm?

David Wells .... *writes about Sergeant Burns*

HE WAS my section Sgt at Arnhem, and was a nice unassuming kind of person. When we were house clearing at Arnhem, he was leading the section upstairs to start clearing and was killed leading this action. The platoon eventually reached the top rooms where we consolidated our positions.

During this time the Germans had surrounded us and brought up small cannon-like guns which they used to rip through the brick and cement. After suffering heavy casualties and nowhere else to go we were taken prisoner. The majority including myself were taken to hospital and then to Stalag 11B.

Previous to joining us at Grantham, Sgt Burns had fought in North Africa and was taken prisoner. He escaped and was placed in charge of guarding Italian prisoners of war. This did not go down too well with 'Robbie' and he volunteered to rejoin the Battalion.

He was a very likeable person and a true Scot who wore his red beret similar to a tam-o'shanter. His leadership qualities were excellent and I remember him for treating everyone firmly but fairly.

158

Ron Holt .... *Cpl Menzies – cook extraordinary*

DURING THE early summer of 1944, a new draft arrived at Easton Hall and amongst them was a replacement Corporal cook. We had not been sorry to see his predecessor go. His one ambition had been to conserve rations for a rainy day and the rest of the rations were mutilated and burnt by his assistant, 'Old Bert'. In those days you ate because you had to, not to savour the meal.

We had no particular expectations from the new Corporal, only the view that it was impossible to get worse. However, we were pleasantly surprised, Cpl Menzies, an unassuming Scot, was great and it became a pleasure to sit down in the Dining Room. Nothing seemed too much trouble and what we fondly imagined was stewed gas cape before, turned out to be cabbage. There was always a good honest brew of tea going in the cookhouse and the pinched hungry faces gradually disappeared.

It was not until the day before Arnhem that we really found out what a truly fantastic man Jock was. The Army Catering Corps, which Jock served with, were of course only attached to the Para Regt. and were non jumpers. On this particular evening as we were talking in the cookhouse, Jock said 'You blokes aren't leaving me behind, I'm coming with you.' We then had to bribe the stick Sgt in the aircraft and smuggle him on board. We were all impressed by this quiet man, who with no parachute training whatsoever, jumped for the first time in his life into what proved to be one of the bloodiest battles in the war. Luckily he escaped death and was taken POW.

Dave Brooks .... *meets an unwilling prisoner*

A VERY crowded railway shed at Zutphen where prisoners from Arnhem were being held. One little old fellow stuck out like a sore thumb, dressed in denims and plimsolls. I said, what are you doing here mate? Whereupon he launched into a diatribe about what he was going to do to the British Army. I should be on bleedin' leave, he said, but they said get on that aeroplane, so I did, next thing I know the bleedin' thing is on fire, and I was told to jump out, so I did, but I should be on leave, and I'm going to sort it out. But didn't you hurt yourself dressed like that? Never mind about that, he said, I shouldn't be 'ere, I should be on bleedin' leave, and its nothing for you to bleedin' laugh at. And that's the story he was telling to anyone who would listen, he was in fact RASC and was on a plane dropping supplies at Arnhem, when he should have been on leave, nothing was going to convince him that he was a POW.

Hugh Levien .... *finds a sick bay attendant gone AWOL*

THE SCENE, the same very crowded railway shed where prisoners from Arnhem were being held. I was curious how the chap in the smart double-breasted Naval walking out uniform came to be with us. 'Oh dear, he said, I'm in trouble. They will have marked me down as absent without leave by now. You see, I only had a weekend pass, in fact it's worse than that because if I don't report back within a fortnight they will book me for desertion.'

He was a sick bay attendant at a Naval Air Station taken into use by the USAF for Market Garden. Being due a 48-hour pass he chatted up a pilot and scrounged a lift for what he thought would be a new experience. He wasn't wrong either! If anyone knows who he was, invite him to a reunion.

Bob Peatling . . . . *seven months living as a Dutchman*

DUSK WAS falling as we approached the north end of the Arnhem bridge on the Sunday evening. It should have been a tranquil scene but instead it was a hive of activity. The enemy was holding the other end of the bridge. Morale could never have been higher in the Battalion, we will soon clear them off I thought. 'B' Coy had not reported in and my platoon officer Lieut JT Ainslie was sent to make contact. I went with him. When Major David Wallis, second in command of the Battalion and an excellent example to his men, decided to reconnoitre, two of us were sent to escort him. I later joined a section from Brigade taking German prisoners to the cells at the Police Station and when I attempted to return to the Battalion lines was ordered by Military Police Lieut Morley to stay with the section, but he left us that night.

While defending the building, we were overrun by the enemy and the Sgt ordered his eight men to surrender. A very painful moment! In a flash I was determined not to be taken prisoner, there was no sensible reasoning behind my action only the fact that the Second Army should be up to us by now and I was going to await their coming, alone if necessary. Amid the din and smoke my comrades, except one, did as they had been ordered and put up their hands. What a humiliating experience for them. I raced for the roof and then changed my mind and settled for the rafters in the attic, it was fitted with shelves laden with confiscated wireless sets. The Germans searched the building firing into every room, but as luck would have it they did not venture up the steep narrow staircase that led to the attic. After about 15 minutes they left with their prisoners and ours. I had won round one!

I watched the sad sight of the inhabitants carrying white flags evacuating the town, pushing prams and handcarts with all their worldly possessions piled high. The water system had stopped so I opened a fire extinguisher, it was foul. I took water from a lavatory cistern and in the process flushed it, so I scooped the water from the pan. It started to rain so I put various utensils under the shattered tiles on the roof, I found some sterilising tablets.

My main worry was food. I had my emergency tin of chocolate and

160

luckily found another left behind by one who was now a prisoner. I searched the policemen's personal lockers and found some scraps of food, cigars and pipe tobacco. I had never smoked before but found that smoking kept the hunger pains at bay.

I settled down to wait for Monty to relieve us, not thinking for one moment that he would let us down. I found a notebook and started to write a letter home and then changed it into diary form in order to keep track of the day. I found a clock in an office below and brought it up to the attic for my use. Many German soldiers came into the building looking for loot, I watched them clear out the shops and a Bata shoe warehouse. October was wet, cold and miserable but I was cheered when the US Airforce visited to demolish the near span of the bridge. They also blew some more tiles from my roof in the process.

I usually went out into the town before 0400 hrs scavenging for food, while it was quiet. At the Victoria Hotel at the end of my foraging one morning I noticed a bottle on the kitchen sink, it was marked Limonade, my eyes lit up, just the job. I raised the bottle to my mouth to take a swig when, with acrid smell, my mouth seemed on fire. I spat out immediately – it was ammonia! Fortunately there was a small water heater above the sink and I used all the water to keep rinsing my mouth, the skin on my tongue was in tatters. I found myself very demoralised and walked back to my hideout in a very low state. Amazingly my mouth healed extremely quickly, but I could not eat anything, nor smoke. I could only drink rainwater, painfully.

On the 30th October I was still waiting to hear the battle moving my way when I had three visitors to my attic. I ignored them as usual but they clambered onto the rafters to look out of the skylight. They caught sight of my washing bowl and other everyday items for living and walked across the rafters towards me. I was not worried for it was quite dark in my corner and I laid covered with a dark green blanket. I hoped I had not been seen. They moved away downstairs but returned very shortly afterwards, as they came towards me I stood up and challenged them. They were surprised. They were friendly, I showed them the card saying I am hungry and thirsty, can you help, etc. I gave them some of our Dutch invasion money. The senior Police Lieutenant, ten Hove said he would not help but would not stop the other man, Lieut Hans van Maris from helping me. They told me that the Division was no more, that 6500 were prisoners and 3500 were dead, and that the army was still at Nijmegen 20 miles away. Lieut van Maris said he would come back alone. He did and suggested that I left in civilian clothes with a Resistance man. About an hour later Johannes Penseel arrived with clothes for me. He introduced himself with the V for victory tap on the door, waited while I shaved and we left for his home at Velperplein 7, an electrical shop. Lieut van Maris walked in front with his cycle, giving the all clear sign at each junction. My new hideout was a void between two rooms and above the two cupboards reached through a trapdoor in the bedroom above. Mr Penseel said he would be back with some food, wonderful! He came back with his two sons, John 24 and Marinus 21. They brought a saucepan of steaming vegetables, coffee, cooking apples and a blancmange. I ate as we conversed. They left and I ate more and more until all the food was gone and lay on my back writhing in pain for being so stupid. Reader, you may judge when you have not eaten a meal in six weeks, have lost about 28lbs in weight from a body with no spare fat and been offered mouthwatering food.

Some days later two resistance workers came to live in the house with me, Klaas Schuttinga 23 and Nico vd Oever 23. We had a supply of vegetables and a meagre weekly ration. I became the cook. They went out daily to do any job that they were asked and because they wore stolen police uniforms they travelled quite freely.

This was quite an exciting time for me. I was informed of all that they were getting up to, what the Germans were doing in the town, their movements, all the time I had a good view of the main thoroughfare in the town. Both lads owned ancient pistols, I showed them how to clean weapons and why. We discussed the use of plastic explosive, I objected to them burning small pieces on our cooking stove, for fun! My English lessons were appreciated. Herman Bresser took my photograph for an Ausweis (identity card). Brother Paul edited 'Worlds Press News' an underground newspaper and was a frequent visitor. All these lads had been sent to Germany to work and had escaped. Fires were deliberately started in the town by Germans and one very near to Velperplein got out of hand and we evacuated. While pushing a handcart up an incline a German soldier came to help and talk, John Penseel quickly changed sides with me. Christmas 1944 was memorable for me with the Penseel family in the vaults of the Amsterdamsche Bank on Velperplein. They had adopted a Jewish girl of seven years whose parents had been taken away, we were great friends for the day and exchanged Christmas gifts.

The Town Major decided not to renew my Ausweis after 31 December and it was thought best that I should leave the town. At 20.00hrs on a cold and frosty New Years Eve I said farewell to the Penseel family and sitting on the carrier of Nico's cycle with Klaas in attendance we presented ourselves at the control barrier on the Apeldoornscheweg. According to my Ausweis I was a deaf and dumb electrician, Nico and Klaas did the talking, we each had a weapon in our pocket to use should it be necessary. I was handed over to Jan Himmerling at Woeste Hoeve for safe keeping and Nico and Klaas returned to Arnhem. The following day we visited various houses at Hoenderloo, Otterlo and Barneveld, eventually I met Herman van Esveld on his farm at Kootwijkerbroek. To my utter surprise I met John Haller, a Glider Pilot and Harold Riley a Brigade signaller. We slept in a hollow haystack with Paul a Dutch radio operator from SOE, like

162

Ref:- NE/REP/*2604*

TO: Officer Commanding,
..."C". Coy...........................
.......No. 1. PARA. REGT.......
         I. T. C.

No.*1436.2066*... Rank *Pte*... Name ...*PEATHING. R*: Unit ..*A. A. C.*:.
                  Repatriated Prisoner of War. *EX GERMANY*

        Please interview the above-named soldier and inform him
that his account has been credited with the sum of £ *1 : 3 : 9* ,
which represents *10 Guilders converted at 3 for 3/9* *and 10*
R. Marks converted @ 6 each = 5/= in full settlement
of the claim for expenses incurred whilst escaping
        The above reference should be quoted in any query on this
subject.

                                              W.O. II
                                              Lieut.
                        for   REGIMENTAL PAYMASTER.

Hawkhill Avenue,
EDINBURGH. 7.
      /1/   194*7*.
--------/-------------
NGJ.

us he was on the run. The haystack contained shelves with British uniforms I helped myself to a pair of trousers. We were too many for safety so I had to move on. Gerritt Munkhoff cycled with me for two days to find another place until Johanvan Dijk of Achterveld said he would have me for a few days until I made the run across the Rhine. I was known as Oome Kees from Limburg to his six children to explain why I did not speak the same dialect as them.

On the 10th January my place to cross the Rhine was taken by a higher rank than mine. Well, quite a few ranks actually.

I had some unexpected meetings with German soldiers, I answered the farmhouse door to be asked, 'Have you eggs?' On another occasion they required labour the following morning in the village for the war effort. Johan van Dijk was well prepared for them, he had been a soldier in 1940. A police officer from Amersfoort, Lieut van Goor heard about me and came to ask that I return with him to his resistance group. Gerrit

Munkhoff was contacted and the Amersfoort man was told that I was part of the Barnevelt group and not for transfer.

On the 16th April rumour had it that troops had turned in our direction. I told Johan that I must leave and not be caught in his house when the battle came to Achterveld. *(Achterveld became 'no mans land' for three weeks after I had left. Eventually on May 5, 1945 the two sides met in the village school to agree the West of Holland Armistice).*

I left at first light with a sandwich from Mrs van Dijk, wearing civvies and carrying the Arnhem Police Chief's 9mm Browning (now in our museum). I set off carefully using cover where possible and after several hours saw some movement on a road. I took cover and waited for it to pass. They stopped short of me and I stood up with my hands outstretched to show I wished them no harm and they descended upon me. I shouted 'Ik ben Engelsman' and then remembered it was time to speak English. It was the 49th Lower Edmonton Regiment who were out patrolling in front of their Battalion. I went back to the Canadian Div HQ, near Arnhem, General McCreery asked me where I had last seen the enemy. I told him, his Signals officer put through a call to the RAF. Within minutes a fighter plane was over us and racing for Achterveld. If only we had experienced that air superiority last September! After telling him my story he said, 'Well done son' – that was praise indeed! Off to Zutphen for interrogation, new uniform, bottle of whisky, medical inspection (B1 malnutrition). Two days later in a Dakota I passed over the white cliffs of Dover, an emotional sight. Landed at Croydon Airport, 'Have you anything to declare?' challenged a customs officer. I rudely answered, 'Where the Bloody Hell do you think I've been this past seven months?' and he stepped back. I had arrived home!

Most of the Arnhem Resistance Group (LKP) that I had joined were rounded up on the 2nd January by the SD and started on their way to concentration camps, they were tortured for knowledge of Bob the Englishman. Toon van Daalen, Johannes Penseel and Nico van den Oever were saved from the camps and returned to hospitals in Holland, all in poor health.

John Penseel and brother Marinus died in Ludwigslust concentration camp in March 1945. Klaas Schuttinga suffered badly from dysentery in February 1945 and was parted from his friend Nico. Klaas died in the camp. The others managed to avoid capture. I will never forget them.

Den Portman . . . . *one of the seventeen to return*

IT WAS with a sense of great foreboding that I boarded the Hamilcar Glider at Fairford to be transported to the battlefield at Arnhem. A few days previously I along with a few others had been sent down to Fairford to take over a few jeeps and trailers with extra supplies for the Battalion. I remember showing some disapproval to the briefing officer

164

when he pointed out the dropping zone at Renkum Heath. Eight miles from the bridge and a whole Division expected to get there intact!

You don't need me to tell you the reply I got. If you think that flying in a glider is 'cushy', let me tell you how it felt to proceed into battle for the first time by this unconventional method. In our glider were two trailers a jeep and five men including the pilots. We moved down the runway towed by a Lancaster, it's engines screaming like a wailing banshee and it seemed as if we would go on forever down the tarmac and finally plough into the trees which were fast looming larger on the horizon. The glider became airborne the pilot struggled to keep the towing cable angle correct through this crucial period before the giant towing plane left the ground. The glider wings bent, creaked and groaned under the enormous stress that our combined weight had put upon it. We held our breath and secretly prayed and finally the plane lifted from the tarmac, we were airborne. We flew around southern England for quite a long time whilst the huge armada gradually assembled to make the North Sea crossing. On quite a few occasions the dial which showed the towing cable angle came perilously close to 'jettison' and the wings of the glider moved like a giant bird and I wondered if they would withstand the journey to Holland.

As we approached the landing area I noticed the flashes of antiaircraft fire as it sped by the nose of our glider and I waited and wondered what a direct hit would do to us. Suddenly the landing area came into view, the ground was littered with gliders, where could there be room to put down? The towing cable released, now the huge weight with no power of its own was floating in space and had to be put down by this very young man. I waited in awe. The pilot picked his spot and seconds later we were diving at an angle of 45 degrees and a speed which seemed about 150mph. We braced ourselves for the impact. The huge glider suddenly levelled out and we ploughed into the soft earth of Renkum. No time to waste off with the back end, up with the ramps, unlash the jeep and trailers and unload. In no time at all we were ready to move off.

Puffs of dirt around our vehicle made me realise that somebody had already taken exception to our being there and was doing his utmost to dissuade us from proceeding. We made rapid progress toward Arnhem, past Div HQ at Oosterbeek and on toward the bridge. About one mile from the bridge, we were stopped by an officer who said it was not possible to proceed further because German Tiger tanks were astride the road. The battle hotted up, shells, mortars, shrapnel and bullets, it was not a healthy place to be. It was here that I received a blast from either a shell or a mortar bomb and I woke up in the cellar of Div HQ, Hotel Hartenstein.

On the third day I was sufficiently recovered to take a party of German prisoners to fetch water from the well in the woods behind DHQ. One of these lads asked if he could borrow a ground sheet to protect him from the drizzle. We came up the steps from the cellar and the one wearing the ground sheet was shot by one of his own snipers and died instantly. Such was the nature of this battle that it was impossible to feel safe anywhere. I was eventually detailed to reinforce the northern side of the 'Cauldron' as it was dubbed by the Germans and a very apt description it was too, because we were constantly pounded with everything they had to throw at us. After nine days the trees around Oosterbeek had been stripped of their foliage, bodies were beginning to smell and lay more numerous around the area. The reek of cordite was everywhere, and we were hungry and exhausted through lack of sleep. The end, whatever it was to be, was not far away.

On the evening of the ninth day a Glider Pilot slid into my trench 'We are pulling out tonight' he said 'The main army has reached the South bank of the Rhine and made a crossing in small numbers'. The plan was that we were to wrap our feet in sacking (where it came from I still do not know to this day) and we had to discard anything metallic that was likely to make a noise (apart from small arms). We would find white tapes marking a narrow corridor down to the river. The artillery to the South of the river had arranged to fire tracer shells every few minutes, red to one side and green to the other. We must stay within these confines at all cost. The enemy was but a few yards away on either side of this corridor. I do not recall the exact time of the start of the evacuation, probably about 21.00hrs. A number of signallers were to stay at their posts and carrying on sending bogus messages in order to confuse the enemy.

It may sound strange but I must have been so elated to learn that there was still a chance to get away from this holocaust that I fell asleep in my trench. The rain began to fall and woke me with a start, I was alone, at the northern tip of this perimeter, everyone was gone, and everywhere was darkness. I prepared myself and slid stealthily from the trench lest I should arouse the suspicion of the enemy who were close by. I made my way toward Div HQ and then on into the wooded area behind where I located a few more soldiers making their way toward the river. I remember thinking that God had been kind in sending the rain at this precise time, because the noise of raindrops falling on the leaves in the silence of pitch black night is quite considerable and certainly it helped the process of our evacuation.

Halfway down through the woods there was a sudden crackle of German machine guns, a sudden cry of pain in the blackness, everyone froze. Minutes later, this caterpillar of humanity started to move again, and eventually we emerged from the cover of the trees on to the flat flood banks of the river. Cows lay about the field like barrage balloons with all fours pointing skyward. Soldiers too, those who had made the crossing to link with our corridor had suffered badly and there was plenty of evidence around this area.

166

We approached the river along a shallow trough and the man in front of me began to talk to his mate (probably through sheer relief at having made it so far). I was so incensed and swore under my breath that I would do the most awful things to them if they didn't button their lips. At the river bank there were many Paras waiting as the boats, manned by Canadians, ferried back and forth. It seemed that it would be forever before my turn came. The eastern sky was beginning to lighten. Jerry had got wind that something was happening and started shelling the river bank from the Westerbowing Heights. I must get across the river before it was too late. I made my decision. Move up the river bank towards Arnhem as far as was possible, discard boots, smock, sling the bolt of my rifle into the water. I entered the water about 150 yards upstream, took a deep breath and struck out for the opposite shore against a strong fast flowing current. It seemed that I had overestimated my staying power. I was weak through lack of food and now I was being carried quickly toward the crossing area but I was little more than halfway across. My strength was giving out. Would I be carried downstream and into the hands of the Germans?

Keep flaying to get across, freedom beckoned at the other side. Suddenly there was a boat in front of me going in the right direction. A hand stretched out. 'Hold on, we are nearly there'. My guardian angel in the guise of a KOSB soldier has scooped me from oblivion and I was delivered to the South bank of the river where, it seemed, our army stood secure. I climbed a steep flood bank and over the other side into a small orchard. Soon a lorry marshal loaded me aboard and we were on our way down the corridor toward Nijmegen. I remember going through a field ambulance for a quick check up, it was daylight now and the men from 30 Corps stood and looked at us as we filed out from the medics. 'Well done lads', said one, 'Sorry we couldn't get to you in time'. That morning brought an event which I shall always remember. Sgt Major Jimmy Sharp had come from Nijmegen to sort out the remains of the 2nd Bn. On this misty field by a small peach tree, he called out in his authoritative voice 'Fall in 2nd Battalion'. Seventeen men, exhausted from their exploits of the last ten days 'fell in'. He looked us over, 'Is this the lot?' he said, and his usually strong expression changed, his chin trembled and his eyes welled up in a veil of tears as he realised that the decimation of our Second battalion had been complete.

Market Garden and why it failed

THE AUTHOR of this book spent seven months after the battle in occupied Holland and saw at first hand the misery the failed battle had caused to the inhabitants. What was the reason?

The source of the following report is uncertain but it certainly gives the answer.

Why did the operation fail? It failed for two major reasons:

1. The Air Plan was bad. All experience and common sense pointed to landing all 3 Airborne Divisions in the minimum period of time, so that they could form up and collect themselves before the Germans reacted. All 3 Divisions could have been landed in a space of 12 hours or so, but FAAA insisted on a plan which resulted in the second lift (with half the heavy equipment) arriving more than 24 hours after the Germans had been alerted. All this evidence seems to point to the fact that this second lift was disorganised or destroyed by the enemy on arrival. Hence, the 1st Division had to fight its battle without a really effective Glider Brigade – a hopeless task.

Who was responsible for this plan which seemed even at the time to be highly dangerous, because it ignored so many of the lessons already learned about airborne. First Allied Airborne Army must take the main responsibility for they settled the plan against advice. FAAA, that unnecessary Headquarters, composed mainly of people who have no experience of airborne or troop carrier, yet given this ghastly power over the lives of the best troops and aircrews U.S. or England can produce.

2. The Ground Army was late on its time-table. Some people in 21 Army Group and below must have underestimated the difficulties of the ground advance to Arnhem for the Ground Forces were several days late in arrival – in fact they never really arrived in sufficient strength to relieve 1st Division. Considerable blame must attach to the planners, and possibly the Commanders and troops, connected with this failure – but I consider the degree of blame less than under (1) because I have always thought an Airborne Division ought to be able to hold out for 8-10 days if it is dropped effectively and is kept supplied. So, if the 1st Division had been dropped effectively, and the air had kept it supplied, I believe it would have held out strongly for 8 days, and the operation could have succeeded. 4 days is a reasonable period to aim at for relief, but in emergency this should be doubled.

Arnhem need not have failed. That it did is due to putting inexperienced people in charge of a highly complicated operation. In civil life, such a failure would result in immediate dismissal; in Russia, it would result in court martial; in Allied democracy, it results in nothing.

No one has the courage to speak openly or to act.

My thanks to the unnamed for putting his thoughts on paper. A brilliant summing up. I agree with him wholeheartedly. RWP

CHAPTER NINE

Dutch Courage and Pegasus

Major A Digby Tatham Warter DSO was captured at Arnhem after he gave the word to the men to make a break for it on 21 September. Once captured he feigned being wounded in order to get into hospital where he thought he would stand more chance of escaping. He did escape, with his 'A' Coy 2ic Captain AM Frank. They met up with the Dutch Underground forces and a month later on 22 October he led 138 evaders back across the Rhine.

He gave permission for his story to be told in this book.

Sadly he died before the book was finished, having suffered a long and painful illness in his adopted country of Kenya.

I HAVE GIVEN this story the title 'Dutch Courage and Pegasus' for reasons that should become clear as the reader progresses. This is a personal account of the four weeks that I spent with the Dutch Resistance after the Battle of Arnhem, culminating in a mass evacuation called 'Operation Pegasus'. There are already historical records of those times and it is not intended that this should be another. I make no pretence at remembering the names of all the people who helped in so many different ways. To recall them would require considerable re-search and would not necessarily enhance the interest of this story. I will, therefore, only mention the names of a few with whom I was most closely involved. Likewise I will describe only the events with which I was personally concerned.

Except for the Resistance fighters themselves, I, probably more than anyone else involved, was in a position to observe the day to day bravery of the ordinary Dutchmen and their families. It is one thing to show courage in the face of danger when you are trained to meet it, or when it is forced upon you, but it is quite another thing to go out and look for it when there is really no reason why you should and when, by so doing, you are jeopardising the safety of your family and others. In any case, at this stage of the war, the Dutch knew very well that the end was in sight and their ordeal nearly over, and it would have been understandable had they opted for a lower profile. To the fact that they chose not to take this path, many Allied evaders owed their freedom and, in some cases, their lives.

Major AD Tatham Warter
(Oxford & Bucks)
organised escape.

Major DE Crawley
(Loyals)
POW Arnhem.

Major Victor Dover
(Royal West Kents)
POW Arnhem.

Captain Francis Hoyer-Millar
(HLI)
POW Arnhem.

Lieut Jack Grayburn
(Oxford & Bucks LI)
Posthumous VC.

Lieut WN Dormer
(The Black Watch)
POW Arnhem.

Captain 'Bombs' Panter
(Royal Fusiliers)
POW Arnhem.

Lieut Peter Barry
(Royal Ulster Rifles)
POW Arnhem.

Lieut Tom Ainslie
(Royal Norfolks)
POW Arnhem.

Memories are not infallible and the events about which I write happened many years ago. So I hope I may be forgiven if some of the details have escaped me. In mitigation I can only say that it took much pressure from my family and a few close friends to induce me to put pen to paper, and I might add, my daughter, Joanna, volunteering her services for most of the hard work. Once the decision was taken it is extraordinary how memories came flooding back.

In and Out

The story, in so far as it concerned me, began on the evening of 21st September 1944. During the previous night and early hours of that day our defences North of Arnhem Bridge had been finally over-run by SS armour and infantry and those survivors who could, tried to make their way to join up with the remnants of 1st Airborne Division, who were themselves desperately fighting to hold out against heavy odds at Oosterbeck, some miles to the West. However, few succeeded and the Germans soon discovered most of us in a thorough search of the area. I myself had a very short run for my money. Duncan McLean, the adjutant of 2 Para, and I had taken refuge in a culvert and, though not an ideal hiding place with the whole area crawling with German troops hunting down the erstwhile defenders of the Bridge, we had hoped it might serve until nightfall. But this was not to be and before long we were unceremoniously winkled out at the end of an SS bayonet and taken to a POW collecting point.

In the late afternoon the wounded were separated from the other prisoners and taken to a small hospital in the Northern suburbs of Arnhem. I thought that if I could include myself among the wounded, there would be a rather better, if remote, chance of escaping. I was lucky to achieve this as, although knocked out for some hours during the battle and battered in appearance, I had in fact suffered nothing which could be called a wound.

Amongst the wounded was Tony Franks, a veteran of North Africa and Sicily, who had been second-in-command to me in 'A' Coy at the start of the battle. He had been wounded by a piece of shrapnel still lodged in one ankle causing him considerable pain and making movement difficult but not impossible. In the transport on the way to the hospital Tony and I discussed possibilities and decided, for a start, to try to stay together when we arrived. We planned to make our stay as short as possible. The first of many bits of luck occurred here when we were put in a small ward on the ground floor. The only other bed was occupied by man with a very severe head wound. Tony and I were told to take off our clothes and get into bed. It may be of some interest that I still had my pistol which the Germans, in their haste, had not noticed. This I concealed in my clothes under the bed.

In the hospital there were so many severe cases that, during our short

171

stay there, neither Tony nor I were examined by anyone. Our unfortunate fellow patient was often visited by doctors, nurses and orderlies as he frequently shouted and became violent. After some time we were given a watery soup which did us little good as we had used up our 24 hour special airborne ration on the first day of the battle and were now extremely hungry.

Apart from this we were left in peace. Lying quietly in bed Tony and I made our plan: as soon as it grew dark enough we would put on our clothes, climb out of the window and crawl away through the laurels which grew alongside the house. No plan could have been simpler but there were two major predictable hazards. Although they had been civil enough so far, we could not be sure that the German and pro-German Dutch staff would react kindly to catching us half-way out of the window. The second was that we could not know where any guards might be situated. A good look through the window just before dark had not revealed any, but we could not assume that they would not be posted after dark. So inevitably a good deal of luck was going to be needed.

As for the details: I first had to move a small table under the rather high-set window so that Tony, handicapped as he was, could use it to climb out. He was to go out first and wait for me in the laurels. If all went well I would first return the table to its proper place and then follow Tony. If I had not joined him within ten minutes it would mean that something had gone wrong and he was to go on alone. As it happened something did go very wrong. When Tony was half way out of the window, he kicked over the table with a horrible crash. This seemed to disturb our room-mate and caused him to have one of his fits, screaming and throwing himself about. I could only lie in my bed watching while a doctor and orderlies rushed in to control the poor man. I imagine that they thought he had knocked over the table himself as they soon departed without apparently noticing Tony's absence, leaving me to follow through the window. We made our departure from the hospital grounds with great caution and without further incident and began our long slow walk towards the West and the sound of gunfire.

Travels and Brave People

We didn't manage to get very far that night, possibly three or four miles. The pace had to suit Tony's bad leg and we kept having to skirt round German positions and bivouacs. Sometimes we were forewarned of their presence by snoring, talking, movement or rattling of accoutrements – quite a lot of their transport was horsed. But the clearest warning of all came from their smell. I am not suggesting that they were any dirtier than any of us in similar conditions. It was almost certainly the spiced food, such as sausages, that they ate and the ersatz tobacco they smoked. Whatever the cause, it was a very distinctive and unattractive smell and this helped us enormously.

172

Some time towards dawn we seemed to be getting out of the suburbs into more open country and we were beginning to feel that we could not go on much longer. It had been virtually impossible to sleep for the last five days and the stress of the battle must have taken its toll of our strength. We were just about done up when we came upon a small seemingly isolated house. Discreet knocking on the door eventually produced a little middle-aged lady, who turned out to be the owner of the farm and a widow. She spoke no English and was obviously very frightened and bewildered and one could hardly blame her. In addition to the awful consequences for anyone caught hiding a British soldier, we must have looked a hideous mess. Also the German army was all around. I fully expected her to shut the door in our faces, but, after talking rapidly for some time in (to us) unintelligible Dutch, she abruptly changed her mind and showed us to a ladder leading to a small loft above a cow stall. A short time after we had settled ourselves in the straw our hostess brought us the most welcome meal of milk, eggs, bread and cheese. When she came back to collect the empty mugs and plates she indicated by gestures that there were Germans nearby and that we should hide under the straw. This we gladly did and slept like the dead for several hours.

A good deal later in the morning we were woken to find the head of a small Dutchman peering over the top of the ladder. This turned out to be a Mr. Van den Ven, a house painter by trade, who had been called by our hostess to help. He had a little English and promised to return later to take us away. We would be disguised as his two sons, also painters and in the meantime he provided us with a razor to make ourselves look more respectable. He also stressed the need for extra caution as some German artillery had that morning moved into the field next to our refuge. Mr. Van den Ven duly returned bringing two pairs of paint spattered overalls and some tins of paint. He told us to follow him closely. First we had to make a small detour round the Germans and then walk a mile or two to Mr. Van den Ven's house on the edge of a small hamlet. He took us to a disused delivery van at the bottom of his orchard and told us this would be our home until arrangements had been made for us to move on.

This delivery van seemed a good place to be. It was well hidden from any road and was quite large enough for our purposes. Mr. Van den Ven gave us food and bedding and said he would bring a doctor to see us later. He then left us to sleep for the rest of the day. The doctor arrived in the evening and cleaned us up a bit. Tony's leg needed attention badly and was not looking too good. The doctor said he would return on the following day, which he duly did.

Our second day in the van was quiet and we had time to take stock of our situation. We had been incredibly lucky so far. The escape from the hospital, in spite of one close shave, had gone according to our plan. We had avoided colliding with the enemy on a number of occasions during our night walk and, when just about at the end of our endurance, had found a very brave lone Dutch woman willing to take us in and hide us. Then had come Mr. Van den Ven to whom we owed our new refuge, sustenance and medical care. But we had no right to expect this sort of luck to hold for ever. Nevertheless we could possibly be forgiven for thinking that the worst could be over and that the future held a fair chance of final escape. For the time being we could only wait to see what our Dutch friends were going to do about us. In fact we were destined to spend another week or so in the van.

I used some of the time to write a fairly detailed report on the action at Arnhem Bridge. With Tony's help I think it was pretty accurate and I also wrote citations for bravery insofar as these concerned men under my command. I addressed this to General Roy Urquhart, our Divisional Commander, and passed it to the Dutch Resistance. I did all this because I thought, as it turned out rightly, that it might be some months before an accurate report could reach the General or higher command. He did, in fact, receive my report soon after he had crossed the Rhine with the remnants of his Division a few days later.

Otherwise the days must have passed slowly as we had little to do except wait for one of the Van den Ven family to bring us our meals and the daily visits of the Dutch doctor. Mr. Van den Ven had a few tobacco plants growing in his garden and used to give us dried leaves which we amused ourselves by rolling into some semblance of cigarettes. We never moved further than the immediate vicinity of the van and probably slept a lot of the time as we were both undoubtedly tired from the stress and strains of the battle and our escape. But by the end of our stay in the van I was ready for anything and rearing to go.

On 3rd October two members of the Resistance movement from the small town of Ede visited us in the van. After looking us over and asking a few questions they said they would come for me the next morning but that Tony would have to be left until later because of his wound. The same two men duly arrived next day bringing me some different clothes and leading a bicycle for me to ride. The Dutch often led bicycles.

I said goodbye to our host with a feeling of deep gratitude for all he had done for us. It was only later that I discovered that he was not, at that time, fully trusted by the Resistance from Ede as he had yet to become one of their members, and after spending some weeks with the Resistance it is easy to see how careful they had to be. Sadly the country abounded in pro-German spies.

With one Dutchman riding two or three hundred yards ahead and the second riding with me I set off. Over the next two or three weeks I grew very accustomed to this way of moving. After what seemed like a good many miles to someone not used to riding bicycles we came to a beautiful house set in its own grounds in wooded country. First I was introduced to its owner Miss Lambert, an elegant and attractive young lady, and then to my surprise and delight found our Brigade

Commander, Gerald Lathbury, relaxing in a comfortable chair in her sitting room. Over some light refreshment, which included excellent sherry, I learnt that Gerald had been wounded early in the battle some way from the Bridge and had later escaped from another hospital. Since then he had been hiding in woods until found by the Resistance and brought to this safe house. From the time of his escape Gerald, like all evaders who wished to survive, had to do more or less what he was told by the Resistance. But, although confined mainly indoors because of his wound, he was always consulted before any major decisions were taken.

Here I should explain that the name 'evader' was given to members of the allied armed forces who, for whatever reason, were avoiding capture by the enemy. If evaders should be caught when wearing uniform they would, anyhow in theory, be subject to the rules of the Geneva Convention and entitled to be treated as POW's. If, on the other hand, they were caught in civilian disguise, they could not claim the protection of the Geneva Convention and were liable to be treated as spies and shot.

At this time I learnt that my guides were no less than "Bill" Wildeboer, the chief of the Dutch Resistance movement in and for many miles round the small town of Ede which was our immediate destination. The other appeared to be his chief staff officer and No. 2. This was Mennor alias 'Toni' De Nooy, a member of a large family in Ede in one of whose houses I was later to discover Brigadier John Hackett. Here Bill told me of his plans for us. Gerald and Tony were to be discreetly placed in different houses in Ede where they could rest and have medical care and start to convalesce. I was to have the honour of staying with Bill in his house on the outskirts of the town. It seemed that he needed some one to visit and coordinate the activities of the considerable number of airborne evaders in the district, and to act as liaison between the Resistance and the Allies across the Rhine. He seemed to consider me suitable for this job.

Sadly, we soon had to continue our journey for a few more miles. Always we could hear the sound of gunfire, now to the South of us. Bill had told us that the remnants of our Division had finally withdrawn across the river. We often rode past units of German soldiery on the move, but they paid no attention to us. After all the Dutch were always riding bicycles and the soldiers presumably had more important things to worry about. On one occasion, however, Toni, our forward scout, had to do a U turn and hurry back to warn us when he spotted a check point ahead. A short detour took us round this and we soon reached the outskirts of Ede and so to the Wildeboer house.

About the Resistance

Before I embark on the next phase of my story it is appropriate to say a few words about the Resistance movement. I soon discovered that they concerned themselves with anything that would assist the Allies and cause discomfiture to the 'Moffen' as they called the Germans – comparable to our word 'Hun'. This included helping and hiding escapers and evaders, sabotage, and the passing of information on German troop movements to the Allies. I have no intention of going into detail of their command structure and organisation which, anyhow, was always a bit of a mystery to me. Suffice it to say that in the Ede district there seemed to be a small cadre of totally reliable officers and a much larger number of members. These latter, although undoubtedly trustworthy, were given the minimum of information about plans and operations and then only about those which directly concerned them. Obviously the less they knew the less they could divulge under interrogation by the Gestapo.

From what I saw discipline and security seemed, and in fact had to be, superlative. I was told that there had been cases of jealousy and treachery in the past, but saw no evidence of this during my stay with the Resistance around Ede. There was also, of course, the very real danger of infiltration by pro-German spies and the Resistance leaders had to be constantly alert against this.

'Bill' Wildeboer, the leader of the Resistance in the Ede district was a solid, shrewd and able man. He was tough physically and mentally, and well liked and respected. Before the German occupation he had been a senior Warrant Officer in the former Dutch army. To say that he, his family and all members of the Resistance, especially the officers, were brave would be too great an understatement. The penalties for assisting the Allies in any way were ferocious and, if a man was caught hiding or helping an evader, his whole family was liable to be shot and their house burned down. I was told of times when this had happened and I have no reason to doubt the veracity of those accounts. I later heard of two cases where this actually happened, during my stay in Holland, in a nearby town. The strain on the women, especially those with young children, must have been appalling.

The Wildeboers

Bill's wife, Mevrouw Hil Wildeboer Voskuil, whom I shall call Mrs. W. for the sake of simplicity, was an exceptional woman. A year or two before I met her, Bill had reason to believe that he had been betrayed to the Gestapo and, to escape their attentions, had gone underground for the best part of a year. This meant that Mrs. W. had to leave her home with her two children, Hilly and Dicky, and go into hiding with trusted friends in the countryside. Hilly, a bright and pretty little girl when I first knew her, was, at the time of their escape, possibly five years old. Dicky was a baby. To complicate matters Bill possessed a forbidden radio which was used to receive communications from British Intelligence and it was most desirable that this should go along too. The curfew was strict and, to move this at night was thought too dangerous. So they hit on the idea of hiding the radio under Dicky in her pram. And so Mrs. W., the children and the radio moved freely through the German check-points around Ede with Hilly pushing her baby sister in the pram. The consequences of discovery are too awful to contemplate.

Not long before my arrival in their house the Wildeboers had hidden a British pilot for several weeks before sending him on his way home. They called him 'Peter' and when I came along they decided to call me 'Peter' too. Theirs was a fairly small detached house with its own little garden in a row of houses on the edge of the town of Ede. It had an outside laundry room and a shed, or garage, used for storing firewood, tools and bicycles.

New Identity and More Evaders

It was now necessary that I should be given a suitable identity so, as soon as I had been introduced to the family, Toni led me off with the usual scout ahead of us to a small clothing emporium where I was fitted out with all the necessities. My suit was a nondescript dark grey colour and seemed to be made of string, wool being scarce in Holland. Thus equipped I was next taken to a specialist in forging identity cards. Here I was photographed and told we could collect the card the next day. I still have the card which describes me somewhat improbably as being deaf and dumb. By this time the day was nearly over so we cycled back to the Wildeboer house to enjoy the first of many most welcome suppers.

Soon after the meal Bill showed me to my sleeping accommodation which had an interesting entrance. First Bill removed a few faggots of firewood and then a board or two in the back wall of the shed. This revealed four or five steps leading down to a small dug-out the dimensions of which were perhaps seven feet long by five feet wide by six feet high. It had been well constructed with the sides and roof lined with some kind of rough timber and Bill himself had used it for several months at times of high risk. The little room was furnished with a narrow bed, small table and chair and there were one or two hooks on a wall for clothes. Some kind of light must have been provided and some ventilation, but I don not recall what. There must also have been a bucket for emergency as no way of getting out existed until Bill came in the morning to remove the faggots and boards which he used to replace after bidding me goodnight. The room may have been a bit damp but was comfortable enough and I had no difficulty in sleeping after my always energetic days.

Providing the coast was clear Bill would call me early and, after replacing the camouflage, I would go to wash and shave in the pantry basin while Mrs. W. was preparing breakfast. Bill and I would be away by 8 o'clock to attend the regular morning conferences. Later, unless there was something special on, I would remount my bicycle for a round of visits to evaders in hideouts and safe houses in the town and outlying farms. After a day to two, when the early discomfort had worn off, I began to enjoy these often long, and sometimes exciting rides around the countryside. As Resistance leader many affairs claimed Bill's time and I would usually be guided by Toni, or another member of the De Nooy clan, and often by 'Flip' Van den Pol, a prominent and daring member of the Ede Resistance.

One of my first calls was at an old barn set among poplar trees far out in the totally flat countryside and accessible only by foot and bicycle paths running along the dykes. It was a desolate and secluded spot to which we were secretively led by the Boer (Dutch farmer) owner. (After the war he presented me with a woodcut of the barn drawn by himself which still hangs in my house). Inside I found a young officer in the RAMC, called Olliff, in charge of twenty or thirty assorted medics. I remember thinking at the time what a nice fellow he was, although both he and his men seemed uncertain and bewildered by the fate that had befallen them. This was hardly surprising as it turned out that they had been wandering, with many adventures, around the countryside for several days, living on raw turnips, after being landed in quite the wrong place, until the Resistance found them. I like to think that they were genuinely pleased to see me and relieved to know that they had not been entirely forsaken. These men were well looked after and fed through Resistance sources but bored and short of exercise as they were never allowed to move out of the barn until after dark, and then only for a breath of fresh air. Olliff was obviously doing all he could to maintain morale. I left them promising to return in a day or two with any news there might be and thereafter visited them as often as my other activities allowed. (Years later I met Donald Olliff when he came to dinner where my wife and I were staying with old friends in Warwickshire. He was then a much respected country practitioner).

Plans for Sabotage

I think it was the same day that I was taken to meet an SAS officer who, with his team of two or three, had been dropped into Holland behind the German lines some time previously. A Belgian named Kirschen; he had been given the code name 'King' by which I knew him, and operated an Intelligence gathering post and radio link to London. His air of efficiency and quiet confidence much impressed me. He had established his post in one of three chicken houses in a clearing in wooded farmland some miles west of Ede, an out of the way spot and one not likely to attract the attention of the Germans.

'King' said that he would be able to arrange for a supply drop of uniforms, food, arms and explosives if I gave him details of our requirements. The first drop was, in fact, successfully carried out a few days later some distance North of Ede. The arms and uniforms were then hidden in a farm nearby until they would be required and the food distributed by the Resistance to help in the feeding of evaders.

178

I should explain here that at this time all of us expected the Allied offensive to be maintained and we were hoping that they would cross the Rhine to join us within days. With this in mind our idea was that, with the numbers we were collecting, we would be able to do useful bits of sabotage behind the German lines once we were supplied with arms and explosives. The Dutch, of course, were more than enthusiastic about this idea as it would give them more chances of a crack at the hated 'Moffen'. They were already doing some effective sabotage themselves. In particular they had succeeded in virtually closing the railway line through Ede by blowing it up when necessary. This, together with strafing of roads by the RAF, undoubtedly hindered the German reinforcement of their defences North of the Rhine.

The next few days were spent cycling round the district meeting more evaders and getting as many as possible organised to operate as small fighting groups under the command of officers or warrant officers when the time should come for sabotage.

Amongst the many I visited were Captain Tom Wainwright and Sergeant Major Robert Grainger, both of whom impressed me as being exceptionally keen and able and were to prove their worth later. Both were Parachutists. After I had been in Ede for three days Gerald Lathbury and Tony Franks were moved there by the Resistance and I was immediately taken to see Gerald. Thereafter we used to meet most mornings at the De Menno house in a street in the town were Gerald was being hidden. These morning conferences were always attended by Bill and Toni De Menno and also by Major Tony Hibbert, Gerald's Brigade Major, who was to play a prominent part in events to come. Tony had been taken prisoner after the battle at the Bridge and had managed to escape in a most exciting way. He used to turn up dressed in a very odd fashion wearing a flashy check jacket, vivid green plus-fours with white stockings. I remember that Gerald and I were horrified by this disguise but it did not seem to worry Tony or attract any attention from the Germans. After hearing the news from the Resistance leaders and discussing plans with them we would disperse for the day and I would continue my round of visits.

In addition to these morning conferences I would attend another with Bill and his lieutenants most evenings. The latest Intelligence would be discussed and Bill would give his orders. Toni spoke English well enough to interpret for me. I also used to visit 'King' twice a week and arranged through him for further supply drops.

Domestic Life

The domestic routine in the Wildeboer house varied little from day to day. Family breakfast in the kitchen was attended by Bill and Mrs. W. and the two little girls. Although very different from the sort of breakfast I was accustomed to, it was always an ample and enjoyable meal consisting mainly of cheese, smoked meats and delicious dark brown bread. Conversation was not easy as Bill had little English and Mrs. W. virtually none. However as I began to pick up a few words of Dutch and Bill a few more of English we managed to understand each other pretty well. Thus sustained, Bill and I would set off on our various affairs and would not normally return to the house until just before dark. The evening meal started with a rich meaty soup, one of the best I ever remember eating, followed by the same assortment as at breakfast.

There were occasional alarms when I was in the house. The whispered "Moffen" would send me scurrying for cover, but the house was never searched while I was there. Usually they were checking for billets.

The Resistance somehow managed to feed their Airborne charges pretty well in spite of the strict and meagre rations allowed to the Dutch people. Many boers were members of the Resistance and used to bring in food to be distributed by Bill's lieutenants and, of course, during my stay the supply drops arranged through 'King' helped as well. I was often given coffee, of a kind, and biscuits at the houses I visited during the daytime and I can never remember going hungry. Twice a week Mrs. W. filled a copper tub in the wash house for my bath with water heated in kettles on the kitchen stove. Altogether I was very well taken care of during the nearly three weeks I spent in that house.

A Change of Plan

Towards the middle of October our situation changed dramatically for the worse when we received instructions from London through 'King' that the Allies had no intention of renewing the offensive that winter. They suggested that we should lie low and hide in the Dutch countryside through the winter months. At our meeting with Gerald next morning it did not require much discussion to decide that such a course of action was quite out of the question.

There were now about eighty Airborne evaders in and around Ede, and thirty or forty more nearer Arnhem who had been contacted by Tony Hibbert, who had charge of that area. Added to this the Resistance knew of many more much further afield. To have asked them to hide these numbers for several months would have imposed an intolerable strain on them and their families.

To make matters even worse the Germans had recently been building up their strength North of the Rhine and there were now thought to be some two to three thousand troops in our immediate vicinity with a formation headquarters in Ede itself. It required only the smallest slip for the whole set-up to be blown, with appalling consequences for our Dutch hosts. We had to get ourselves out, and the quicker the better.

The question was how and where could we hope to cross the river with such large numbers. The established escape routes many miles down stream to the West were very fragile, and could at best handle only one or two men at a time. Our only hope seemed to lie directly South of Ede, but this might mean that we should have to fight our way through the German river defences. At least there was some wooded country fairly near the river to give us some cover.

Our first priority was to get a British officer across the river to explain our circumstances and plans. It was at this time that Colonel David Dobie, the commander of 1st Parachute Battalion, turned up after a very exciting escape which is a story of its own. He was brought to Ede by the Resistance and at once I took him to see Gerald Lathbury. It did not take Gerald long to decide that David was the perfect agent to send across the Rhine. His resourcefulness and determination would give him a better chance than most of getting through and his rank, experience and ability meant that he would carry weight in expressing our situation to 2nd Army and making a good plan. And so, after long and detailed briefing by the Dutch and ourselves, David set off with Resistance guides on 14th October.

This marked the beginning of the final phase of my adventures. It was now obvious that we would need a very great deal more than ordinary good luck if we were to get across the river without heavy casualties to ourselves and disaster to our Dutch friends, and I am not ashamed to say that I began praying very hard in my dug-out every night.

The Telephone

For some time we had known of the existence of a secret telephone link which the Resistance used to talk to their contacts in Nijmegen, to the South of the Rhine, and other towns in Holland. This was a remarkably convenient means of communication which the Germans had so far failed to learn about. It seems that a great many power lines in Holland ran underground, and the engineers who installed them had wisely incorporated a telephone line with the power cables. The only snag was that the telephone terminals were inside the power stations and these were guarded day and night by supposedly pro-German para-military Dutch. In fact some of these were not pro-German at all but reliable members of the Resistance, and Alex Hartmann in charge of the station at Ede, was one of Bill's most trusted men and could let him know when it was safe to use the telephone. Up to now I had not made use of this service as, for various reasons, we had thought it more secure to use 'King's' radio link to London, and this had so far served our purpose well. But from now on we would be discussing and reviewing the detailed plans for evacuation, and it would suit us far better to have direct communication with XXX Corps Headquarters at Nijmegen.

The Dutch thought that they could, with luck, get David across the river in two days. So, before he left, we arranged to talk on the telephone two nights hence. As this occasion was to be the first of many nocturnal trips to the power station, I will describe it in some detail. I had by now

181

become very used to cycling around in daylight with my two watchdogs, continually passing German soldiery apparently uninterested in me. There was really no reason why they should be suspicious, and I had complete confidence in my advance scout giving ample warning of any check points. These had to be avoided at all cost, but otherwise there seemed little danger of detection. The prospect of moving at night, after the curfew, seemed to me a different kettle of fish, and I can remember feeling some apprehension.

After supper on the appointed night Bill said that the right guards would be on duty at the power station, and it was time to go. We left the house through a hole in the fence at the back and followed a footpath through woodland to a railway line. There seemed to be little risk here and we moved fast along it for some way. After a mile or so Bill stopped to listen and then gave a low whistle. When this was answered from somewhere ahead, we knew that the coast was clear and it was safe to go on. Shortly afterwards a large building loomed up in the blackout. Alex Hartmann met us and led us in through a side door into a little room which contained the telephone, the odd table and chair and not much else. The guards remained outside to warn of approaching danger.

On the telephone Bill spoke to someone in Dutch for a minute or two and then handed the instrument to me. There to my relief and delight was David's voice as clear as if he had been sitting in the room beside me. He did not waste words in describing his many adventures crossing the Rhine, but did say that everyone over there seemed enthusiastic about getting us back. He had not had time to discuss a plan with XXX Corps and suggested we talk again the following night. After consulting Bill I agreed a time.

Plans for Departure

I continued to visit evaders, many of them for the second or third time, and was now able to give them the welcome news that plans were being made for their evacuation. Although all of them were well looked after, inevitably morale was low and I like to think that my visits cheered them up.

One such visit that stands out in my memory occurred when I was taken to one of the De Nooy houses in the middle of the town to see Brigadier John Hackett. He had commanded 4th Parachute Brigade, had been very badly wounded in the battle and was lucky to be alive. He, like several others, had been spirited away from the St. Elizabeth Hospital at Arnhem. Now in the capable hands of three old De Nooy ladies, he was receiving regular visits from a Dutch doctor and, although in bed, seemed in good heart. He did not seem too concerned by the presence of a German headquarters in a house just down the street. The Brigadier has written the story of his sojourn in Holland and eventual escape, and I will only say here that, because of the severity of his wounds, the

182

Resistance tried to arrange for a light aircraft to land at night to take him to England. For various reasons this proved impossible and the plan had to be abandoned.

Piet Kruyff headed the Resistance in the Arnhem district, and worked closely with Bill Wildeboer of Ede. A very bold and enterprising leader, he was responsible for some brilliantly planned and executed missions during my stay in Holland. Like other Resistance leaders he derived inordinate pleasure from outwitting the "Moffen", and he was certainly good at it. Somehow he had access to some ancient wood-fueled vehicles that had so far escaped the German net and he used these when the occasion demanded for transporting evaders. The Brigadiers Lathbury and Hackett, and Tony Franks were amongst those he conveyed to Ede.

When I spoke to David on the telephone the following evening, he told me of the plan being made for our escape. This, although sounding simple enough, was obviously not going to be easy to execute. We were to make our own way to the river at a point given the code name "Digby". Here boats would be sent across to collect us. The exact position of "Digby" would be indicated to us by a Bofors gun firing bursts of tracer shells low over the river some time after midnight, and we were to signal our arrival by flashing a red torch. The whole operation received the code name "Pegasus". The exact time and date would be fixed later, probably during the last week of October. David then told me that my main telephone contact in future would be Major Hugh Fraser of the SAS, the staff officer assigned to the operation by General Horrocks, the Corps Commander.

South of the Rhine the team responsible for planning "Pegasus" consisted mainly of David Dobie, Hugh Fraser and Airey Neave. The latter had himself escaped from Colditz and was now working in the British Intelligence service. North of the river the planning was done at our daily morning conferences in Gerald's house. My nightly talk on the telephone formed the link between the two.

Our first objective was to concentrate as many evaders as possible close to the river and for this we decided to make use of the extensive woodland near Bennekom to the South of Ede. A day or two before the date appointed for "Pegasus" the Resistance would start concentrating evaders from outlying areas and bring them closer to Ede. On the day itself we would all somehow have to rendezvous in these woods. It was obviously going to be an extremely difficult and dangerous operation for the Resistance, with the countryside now milling with German soldiery.

Except for those coming from far afield, who were to be moved at night by Piet in his lorries, evaders would have to move from their hiding places to the RV in daylight and in civilian disguise. But, for the final move down to the river through the German defensive line, where we expected to have to fight, we would need to be in uniform. As a result of supply drops arranged through 'King' there was now an ample supply of arms and uniforms hidden near Ede, but these too would have to be transported to the RV by the Resistance.

While Bill and Piet made their arrangements, I tried to see all the evaders near Ede to give them some idea of what was being planned for them. Tony Hibbert was doing the same in his area around Arnhem. Moving around the country I was impressed by the increased troop activity as the Germans were obviously building up their river defences. During those few days I covered a good many miles, usually guided by Toni or Flip but sometimes others. There was an attractive girl who often came with me, usually acting as a forward scout. She was with me one day when an amusing incident occurred. A German staff car overtook us at high speed and then skidded off the muddy road into the ditch. As the officers seemed to be in an excitable state, we thought it wise to help push their car out. They were gracious enough to thank us for our help and went on their way, leaving my Dutch friends and me to have a good laugh.

Unwelcome Guests

However, life was daily becoming more difficult as, apart from regular German troops, the number of Gestapo, Green Police and Dutch SS operating in the vicinity had increased considerably. It was even rumoured that they knew of the presence of a number of Allied evaders, so greater care than ever was needed.

The Wildeboer household had to suffer the inconvenience at this stage of the billeting of four men from a Panzer unit. However, they seemed decent fellows and confined themselves to their room upstairs, leaving the downstairs for us. After Mrs. W. had given them supper they always departed for some canteen and did not return until late at night. Occasionally we would meet coming in and out of the house when they would usually stand aside to let me pass, sometimes giving me a friendly pat on the back. Altogether, their manners were excellent and, although a constant worry, gave us no trouble. Hilly, who knew all that was going on, just ignored them and Mrs. W. treated them politely, but with ill concealed scorn, while Bill very wisely went out of his way to appear friendly.

The evening conferences with the Resistance leaders were usually held at Toni De Nooy's place. Bill would receive reports and give his orders for the night and the following day. Toni was a member of the large De Nooy family clan and ran one of the family businesses, a paint factory. As people were always coming and going on paint affairs, a few extra visitors would be unlikely to attract the attention of the Germans working at a depot next door, and this made it an ideal place for the Resistance to meet. The factory was allowed a ration of industrial alcohol for the manufacture of paint and, with the addition of some kind of fruit flavouring. Toni made a very passable liqueur. Although probably lethal if taken too freely, it

184

provided a very welcome and refreshing drink at the end of a long day, and Toni usually gave us a nip after the evening meeting. Bill and I sometimes had a nightcap on our return from the telephone. Otherwise alcohol did not seem to be available to the Dutch at Ede.

Good News

On Friday evening, 20th October, we received the stunning news that the Dutch had been ordered to evacuate the entire village of Bennekom by Sunday 22nd. There had been for some time a prohibited zone extending two kilometres North of the Rhine, but this was altogether a different matter. Bennekom, then quite a large village, lay some three kilometres from the river and its evacuation meant that all the roads and tracks leading to it would be congested with Dutch families coming and going with their household belongings. It was sad for the villagers but wonderful news for the Resistance and ourselves as, for the next two days, it would be almost impossible for the Germans to know who was who.

Furthermore Bennekom was near the woods we had selected for our RV. Although it gave us very little time, we had to make use of this opportunity.

Luckily we had already made a number of preliminary arrangements. Members of the Resistance had been allocated to lead all evaders to the RV when the time should come, but of course had not been told where this would be. I had done a daylight reconnaissance with Wainwright, Grainger, Toni De Nooy and the local farmer, and had decided on the best approach route to the river. We had been led to the edge of the thick woods overlooking the flat river land from whence we could see the German defences set back some 300 yards from the river behind what was called the winter dyke. At this point we could see a gap of some 300 yards between the posts, and this seemed our best chance. Furthermore, we had found a clearing in the woods South of Renkum, about two miles from the river, and far enough from any of the numerous gun positions to make it reasonably safe as the RV.

Final Arrangements

My first priority that Friday evening was to see Gerald, who immediately gave the green light for the crossing on Sunday night. Bill and Piet then put their mobilisation plans into immediate effect at Ede and Arnhem respectively. On the telephone that night I explained to Fraser the new urgency of our situation and he agreed to Sunday night for "Pegasus" and told me that arrangements on his side would be made accordingly. On Saturday morning Wainwright, Grainger and I did a further reconnaissance to confirm that the RV and the proposed route through the woods was still clear. They would do a patrol that night to find the best line from the edge of the woods to the river.

Sadly, the short time left to us meant that a number of evaders who were in hiding too far afield could not, as had been originally intended, now be included in "Pegasus". However there were eighty to ninety in the vicinity of Ede and another forty or fifty near Arnhem, and this was really quite enough to handle. The Resistance plan was to concentrate the evaders scattered around the Arnhem district in some woods at Oud Reemst, several miles to the East of Ede and some 20 miles by road from the RV. Here Hibbert was to take charge of them and they would be equipped with arms and uniforms brought there by the Dutch. From there Piet undertook to bring them by night on the final stage to the RV in his lorries. Meanwhile the Ede contingent would move by foot, bicycle and horse drawn carts on Sunday morning, with the whole party hopefully assembling at the RV soon after dark that night.

Such was the plan; but the chances of us all reaching the RV undetected did not look good to Gerald, Tony Hibbert and me. The Dutch, however, appeared quite confident and, anyhow, what alternatives did we have other than to give ourselves up or expose our Dutch hosts to hideous danger through the long winter months?

That night I had my final telephone talk with Fraser and confirmed the plans for the next day.

Pegasus – The Concentration

Sunday dawned bright and sunny, though bad weather would have suited us better. From early morning, evaders led by their Resistance guides, men and women, boys and girls, started to make their way in ones, twos and threes along by ways and footpaths to the edge of the woods at Renkum. Here new guides met them and took them to the RV in the clearing. All travelled in some kind of civilian disguise. Even Olliff's non-combatant Field Ambulance men, who had remained in uniform from the beginning, had to look like Dutchmen, while their uniforms were brought to the RV by the Resistance in a covered horse drawn cart.

Having said goodbye to Mrs. W. and the children I left their house in mid-morning and, with Bill and Toni De Nooy, called round to collect Gerald and Tony Franks from their houses in the town. Both had now more or less recovered from their wounds, but, like most of the evaders, were very unfit from enforced inactivity. I remember being somewhat doubtful about Gerald's similarity to a Dutchman. He was abnormally tall and, looking a bit seedy in a dark clerical suit, did not quite fit into the landscape. He didn't look too happy on a bicycle either.

The peaceful Dutch countryside became the scene of abnormal activity today. There were many people on the move, some on foot and others on bicycles and some with horse drawn carts. Among them we recognised several evaders with their Resistance guides and we also passed German troops on the march, or resting by the wayside. More than once we came

186

upon emergency first-aid posts that had been established by the Dutch Red Cross, ostensibly to provide help and refreshment to tired refugees from Bennekom. But it so happened that all the nurses, some of them quite young girls, were members of the Resistance and had been positioned and briefed to give warning of unusual enemy activity and point evaders in a safe direction. Bill and Toni had a quick word with them as we passed by.

At the RV in the woods we found that many of the evaders had already arrived and had changed into the uniforms smuggled in by the Resistance. Many of them, tired after the unaccustomed exercise, were soon asleep. It must be remembered that most had been confined to their hiding places for nearly a month now. However, now in uniform, we had to become a fighting force, albeit not a very good one, and we soon got everyone armed and oganised in platoons and sections under officers and NCOs, with fire positions and sentries posted. A hot meal prepared by the Dutch helped to put heart into us all.

Bill had other arrangements to make and had to leave us now. It was a sad moment for me, as I had grown to like him enormously during the few weeks we had been working together. Toni and one or two others, including the farmer whose local knowledge had been of such value, remained with us. Wainwright and Grainger had reported favourably after their very bold patrol the night before, and now there remained nothing more we could do but lie low until after dark, and await the arrival of Tony Hibbert's party from Arnhem.

It was to be of such importance to us a few hours later that I must digress here to explain another of XXX Corps plans for our evacuation. This was the softening up of the German defences through which we would have to pass. To achieve this they had been sending strong fighting patrols of about a hundred men over the river for several nights previously. The patrols were provided by 101 American Airborne Division, under command of British XXX Corps, who were holding that sector of the front. These comprised soldiers of the highest fighting quality. The idea was partly to scare the wits out of any German patrol they might bump into and also, to draw fire from their defensive positions. This in turn would provoke the return fire of a fair slice of XXX Corps artillery, and they hoped in this way to teach the German defenders the advisability of keeping a low profile.

To return to the RV: shortly after dark Toni led me to a road running through the woods where it had been arranged to meet Piet Kruyff with his lorries bringing the Arnhem contingent. We did not have to wait long for the welcome sound of the ancient vehicles clattering towards us. I don't remember the details, but I do know that there had been one or two narrow escapes on the twenty mile journey. Piet had brought them through by the sheer audacity of his plan, and the clever positioning of Resistance members at crucial points along the route to give forewarning of danger. Tony Hibbert's party, now about forty strong, had been equipped with arms and uniforms before leaving Oud Reemst and had travelled crouched in the back of the lorries, ready to fight their way through should it have become necessary. There was a nasty moment when these men were clambering noisily out of the lorries, and a German bicycle patrol came down the road. We had to take cover quickly, but some men were a bit slow and the patrol had to slow down and ring their bicycle bells to clear a path. It seems that they noticed nothing to make them suspicious, and we heard no more of them.

Pegasus – The Execution

When we were all assembled at the RV I gave the final orders for the move to the river. The first two miles or so would be through the woods and, with so many virtually untrained men, there would be a real risk of losing some on the way. So, I ordered double file with frequent stops to allow the men at the back to close up. After that would come the really difficult part of leaving the cover of the woods and crossing completely flat, open farm land for several hundred yards to the river bank passing between the German defences on the winter dyke.

At the final count we were about 150 strong. In addition to some 120 airborne, we had been joined by several Allied airmen who had been shot down at some stage, and brought to us by the Resistance. There were also a few young Dutchmen who wanted to join the Allied forces and, for some reason that I never understood, two Russians. It was a strangely assorted lot and not one I would have chosen for what lay ahead. However, Gerald had delegated command of the party to me, and at 9.30pm when the moon rose, I gave the order to move off with Wainwright and the Dutch guides leading.

Although the importance of moving silently was obvious, and I had stressed this at the briefing, we were soon making far too much noise, and the further we went the worse it got. The morale of these men was low anyhow after several weeks of confinement to one place, and most of them had never set eyes on the officers and NCOs appointed to command them. And, of course, many were totally untrained and unsuited to this kind of adventure. Be that as it may, I was utterly horrified as it seemed that the Germans could not fail to hear us coming a mile away. As the men grew more tired they strumbled into each other and over roots in the woods and fell into holes and ditches. To make matters worse, all this was accompanied by low mutterings and oaths which no amount of admonishment from their officers seemed able to control.

In spite of everything we reached the edge of the woods overlooking the river flats at about 11.00pm without incident. As there was no call for our Dutch guides to come any further, and to do so would have been an unnecessary risk, we shook hands with whispered thanks and farewells. For the final stage to the river we adopted the formation that I

188

had previously ordered for the open country. We would now move in a compact main body with Gerald, Tony Hibbert and myself at the head and Tony Franks bringing up the rear. Ahead and on either flank were strongly armed sections with picked officers and men. I thought that this formation should give us some all-round protection if we bumped into trouble.

Wainwright, who had reconnoitred the route the previous night, led the advance guard for some way along a series of drainage ditches, which at least provided a little cover should we come under fire. But for the last 200 yards or so we had to crawl across a completely open meadow in full view of the enemy. By some miracle just before midnight we reached the river without a shot being fired, and turned West downstream on the last leg to "Digby".

The going was better now and we were making much less noise. I think that everyone appreciated the danger of our situation, out in the open and only about 300 yards from the German defences. And luckily there was now some cloud cover, and the night had become appreciably darker. We could just make out the far side of the river, here some 300 yards wide.

We had not gone far along the river bank when what we had all been dreading happened. The silence was shattered by several bursts of a light machine gun from close in front. Our advance guard returned the fire while we all went down ready to defend ourselves, expecting at any moment to be lit up by star shells and plastered by mortar and machine gun fire. But apart from a few Very lights over the forward posts nothing happened, and with a sigh of relief we went on our way.

Pegasus – Trouble With Digby

When the Brigadier, Hibbert and I thought that we must have reached the right place we decided to call a halt and wait for the boats to come over. But after twenty or thirty minutes had elapsed and there was still no sign of them, we began to think that something had gone very wrong. Either we were in the wrong place, or the boats were, for some reason, unable to come. There had been no answering torch signal from the other side and there remained at least another half hour before the next Bofors tracer signals were due. Meanwhile, if they were to light us up, we would be sitting ducks on a totally exposed river-bank in full view of the enemy. The outlook was not good and the choices open to us limited. If we were to stay where we were we would be finished off at dawn or earlier. If we were to turn back there was nowhere to go to, so our only line of escape lay in the river itself, here cold, wide, deep and fast flowing. Without boats very few of us would have made the far side.

It can be imagined what a very worrying time this was for us all, especially for me, as I had agreed the plan with Dobie and Fraser on the telephone and so felt that the responsibility for our situation was largely mine. Were all our efforts and the bravery of the Dutch to be wasted at the last minute? And then out of the night came what must have been the most welcome words I ever heard, "Are you people by any chance looking for some boats"? Had I been a modern footballer I feel sure that I would have hugged and kissed the owner of this voice, such was my joy. As it was, I am reputed to have said something like "Well, actually we are rather". We then wasted no time in following this Canadian, as he turned out to be, a short way down the river to where we found David Dobie waiting with the boats.

Pegasus – The Finale

On either side of the crossing point the Americans had set up machine gun posts to protect our flanks. This had been a wise precaution as the British sappers paddling the boats had to make three crossings to carry us all over, and this, with the fast current to contend with, took some time. At the final count we had lost only one man, one of the two Russians who had disappeared somewhere along the way as mysteriously as he had arrived. It was, without doubt, a remarkable achievement for which the Dutch Resistance were mainly responsible. We had, of course, been blessed with incredible luck and it must also be recorded that we almost certainly owed our survival in the final stage to the preparations made by XXX Corps. Their foresight and planning had left nothing to chance. General Horrocks had personally visited the scene the previous day to satisfy himself that all was ready, and there is no question that the softening up by the American fighting patrols had saved us when the Germans, although probably having no reason to suspect a mass escape, must certainly have been aware of the passing of a large and noisy body of men through their defences.

As I stepped out of the boat on the southern shore I was greeted by the two Majors, Hugh Fraser and Airey Neave, who had been anxiously waiting and watching most of the night. I also renewed my acquaintance with our Canadian saviour, Leo Heaps. As he has recorded his own exploits elsewhere suffice it to say here that he was a very bold and enterprising officer who had, early in the battle of Arnhem, while attached to David Dobie's First battalion, was captured and escaped across the river. And now, after a long and exciting escape experience, he had involved himself with the "Pegasus" operation. It was he who, standing on the river bank with Dobie, Fraser and Neave, and happening to glance upstream at the right moment, had spotted the dim flashing of my torch and had immediately come across with Dobie to look for us. Not seeing any sign of us, he had walked alone upstream until he found us and introduced himself in the manner I have described. We had owed a lot to Leo Heaps.

Now, with all the worry behind us, we followed a white tape that had been laid to guide us across the river land to a farmhouse where the

190

American Parachute Battalion had its headquarters. Here we were given very welcome tea and buns before climbing into and onto an assortment of jeeps and trucks, which were to take us further back. It was then that the only tragedy of the night occurred. Not finding space inside, Tony Hibbert had climbed onto the front of a jeep which, in the black-out, rammed a jeep coming from the opposite direction, crushing both Tony's legs between the two. It was a sad ending to all that Tony had done, both during the battle at the bridge and the escape. He was destined to spend many months in hospital and, when I saw him last, in 1984, he was still walking with a pronounced limp.

The rest of us ended up in the very early hours of the morning in a casualty station that had been prepared for our reception, and where David had had the foresight to provide refreshments more appropriate than tea. I can still remember how good that champagne tasted.

The next day we were debriefed and I was interviewed by Generals Dempsey and Horrocks. Then, after more celebrations that night, we were flown back to England, to the very airfield in Lincolnshire from which we had set out so full of hope five weeks earlier.

Epilogue

The success of the "Pegasus" operation tempted British Intelligence to mount a second operation to bring out some more evaders about a month later. This was given the name "Pegasus II", and the plan was very similar, perhaps too similar, to ours. Sadly, it proved a total disaster resulting in the loss of a number of lives, both of evaders and Resistance. Luckily for them, most of my friends in the Resistance had been on the run from the Gestapo ever since our escape, and so played no part in "Pegasus II".

A happier sequel was the eventual escape of Brigadier, now General Sir John, Hackett in early February. He had remained hidden and convalescing in Ede until the Resistance were able to smuggle him across the Rhine by a long and hazardous route many miles to the West. They successfully used the same route to bring out a number of other evaders.

When the Allies resumed the offensive and crossed the Rhine in the spring of 1945, I at once asked for and received permission to visit my friends at Ede. After flying to Paris I was lent a jeep and told to help myself from army supplies. Filling it with everything that I thought would be most welcome, I drove through France and Belgium into Holland where I spent two happy days staying with the Wildeboers and renewing old acquaintances.

The next opportunity to visit Ede came in 1955 when my wife, Jane, and I stayed with the Wildeboers in Lunterensweg and were shown around some beautiful parts of Holland by Hilly. This was the last time I was to see Bill as he died not long afterwards. But we kept in touch with the family over the years, and Hilly and Dickie stayed with my mother in England. I last saw them in September 1984 when Jane and I with our youngest daughter went over to Holland for the 40th anniversary commemoration of the Battle of Arnhem.

During this visit we stayed with both Hilly and Dickie in their new homes and called on Mrs. W. in her retirement home. We also attended a huge reunion party for ex-evaders and former members of the Resistance and their families in the town hall at Bennekom. This had been organised largely through the initiative of Tony Hibbert, who persuaded me to give a short account of 'Pegasus'. There were many familiar faces there and amongst them I was especially pleased to see the farmer's widow, then an old lady, who had taken in Tony Franks and me after our escape from the hospital. Altogether a great occasion bringing back many happy memories.

Nanyuki, Kenya
December 1990
© 1991 by Digby Tatham Warter

CHAPTER TEN

1945 – the Prisoners return

IN APRIL and May 1945 approximately 800 ex 2nd Battalion men were returned to the UK from German Prison camps. After documentation, a medical, and a new uniform they were given a six week pass, ration cards and some of the back pay they were in credit. Later, most were given six weeks extension of leave and were then called to a depot for another physical check. Some were discharged, others went back to their parent Regiment, keeping their Parachute wings on their left arm but not receiving any jump pay. All were asked to return to the 2nd Battalion, some did and in January 1946 were sent to Palestine.

Our Colonel, John Frost wrote some years later.
"I wonder how many of us look back to the time we spent as POW's? Possibly the most unpleasant episode in our lives. Fortunately we tend to remember only the nicer things but I still think that losing ones freedom for whatever length of time will make one value that more than anything."

John Measures . . . . *in captivity since recapture on the Sangro*

AFTER HIS recapture in the minefield on the Sangro river, Italy, John was taken to an Oflag in Germany and issued with a Log book. He entered the title of every book he read and enjoyed, he entered his favourite recipes, and he kept his cricket team score card with names that seem familiar, Mountford, Ross and Tite. His diary proper, commences on Sunday 15th April 1945, the Boche marched everyone out of camp away from the approaching front, John hid himself in the camp and then joined the French in their Stalag.

Monday 23rd April 1945

'Parcels at the station' was the cry today! Old Kriegie rumour, but it was true. Two waggon loads rolled up, with the fighting going on about 15km away. Extraordinary. There was a distribution of the remaining bulk among the Camp this afternoon; a few tins and lumps of sugar to each mess of four or five. This evening numerous explosions were taking place in and around the town, and a lot of German traffic is on the road going eastwards. Air activity nil today except for two small air OP's which came over at lunchtime. Can this be the end? They can't move us now, and the gunfire is very distinct today; heavy shelling going over our heads. One can hear each shell pass by.

Tuesday 24th April 1945

Last night at 10pm, four terrific explosions took place just nearby and the whole building moved out of alignment about an inch or so. The Russkies went mad, thinking the Americans had arrived, but when we awoke this am we found that it had only been this small girder bridge over the stream down in the fields at the bottom of the camp. Why they've blown that, God knows. Numerous smaller explosions taking place in and around the town and large columns of smoke in the town itself. A little shelling over our heads and a litle air activity. The Americans are about 10km away and the SS are engaging them hard.

Another Red X truck came in from Moosburg today and the driver stated that he had been stopped by the Americans at Ingelstadt yesterday! Parcel issue this evening of ½ per head. We looked at ours and the cook kept all the chocolate to make brews with, in accordance with their custom, so there was no chocolate "bash" for me. The Russkies are mixing everything in together, sardines with porridge, honey with salmon, etc. Also, a terrific amount of bartering is going on. 3 cigarettes will get one a packet of tea, 10 will get one a tin of milk or cocoa.

Am afraid the poor blighters in their anxiety to get something to smoke will forget their stomachs. Everything is still filthy; piles of stinking rubbish several feet high, latrines blocked, people spitting all over the place. God! Sound of the approaching battle this evening; at least, I hope it's approaching. I cannot believe they'll be here inside a week, but I do believe that the Goons will keep us here. Only one officer left in the Guard, a few NCO's and 100 odd men.

Wednesday 25th April 1945

Definite signs of battle just the other side of the town; not much rearward movement on the road tho' and the bridge seems still unblown. Little air activity; gunfire heavy to W, SW, E and ESE. Very fine weather today! Went out to brew with some Belgian blokes this morning and at 11.30am the astounding news came round that two American officers were at the gate and that the keys had been handed over. I certainly saw several white flags being put out at various strategic points, and all the nationalities are now putting out their own flags. God, I can scarcely write, I'm so, well, not excited but sort of dumb and numb. I can't describe the scenes which are now taking place; press photographers are here, reporters, Russians are crying, tanks are going past on both roads, Americans are waving at us and I'm nearly crying myself. Have just seen Col Trendle and he says we might as well get dressed as British Officers now. God, I can't believe it. Are we really free? Or is this a dream? It can't be. GOD, WE'RE FREE!

194

Dave Brooks .... *three weeks before Freedom*

STALAG IIA situated at Neubrandenburg was an International Camp, made up from Russians, Poles, Serbs, Dutch, French, Italians and after the Ardenne offensive, Americans. The British contingent was 200 strong, all corporals and upwards, all taken at Arnhem. Our senior man was the RSM from the Airborne Medics.

On route to the camp we had all made a pact that we would not work for the Germans, as was our right under the Geneva Convention, unless we intended attempting escape; only a few tried, all unsuccessfully. Our pact was not accepted well by the authorities, as IIA up to then had been a working camp with no exceptions. Consequently certain pressures were brought to bear on us; certainly very inferior rations, and a week or so after we entered the camp, our hut was segregated from the rest by a wire fence, including a 'no go' zone, with a guard on the entrance to our small compound and many other smaller irritations. Incidentally the wire did not stop us mingling with other nationalities once darkness fell. This was essential if we were to continue trading (bartering) to augment our food supply. We did have a shipment of Red Cross parcels 500 I think came to us during December 1944, which were distributed one to two men per week for as long as they lasted. These parcels made a tremendous difference to our trading potential, as they contained cigarettes, coffee, chocolate and soap, all of which were in short supply with the local German population.

To escape from our compound, we organised a party to lift the lower strand of wire, "traders" representing groups of POWs went under the wire, others erased their marks in the sand with twig switches, with the same procedure for the return of the "traders", we changed our exit point each night of course. As I recall we were discovered just the once. Those caught were placed in the cells and next day charged with "attempting to escape". They were sentenced to 14 days hard labour and were put to work with women slave workers who were digging the biggest tank trap I ever saw. However, all this is just to set the scene, as the title says this is about the last few weeks of the war at Neubrandenburg which I think are worth recording.

During April of 1945, some 200 British prisoners were dumped at the gates of Stalag IIA. Our senior man was summoned to the Commandant's Office to be told that these men were to be our responsibility and the restrictions on our hut would be lifted. These extra men had been marched from their camps in Poland for weeks, maybe months, away from the advancing Russians. All were very sick and unable to continue further; there was a lot of serious frostbite and dysentery. As I have said, our senior man was from the Airborne Medics; we also had with us the RQMS, and about six staff sergeants from the medics. They of course took on the nursing duties aided by a Serbian doctor who from all accounts worked like a Trojan with little or no help from our captors. Bad frostbite often leads to amputations, I believe, or the sufferer will perish from gangrene. Of the 200 sick men, some 39 died before VE Day. All these men had been taken prisoner either at Dunkirk or Dieppe; very sad I think to get so near to freedom, and then lose your life through German callousness.

The remainder of the Arnhem POWs did all they could to help these poor devils. I went on the burial party. I remember when the first death occurred, we had a terrible tussle with the Germans, who thought we would accept brown paper as a shroud, whereas we said they were entitled to a proper coffin. I think we would say we won the day as timber was supplied, and we made the coffins, a blanket was turned into a Union Jack, a bugle was borrowed from the French and all the men who died had a decent military funeral. A week or so after these sick men arrived at IIA, a remarkable thing happened; I think I would say a very British happening. In the middle of the night we heard the sound of aircraft engines, the aircraft were flying very low; I recall it was a clear moonlit night. Very shortly we saw, would you believe, a number of Lancaster Bombers, then parachutes. For a few seconds we thought it was "the lads" come to release us, then we saw the wicker baskets below the parachutes; the baskets contained many things to assist with the nursing of the sick men including food. Of course we were not allowed to collect those baskets, there being an air raid situation in force, but to the Germans credit, they were handed over in the morning, at least, enough were to make all the difference to the sick men. I've often thought of those Lancaster crews, hoping they all made it back to "Blighty". They had had a very long journey, as Neubrandenburg was very close to the Polish border. I believe the news of IIA's problems had been relayed by the International Red Cross who were very active in the area, travelling around in white painted trucks.

Meanwhile, the war was rumbling on to its inevitable ending; the German nation was collapsing. They had been for some time, trying to persuade prisoners to join their cause; at IIA they only succeeded with the Russian POWs, they joined the Germans certainly in their hundreds, in mitigation, they had suffered terrible hardships as prisoners, worse than any other nationality, and had been dying at the rate of five or six per day all the time we were in the camp. By early May the sounds of war could be heard very close now.

All the guards were marched out to fight their last fight, except six medical orderlies and one old officer, we were virtually free again. The senior men, called "confidence men" by the Germans, got together and reached agreement that all prisoners would remain in the camp in a disciplined manner until the Russian Army rolled through. The British were asked by the remaining Germans if we would look after their families until the Russians came, as they were afraid of reprisals from within the camp and we agreed to their request. I myself spent the last night in the office that housed them; I don't think I have ever seen women so frightened before or since.

Around 2am in the morning, a Russian tank rolled through our wire, to a great cheer from the inmates. When daylight came we were surrounded by a formidable tank force. Fighting was still going on in nearby Neubrandenburg, but for us "kreigies" it was over. We had survived, I think, or should I say hope, with honour and some dignity, which is more than I could say for the Germans, they were crushed, and by now fawning on their Russian captors.

We were to remain in that area for three more weeks, so I got a good look at the Russian Army. They appeared to me to be disciplined and efficient. I found it strange that about half their tanks had women drivers, very handsome girls they were too, and all their military police on traffic duty were women. I did not witness any atrocity committed by them, except one on the first day and there were mitigating circumstances connected with that. In general I would have to say the Russians behaved properly according to their system, which differed vastly from the British way of doing things.

Soon after dawn on the day of release, the senior men were called to a meeting with a Russian Brass Hat, who gave us bounds that we were free to move in approx. five mile radius of the camp. It was made clear we would have to look after ourselves, and to that end we were free to take whatever we wanted from the locality, providing the Russian Army did not also lay claim. In fact they and us were to live "off the land", a creed very alien to the British soldier. Very soon the camp was a veritable butchers shop. I would say the Serbian contingent were easily the most proficient in this department, and to my mind the Serbs were the people I liked the most, nothing seemed to get them down. German prisoners taken in the area, including those remaining at IIA were stripped of badges of rank etc., and immediately put to work mainly tending the Russian sick of whom there must have been hundreds.

On the first day of freedom, an Air Force officer arrived and arrangements were made to move these people by road, I think on the same day, but I don't know where to. Meanwhile, all the roads in the area were choked with people, the majority going westward, a few eastward, it was impossible to know who they were, obviously a lot more Germans, probably some slave labour, and other people trying to get home. It seemed to me they were totally disregarded by the Russian Army. Together they left me with a picture of poor suffering humanity, conscious that I could do nothing to alleviate their plight.

As soon as we realised we were not to be repatriated by the Russians, we took steps to alter this situation. I don't think the Russians repatriated any of their own ex POWs. I think they solved the problem by inducting them into field units in the area, according to their training; infantrymen to infantry, tankmen to the tanks and so on. We found the nearest allied force (Americans) were at the town of Schwerin some 70 miles away, so that's where we made for. When we arrived it was just dark. Already there was a "no mans land" between the Russian check point and the American one of about 100 yards.

The Americans at their check point directed us to the Town Opera House, which had been commandeered for returning POW's. What a sight the foyer was, a veritable Aladdin's Cave, food and clothing galore, everything a returning POW might need, and the instructions were, "Don't take a packet bud, take the carton", yet another illustration to me how very affluent and efficient the 'Yanks' were.

We settled down for the night with the assurance that the 'Limeys' would be moved to Luneburg the very next day. Sure enough the next morning we were taken in their troop carriers to Luneburg and into British hands where the welcome was very genuine, but austere by comparison with the 'Yanks'. We were told that we would be on our way to England just as soon as air transport became available, meanwhile we were accommodated in a local barracks.

The wait was not long as I recall and I was instructed to board a Dakota. Before take off, a member of the crew came back to the passenger area and singled me out to go up into the cockpit, apparently they were to fly without a co-pilot, and I was to take the vacant seat in order to balance the 'plane. This I welcomed as I had never had the opportunity before to travel at the business end of an aircraft. The Navigator gave me a map with the route marked on it, and the pilot pointed out that I would get a better view of the ground by looking down through a square lens at the side of the seat.

As we flew over Germany, the utter desolation of their towns quite shocked me. Town after town seemed to have very few intact houses left, ruin was everywhere, even woods looked grotesque where they had been ripped by shells, many bridges were down, including those across the Rhine. The German race had paid in full for their political follies of the 30s, just as Winston Churchill had said they would. Our route took us over Dunkirk, docks still flooded, over to Folkestone. What a lovely sight those white cliffs were, on over Kent and right over my home village of Wateringbury. I was able to see the house where I had lived, and a good view of Mereworth Castle from the air, on to the outskirts of London at Croydon, to touch down at Dunsfold.

We were escorted off the 'plane by girls of the WAAF, up to a small hut, where we had to be deloused, or rather they poked the nozzle of a bellows like instrument up your trouser legs, then pumped away, God knows what it was, but for sure it wasn't talcum powder. Then to a hanger set aside where a very passable meal was laid out, the WAAF's sat with us and had a good chat. Yes it was good to be back. On to a hutted camp at Haywards Heath, which was remarkably well organised, your old clothing was taken away and new issued. WVS ladies were on hand to sew on badges of rank, Para wings and flashes. I didn't really like parting with my old battle dress, shirt, drawers cellular, socks and boots (they didn't get my beret), that's all I'd lived in for the last eight months. New Pay books were issued, and paymasters were present, leave passes were issued and off we went. It was Whit Sunday, I was now living in London, quite a short hop from Haywards Heath. I was somewhat apprehensive, as I had to approach my wife's home through a railway tunnel. I had sat with the driver en route from Dunsfold to Haywards Heath, a somewhat pessimistic man who had described in detail the damage that V2 rockets had inflicted on London, and those of you who were POWs will remember how clever the Germans were with their constant propaganda, which one had to weigh against your own 'grapevine'. So this tunnel was something of an ordeal. When I emerged, to my relief there stood the street just as I had left it, the house was bedecked with bunting and flags to welcome me home, along with all the family. Home came the wanderer, to the best leave ever. My enlistment for the duration was over, but never forgotten, particularly my time in the Paras. I can still see those mates of mine who were cut off in their youth, and it is always a pleasure to see those who survived, at the Stoke Rochford Reunion.

Tom Ainslie .... *remembers the summer of '45*

WHILE AT Ringway in January '44 I dislocated my shoulder on a night jump. I think I was the last one of the whole course to jump that night, which was a marginal one as far as jumping was concerned. As I was nearing the ground a gust of wind hit me and blew me up sideways. I was too near the ground for the swing to be corrected and the first thing that hit the ground was my right shoulder.

It wasn't too bad until the starvation diet in POW camp caused a lot of deterioration through muscle wastage and so on. In the late summer of '45 I was at the depot on the Isle of Wight and the thing would dislocate itself on the slightest provocation, such as forgetting and washing my neck with my right hand. It was obvious that an operation was necessary so I was sent off to hospital in Shaftesbury. The day I went turned out to be VJ Day and we got the news on the train. Everyone got off at the first stop and went to the nearest pub to celebrate. I don't know whether anyone else was actually going to hospital with me but I know I was feeling no pain when I got there. It didn't make much difference because most people at the hospital seemed to be that way too. I didn't have the operation until two weeks later because I'd got a cold and they couldn't give me a general anaesthetic till it was gone. Let me say right now that it was a masterpiece of surgery and every doctor who has seen it since then has said that it's the best piece of bone-grafting he has ever seen and I don't even know the name of the surgeon who did it. What they did was to take a slice of bone off the outside of the hip joint and graft it into the shoulder to form a cup and thus prevent the arm from slipping out of the socket. It has never been the slightest trouble and I was able to play squash till I was fifty. I only gave it up then because I'd run out of partners of approximately my own age. Although the hospital was medically first-rate, it was pretty chaotic administratively, for it had accepted a lot of poor fellows who had been prisoners of the Japanese and who were in pretty bad shape. In short, as long as you were medically OK, no one worried about anything much else.

We would have breakfast in bed because we were patients and entitled to it, then we would stroll up to the pub and stay there until closing-time. Then we would come back to the hospital for tea and then head back to the pub for the evening session. After starving for six months in Oflag 79, I must have had proper meals some time but I can't remember where or when. I mean, the fascination of food can't have worn off that quickly! We soon got the ex-POW's from the Far East to join us and I'm sure it did them far more good than harm though I did sometimes feel a bit alarmed at seeing chaps with missing limbs, pissed to the wide, literally rolling down the hill to the hospital. I don't know exactly how long this went on but it was weeks, if not months.

Finally I went to the adjutant and begged him to discharge me. It was a real relief to go on a sober sick-leave and I was the only one who knew that it wasn't the operation I was recovering from. It was a memorable summer. Even the weather was great.

. . . . uses his knowledge of German and asked about flying bombs

IN ANSWER to your question as to whether knowing German made any difference when we were captured, it was certainly useful immediately after we were captured. The first person in authority that my little group came in contact with was a sergeant. When we were escorted in, he said, "Good evening. That was a good fight, a really good fight. Have a cigar. We're human too." So we all lit up Dutch cigars about a foot long and had quite a matey chat. One chap whose name I don't remember had been hit in a rather awkward place. I just couldn't think of the proper word but I knew the slang word. This amused our captors very much. "Hit in the arse, you say? Oh, you speak very good German." Later that night I was perhaps of some use to Jimmy Logan in trying to impress on the Waffen-SS officers the urgency of getting the severely wounded to a place where they could be properly looked after. It was somewhere about this point that someone was kind enough to say that things would have been a lot stickier if I hadn't been there to help out. Next day I was formally interrogated at Zutphen by an interpreter who spoke English. I then had an informal conversation in German with one of the Div. or Corps intelligence officers who was supervising the interrogations. Like quite a lot of Germans to whom I spoke in the next few months, he was very interested in the effect of V1's or flying bombs.

He was quite annoyed when I told him that, while they were very unpleasant for civilians in target areas in London, they were otherwise militarily useless.

So far, knowing German was certainly an advantage but this ceased when we got to the 'permanent' camp. Oflag 79 was an old Luftwaffe barracks where we were about 10 or 12 to a room. Most of my room-mates were New Zealanders or South Africans who had been captured in North Africa and whose morale was very low indeed. I was regularly asked for translations of German newspapers, a singularly boring and futile exercise as no German newspaper ever contained any news. We got the real news from the BBC on one of our secret radios.

George Stubbs . . . . *helps dig a mass grave at Halle*

WHILE LISTENING to Radio 2 on Sunday morning 3 September 1989 50 years since war was declared, Cyril Fletcher requested 'The Hallelujah Chorus' from Handel's Messiah. During this stirring rendition my thoughts were taken back to the winter of 1944/45 where I, together with other 2 Para mates were in the Arbeits Kommando RE 113 in the city of Halle the great composer's birthplace.

These names come back to me, Ken Wadsworth who was Lt McDermont's batman, Georgie Barnes, Jack Dimond, Ray Delano, Smith 48, Needham, and of course Charlie Barraclough, the only one I have seen in the past 45 years.

It was a hard winter that year, they say the coldest they had had for 30 years and we were rising at an hour when it was still dark, a mug of acorn coffee, slice of 'brot' and off to work, where we had to light brush-wood fires to try and thaw the earth out before we could use 'hacke & schippe'. Our camp which held only 200 (quite a lot of us 1st Airborne) was almost alongside a huge railway bridge which spanned several lines and was the target of night and day air raids by both Air Forces. On Good Friday we had a day off work but luckily were sent out shifting bomb rubble at Merseburg. The RAF bombed Halle and we had to march back to camp through the city which had received much damage and many casualties, many of whom we saw on our journey, and we were stoned and abused and relieved to get back to safety. However some bombs had hit our camp and some French POWs killed, they were cooks.

The Germans soon found a job for us digging mass graves only one metre deep to bury the raid victims, side by side, men, women and children, quite a harrowing experience. During this time I remember hearing the first German jet aircraft flying over. Very soon after this we were on the march heading eastwards. Luckily it wasn't as bad as the notorious Death March that some POWs experienced and after five days a column of Yank Shermans came along throwing 'Camels' and 'Luckies' out of the turrets, most of our posterns scarpered, those that stayed were terrified they would be shot but we persuaded the Yanks that they hadn't ill treated us. The following day some Russian POWs in the same village killed and roasted an ox, and we had quite a feast, and soon were taken to Naumberg and fed on 'K' rations for 2-3 days, then to an aerodrome at Kholleda and flown to Brussels (most of us were air sick over the Rhine Valley). Then to delousing and a night in the city, then out to the 'drome (where I met Lt Vlasto of 1 Plt) where scores of damaged allied planes were stacked, shot up during the Ardennes Battle in a raid which caught them by surprise. Then in a Dakota to Aylesbury to be welcomed by WAAF's, and a meal, new uniforms etc, particulars taken, rail passes issued, and after one or two days we were on our way home on 56 days leave. VE day I spent in my home town, leave was extended by 14 days three times. I finally got back to 2 Para at Oakham and went to Palestine.

Sid Elliott . . . . *for you the war is over Tommy*

IT WAS in the early morning of Friday 22 September, myself and three or four others were holed up in the cellar of a Dutch house. The door was flung open and standing there were a couple of Germans. The one who appeared to be in charge said, "For you the war is over Tommy." I must say he spoke better English than I did.

By this time I was in a state of considerable discomfort having had a lump of shrapnel hit my left forearm on the Wednesday. I had placed a shell dressing on the wound and by now it was swollen up like a balloon and certainly not smelling of violets. I therefore made some remark to him like "bloody good job".

We were then taken out to the roadway where he looked at my arm, called up transport and had me taken to what appeared to be a Church Hall. I was quite pleased to see Doc Logan there. While he was cutting off the shell dressing someone came over and said to Doc, "cover the wound" and for me to follow him. He took me outside put me onto a vehicle and told the driver where to take me. Eventually I arrived at a fantastic looking building (later found out it was the Royal Palace at Het-Loo). On entering the main door I noticed straight in front of me a lovely stairway. On my left a rather large door way, I was taken through and what a surprise. Along the outside flank wall stood two or possibly three operating tables, along the wall opposite about six chairs all taken except one. My throne – my Royal blood had at last been recognised. I suppose many of the lads have experienced similar situations. But I must admit that it is a memory I shall carry with me forever.

As one patient was finished and carried out, the next patient would step up. I am sure even Henry Ford would have been pleased with this production line. While waiting, the lad next to me was asked where he was wounded and he said, "In the backside – near the base of the spine". Drop your trousers said the orderly, and staring me in the face appeared

202

a fellow with two rectums. He and I exchanged a few quips, and I had met Dusty Milner, 156 Bn, a fellow that helped to care for me while a patient. Eventually both of us were together at Stalag 7A just outside Munich.

They eventually got me onto the table and it was a German doctor who I am given to understand sorted me out. He came up to me later in the day and explained that my arm had been opened up, cleaned off and was being left as an open wound to allow the poison to drain. It was hung up like a ham in a butchers shop and Bernard the German orderly cleaned and attended it every four hours. He was another German I met whose command of the English language was exceptional.

The Doctor had a name that from memory sounded like Hansler or Hassler. It was said that he played football for Germany in 1936.

While at the Palace a Sgt Mahoney, a glider pilot, engineered an escape. It was arranged that some of the lads would pull up the fire hose they used to get out, and then hang on for 15 minutes in case they had to call it off and get back in. Dusty Milner was one of the lads and Jim Sims in his book was also involved. By the way, the glider pilot Pat Mahoney managed to make his escape with the help of the Dutch underground and came out on Pegasus 1. I know this because soon after moving to Westgate on Sea many years ago I was pleasantly surprised to find that our gardens were back to back. So needless to say we have some very pleasant memories.

Ginger Jonas . . . . *meets some friendly Russians*

WE WATCHED from the neighbouring Oflag as they marched the lads away from Stalag 8c early in 1945. We had buried ourselves under the floorboards while Jerry searched the area and stayed like it for two days not daring to show ourselves to search for food.

When we did surface we knew the camps were empty and we scrounged to find anything that would be handy on our journey to fredom. We found bottles of Cod liver oil and malt and a jar of fag ends in the Officer compound, it seemed like Christmas! Breslau seemed the best place to head for so we just kept moving. As we approached the Russians were pounding the city, a Russian soldier challenged us, we got him to understand we were escaped prisoners, he called for an interrogator who spoke a little English.

Next day we were given bread and a thick slice of fat bacon and sent on our way, south, as escort to German prisoners being taken back. At Cracow we had our first encounter with rape, on entering a house we saw a dead woman, her clothes up around her waist. The husband at the side cleavered in two nearly. I was stricken with a cold and all I wanted was to sleep, although that night it was below zero, I laid down in the road. I was rudely awakened and told to get moving if I did not want to die. We found some spuds in a field and got fired at for stealing. We came across a farmhouse with a water pump, we stripped and had our first bath with our sentries laughing like hell at us. I thought the lice on us had enjoyed a long enough ride on us from the Stalag. We had a large fire going but still had to put the same clothes on again, at least it made us feel like humans.

A young Polish girl came in to the barn and begged to be allowed to sleep in the straw by our side for the night, she was about 17 years old. Two Russians came in during the night looking for her but we kept her head down and shouted at the soldiers for waking us up. Next morning a large pig was killed by the guards, they laid straw under and around it and set it alight. When it was well alight the women poured water over it and scraped it clean. A novel way of removing bristles. We were now told to get on a train, the open trucks for the guards and us, the prisoners to be locked in the goods waggons until the end of the journey.

German prisoners were sometimes allowed out to chop firewood for the engine. It was at that time we found about a dozen prisoners had committed suicide using the small blade of a penknife in the ear.

They were just pulled out of the waggon and dumped on the side. They had been told it was the salt mines for them!

One day we stopped and women Tank drivers called out callously to us, put them under our tracks and we will get rid of a few for you.

At last we came to Odessa, a Crimean port, the guards shook hands with us and said goodbye.

We paraded in barracks and were met by an English Colonel, with stick and monocle. He said we were not allowed out, if we did then mind the women for there was a lot of it about!

I was given the job of bodyguard to a Wren officer and had to go everywhere with her. I escorted her back to England.

Alan Johnstone . . . . *sees a vision, Beauty and the Beast*

ON A lovely spring morning in 1945 I was stumbling across the tracks at the marshalling yard in Luneburg in North Germany, having ridden in comparative comfort all night on a large truck-load of flax from Elster-werde near Stalag IVB from which, along with other restless souls I had escaped.

I was barefoot, hungry, unshaven and clad in denim overalls stained by some days of skulking in the heathland and pine-woods near Elster-werde. Across the tracks I had seen a thin line of small trees through which I could discern the buildings of a fair sized town at a lower level than the railway. When I reached the trees, I wandered along them until I came to a bridge spanning a quite busy street. For a while I lounged listlessly looking at the scene below until suddenly the apathy vanished and my senses awoke to a half-forgotten thrill as I spotted coming down the street – her figure silhouetted through a diaphanous summer frock, a gorgeous German blonde, an ideal Hitler-maiden, with the voluptuous

204

proportions considered essential to future mothers of Nordic supermen. My debilitated, sex-starved, Anglo-Saxon senses rose to this goddess and I was suddenly aware of gripping the railings and goggling down hungrily at her. The humour of the situation struck me and I had a cinematic flash of myself, a barefoot, unshaven, haggard, wretch, goggling wild-eyed down at this vision.

'Beauty and the Beast' I cackled to myself, and for the first time in some hours I felt really cheerful.

Ron Holt . . . . *three month Death march*

WARTIME SERVICE life can be divided into three separate parts. Recruit training and service in the home country. Then as a reinforcement to a fighting unit and an entirely different type of soldiering, where skill at arms and good basic training plays such an important part in your life and that of your comrades. There you can remain until the cessation of hostilities, unless as in the case of Arnhem with impossible odds, you are then into a third situation, as a Prisoner of War.

This will be the most emotional part of your service. One minute you are a fighting soldier with a crack unit and the next you are a nobody.

The first few moments of capture are dangerous, emotions are high and trigger fingers are nervous. Luckily front line soldiers of most countries have a respect and understanding for each other.

You part company with your original captors who at least respected you, shared their food and cigarettes and you go back to face the army misfits, the cripples, the sadists and general untrainable rabble. For the duration of the war their sole aim was to make life as miserable as they could.

I was thrown into this sort of life after Arnhem in 1944 and it was my misfortune to get sent to a stalag in Poland. It was colder than I have ever known in my life, the snow was four to five feet deep and our knowledge of Poland at this time was restricted to what we could see from the perimeter wire. The "kreigies" were a mixed bag, South Africans, Indians, Gurkhas, Americans, Australians and New Zealanders, mostly from the desert war, and British 1st Airborne and Polish Para Brigade.

Just after Christmas the Russians were getting near and it was arranged that we march to Leipzig. All we had to eat was one slice of bread and half a sugar beet. We carried extra blankets and personal belongings but, after a very few miles in our weak condition they were discarded and the next few nights were spent sleeping in the snow. Needless to say Leipzig could not accommodate us so we set out for Western Germany and hopefully the British front.

This was the beginning of the notorious death march and by April we were destined to travel well over a thousand miles. This would have been quite a challenge to fit healthy young soldiers, but stumbling along with the blood from dysentery running down your legs or dying of starvation was a different story and the toll in human lives averaged over twenty per day and, at one period the sick column was twice the size of the main column.

One night we slept in a disused brick factory and after an hour or so a column of Russian POWs arrived. Afterwards we found they had left us a present in the form of lice, we added this to our list of ailments.

The survivors of the original column arrived in Brunsweg in rags, exhausted, starving and sadly depleted, they were met by a British army hygiene unit who made a canvas tunnel. You took off all your rags and walked through the tunnel and were sprayed the whole length with DDT powder. The relief was instant, you were given a brand new uniform and once again rejoined the British Army and the human race.

CHAPTER ELEVEN

And fifty years later

IN 1969 Ron Holt then living in Chester, thought that it would be a good plan for the Old Comrades of the Battalion to have a get together. As we had been stationed in Grantham in 1944, he decided that it would make a central meeting place. Word spread quickly and at our first evening dinner there were forty men, some with their wives, to meet the Colonel and Mrs Frost. It was a most successful gathering and has become an annual event. I quote the first line of Nancy Mayhew's poem, 'You belong to a most exclusive Club, unique in every sense'. We do!

Many who attended that first meeting have now passed on, including Ron Holt and the Colonel. At our last reunion just a few Bruneval veterans attended. The men who dropped at Depienne may number double figures but the reinforcements for Sicily and Arnhem were younger men and so make up the majority of Para 2 Club members.

Ron Holt started a newsletter which has been continued, items in this book have in many cases been carried in that newsletter. For permission to reprint their writing of personal stories, I thank them.

Dave Brooks . . . . *we meet our successors*
THERE COMES a time when I am asked to write about something that requires the skill of one more gifted than me. Such was the case on Friday 2nd August 1991, when the Parachute 2 Club was entertained to lunch by the 2nd Parachute Bn. We could not have imagined how successful the day would be when the forward planning started 18 months previously. It almost beggars description.

On reflection the operative word was 'Welcome', As you get older you get an instinct for knowing if your hosts are just performing a chore, or really want to get to know you. All those present will know that the latter was the case. Lt Colonel Hicks put us at our ease in his opening talk. It was clear that the 2nd Parachute Bn do regard us as the founders of a Battalion that has gone from strength to strength since 1941.

On arrival we were taken to the lecture hall in the Depot, where we had tea and coffee, followed by interesting talks on the make up and equipment of a Para Bn, their different roles in defence of the realm, and frequent tours of Northern Ireland. They are able to make good use of modern technology, though when questioned we learnt that wireless sets can still be a bit contrary, so some things do not change. They can be deployed by air very quickly in aircraft that can carry far greater loads than the planes used by us. Operational jumping height is still 800 feet, but that could be halved if necessary, and a 'chute' is being developed that will allow troopers to exit at 250 feet in safety. We were also given an insight into the rules that govern soldiers serving in Northern Ireland, which is called the yellow card.

From the Depot we were taken to the playing field, first to see a free fall by the Red Devils, from a great height as the day was so clear, then the Bn demonstrated their wares and skills, all most impressive. Since our day there have been advances in weapons and firepower, all the soldiers I spoke to thought their weapons were the best available, they have faith in their modern carbines, all fitted telescopic sights which are accurate despite being shorter in the barrel than our Enfields. There has been great improvement in clothing and equipment, though I was somewhat shocked to learn that soldiers are allowed to purchase and wear items of footwear and clothing, similar in design, but superior in quality to that which is issued. I was shown boots that cost £115.00, whilst one can applaud the keenness of a soldier to be as effectively clothed as possible at his own expense, I feel they should be equipped with the best available in the first place. Emergency rations have improved out of all recognition, very compact indeed. I was treated to a swig of tea that one of the soldiers was brewing in his Billy, it tasted good, same as it did in my day. We had a first class barbecue lunch and a welcome glass of beer, followed by a display by the Drummers resplendent in their Dress uniforms, quite magnificent. The presentations were made in a simple ceremony. Men of the Bn formed two sides of an open box, and the Club members the third.

General John spoke of our formation days and of his and many other doubts that Parachute soldiers would be required in peacetime. In fact they have gone on to become the elite of the army, bar none, renowned and copied throughout the world.

The Bruneval Cup is spectacular, fully 2 feet high, the new plinth is neatly engraved, with details of the occasion. The Bell and its companion engraved plaque will be housed in 2 Para Officers mess. Both will be tangible reminders of our existence long after we are gone. We were all invited into the Sgts Mess by RSM Fred Toland, some of us accepted his kind offer and were received most hospitably.

A never to be forgotten day, thanks to Lt Colonel Hicks and his men, and a splendid turn out by Club members. I can best sum up the feeling of this day by using a verse by V. Lumb of 3 Para Bn. 'The spirit that's within me lifts my head in silent pride Recalling days behind me and the men I've marched beside'.

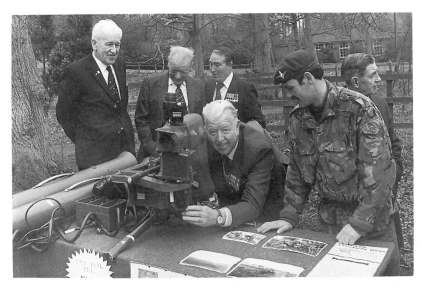

The Bruneval veterans join the present 2 Para at Aldershot in February 1982 and inspect the new weapons. L to R, Alex Reid, Charles Cox MM, Jack Grafton, Bob Dobson and Stan Halliwell. Photo: Soldier Magazine.

John Judge .... *a Bruneval veteran wishes he was 20 again*

I ARRIVED at Aldershot by train about 2pm to attend the Bruneval visit and as requested phoned the barracks when a truck was dispatched to pick me up. On arrival I was given my room for the 2 nights and then sat and talked with some mess members present. I had a drink of tea and later was told I could have something to eat, but refused, as there was a buffet laid on for 5.30pm. After our instructions for the next day we had our buffet and a very enjoyable one it was. For the rest of the night we sat drinking and yarning over old times. Although we knew reveille was at 2.00am none of us was eager to make the first move and it was after 10 before the first one went to bed.

At 2.00am we were up and showed no signs of the late night (that was to come later). I was lucky I knew where the kettle and coffee was kept so I made myself one and got into trouble as no one else did. It seems the army doesn't believe in 'gunfire' Sgt Majors tea anymore. At Lyneham we embarked on 2 Hercules eight men to each after we had had our breakfast. We sat in the tail and were able to watch the jump from the inside. It amazed us to see how the jump masters nearly threw them out of the door but the reason for this was explained to us and made sense. There wasn't room in Whitleys for a jump master but with the present day situation I can't see anyone being able to refuse to jump. On arrival at Le Havre we were helped into trucks and off to the DZ where we met up with the Coy. As expected with French organisation the service was long winded and also in French, so not understood by us.

The place where we operated in 1942 was an eye opener to me and I wonder how we got down the hill in the dark with snow on the ground and with no casualties. We had a look round the DZ and chateau and were asked to give a little speech on our part of the raid then back for a first class barbecue. We then went back to the memorial and had our pictures taken with the Coy before going back to the plane.

On landing it was back to barracks and a first class meal waiting for us. The rest of the night again spent with memories in the mess. Monday morning it was breakfast and we left about 9.00am.

Altogether we were treated like royalty by one and all including the RAF. People couldn't do enough for us and the meals were first class. Made me wish I was 50 years younger and still serving.

Dennis Rendell . . . . *The Leaping Seventies*

THE WHOLE thing started at the May 1989 Parachute Regiment Officers' Dinner, at RMA Sandhurst, when Major Jasper Booty TD, late 10th Bn, after several drinks suggested to General Mike Gray that if a number of old codgers of seventy and over could do a parachute jump, they could hardly fail to raise less than £50,000 for the newly-formed Airborne Development Trust.

It was decided that we had best drop into water, softer for our old bones, and Studland Bay in Dorset, near Poole, seemed the ideal place. The Royal Marines stationed nearby readily agreed to pick us up.

The chutes we were to use would be sports round main parachutes and a standard reserve chute. Lifejackets (Mae Wests) and dry suits would be provided by the Royal Navy. The main chutes were of 35ft diameter, a long way from our old X chute of 28ft. As we were to jump from 2500-3000 feet, we would have over two and a half minutes in the air, and bags of time to look around. The medical risk of jumping into water is the shock to a seventy-year-old of meeting cold water, and we wanted no accidents from hypothermia – hence the dry suits. As a result of this, we all had to have a medical with a certificate signed by our own quack to say we were fit to jump. Mine said I was perfectly fit to drop, but doubted my mental state! Nevertheless, he agreed to sponsor me!

The training given by the Red Devils was superb and, though hard, enjoyable. They are a splendid bunch under Captain Muir, with CSM Whittle as our Chief Instructor. I was delighted to have the personal assistance of Corporal John Dyer, RMP, the only Redcap ever to have served with the Devils.

Thursday 7th August dawned bright and clear, with a windspeed of about 15 knots, with the wind scheduled to drop – near perfect. The first stick departed for Farnborough at about 7am and the second Stick left for Bournemouth soon afterwards. I was to drop No.1 of the second Stick, and on arrival at Hurn at about 0945 went to the Control Building for coffee; and after spending pennies went out on to the tarmac.

Those dry suits could be a real problem for the more incontinent among us oldies the Devils had laid out our chosen kits. At 1030, helped by our minders, we started to dress; it takes quite a time to do this.

Dry suit first, just wearing light slacks and shirt, no shoes, and bags of French chalk on collars and cuffs, all uncomfortably tight, but hopefully waterproof, then zipped up at the back by a gi-normous zip. Next the Mae West, followed by the main chute on your back. All webbing D's well tightened, and the reserve chute clipped on in front. Finally a plastic helmet not unlike the old rubber ones of 1940-41. You'll remember it was supposed to stop you 'ringing the bell' and suffering a bloody nose! The full kit weighed just over 40 pounds.

We emplaned as instructed, all sitting on the floor, reminiscent of those ghastly old Mark V Whitleys, but this time no dreaded hole, just a small door which one can comfortably sit in and easily push off from, although it did seem to me that my exit might be a bit close to the port airscrew!

I felt the motors being throttled back and the CSM beckoned me to the door. I slid over on my behind, and sat with my legs hanging out, surprised that I couldn't keep them straight. A gentle shout of 'Go!' from the CSM and a light touch on my shoulder, and I was away. I counted – 1000-2000-3000 – and then felt the satisfying pull of the lift webs on my shoulders as the chute bit the air; I looked up and saw that lovely great canopy.

I had three twists in my rigging lines, probably due to a poor exit, but I soon had these out and felt for the toggles above. Placing my hands on these I found I could control the chute very easily and accurately. The view was marvellous, the silence golden and the sun restful and warm. I had been told that there was a nudist camp on the Sandbanks spit, and so directed myself to that area – I couldn't see any nudes, male or female, and suddenly realised that my fruitless search had brought me unwittingly down to about 800 feet. I located the Royal Marine landing Craft and saw the yellow smoke marker, so headed in that direction, turned into wind and made a perfect (that's my claim anyway!) backwards landing as instructed by the CSM.

I noticed a Royal Marine Dory boat nearby as I hit the water, inflated my Mae West and sat there floating completely dry and feeling like a rather helpless Michelin Man. I must have opened my mouth, because I found that seawater tasted salty; I'd forgotten. In next to no time I heard a voice say 'Hold on, sir, we're coming' and then 'We'll pull you in backwards', and I felt myself being hauled in to the Dory. It took some time for the two chaps aboard to get all my kit off, and I could not release my helmet; willing hands quickly remedied that. 'Thank you, Royal Marines' I said. 'Well done'. 'Not forgetting the Parachute Regiment' said a quiet voice, for one of the men in the Dory, was a Para. As they were both in camouflaged suits and not wearing berets, it was not possible to identify them, but between them they did a wonderful job. They took me to the landing craft and helped me aboard, where I rejoined my friends of the first Stick. A Para doctor asked how I felt, and having told him I was fine he produced a welcome dram of whisky offered by Jasper, and later a scalding cup of coffee, courtesy Royal Marines.

When all were down and safely aboard, we set off for the Royal Marine Depot, being saluted on the way, by our lined-up rescue craft – nice touch, that. We waved and shouted our thanks, and then got down to finishing a bottle of the hard stuff kindly provided by Arthur Kellas CMG, late of 1 Para and SOE and our one-time Ambassador to Iraq! After changing in Poole, on to the Sandbanks Hotel, for a tremendous party with families, friends and Press. In all a most splendid day, enjoyed by everyone including our mentors, the superb Red Devils. I personally was sponsored for £4,600 and so on behalf of the Airborne Forces Development Trust I sincerely thank all my sponsor friends; we are most grateful.

We haven't quite reached our target, but we are not far off it at £46,000. I personally thank you all again for your generous support. We are now planning 'The Leaping Eighties' and inevitably 'The Jumping Nineties'!

Joe Beckett . . . . enjoys Pilgrimage hospitality

I WAS lucky enough to be one of five 2nd Bn men chosen for a five day trip with all expenses paid, by the Silver Cross Medical Co. The others being Fred Kidds, Arthur Letchford, Bill Avery and Ron Youngman. An early morning start from my home to Norwich for the train to Liverpool Street Station, then across London to Heathrow in time to board our plane for Schipol, Amsterdam.

We were met and taken by minibus to the Kievitsdel Hotel, Doorwerth just outside Oosterbeek, where we were made more than welcome. Food, accommodation etc, first class. We were given 50 guilders spending money. The minibus was at our disposal for the five days. A programme of the Commemoration of the Battle was arranged for us and places visited were: Koning Willem III Barracks, Apeldoorn, Reunion at St Elizabeth's Hospital, Arnhem, a Battle Tour, Airborne Museum, wreath laying Airborne Memorial, Oosterbeek, silent procession and wreath laying at Memorial in Airborne Square by the John Frost Bridge, the 10th Bn Parachute descent, Driel and evening tattoo by the Royal Band, Oosterbeek. Bill Avery and myself did not go to the boat trip on the Rhine, instead we retraced our footsteps of 1944. We also managed to find time for shopping for gifts for the family.

Sunday was the climax of the pilgrimage with a most moving memorial service at the Airborne War Cemetery, Oosterbeek. Although the weather was wet, it did not stop the people from turning out and paying their respects. Although the years have passed, seeing the graves of friends and comrades left me with moist eyes and a lump in my throat.

The Dutch people were wonderful treating us like royalty. I cannot remember having my photo taken or signing my name so many times. The last evening at the hotel ended with a sing-song of all the wartime songs, the Dutch people thought it great. We were given a very nice Silver Cross tie and a bottle of the Hotel's best wine. Monday morning time to leave. After such a wonderful time it was hard saying goodbye. A good flight and rail journey home. Five days I shall never forget, and to all the people who made it possible I cannot thank you enough. To the other nine chaps, thanks for being such great company.

Matthew McAllister MM . . . . *sends a tie to HRH Prince Charles*

DURING THE Airborne Forces Day at Aldershot I was fortunate to be one of those who were spoken to by HRH Prince Charles. During the conversation he noticed I was wearing the Club tie and asked if it was a new type of Regimental tie. Knowing I only had a brief minute before he moved on I explained very quickly about Para 2 Club. Later I decided to send one to Prince Charles with a letter giving more details about the yellow stripes and the hunting horn and its use in battle.

BUCKINGHAM PALACE

From: The Assistant to The Equerry to H.R.H. The Prince of Wales

13th August 1990

Dear Mr McAllister

The Prince of Wales has asked me to write to thank you for your letter together with the Parachute 2 Club tie.

His Royal Highness was most grateful for your kind thought in sending this gift and has asked me to convey to you his sincere thanks and best wishes.

Yours sincerely

Susanna Perkins

Flight Lieutenant Susanna Perkins, WRAF

Hugh Levien .... *Prince Charles at Oosterbeek*

MOST OF our members have visited the Cemetery at one time or another and cannot fail to be aware of the tangible atmosphere of reverence which is present. No description of the memorial service on the 40th anniversary can be complete without reference to this feeling which struck especially strongly this year. The Cemetery was crammed and overflow crowds could be seen peering over the boundaries and on top of vehicles parked outside.

The first few rows of chairs in the central aisle were reserved for VIPs and the front row included Prince Charles, The Queen of the Netherlands, the Dutch Ministers for the three Services, Gen Urquhart, Gen Frost, wives and ADCs.

After they had taken their places the three National Anthems were played by the excellent large band of The Royal Dutch Air Force, and then the numerous colour-parties filed in with the OCA branch standards and took post either side of the Memorial Cross. The service of prayers, hymns and addresses was conducted by Padre Phillips (3rd Para. Bn. during the Battle), an R.C. priest and a senior representative of the Dutch Reformed Church. At the end of the latter's address, which was in Dutch, school children from Arnhem and the surrounding villages filed in with bunches of flowers and took position facing each grave stone.

Then followed the Last Post, the ending of which was the signal for the children to place their flowers at the base of the graves, then Reveille, during which the sun broke through as a fitting addition to a moving and solemn occasion.

The next ceremonial was the laying of wreaths by Her Majesty, our Colonel in Chief, Commanders during the battle, Heads of Service, Ambassadors, numerous others not easily identified and the OCA branches. This was rather a protracted business but unavoidable in view of the 40th Anniversary resulting in many more wreaths than usual, and fortunately it was not too cold and kept dry.

After the final prayers and hymn we were requested to keep our places until after the Royal parties had left. At this point Prince Charles was marvellously considerate. He moved among the veterans shaking hands, asking questions, posing for photographs and chatting away for half an hour or more without any sign of impatience. One heard his praises being remarked on all sides.

Bill Aldcroft .... *in Australia remembers Lieut Richard Spender*

SINCE WEARING the Para 2 Club tie I've met up with the families of two ex-Paras who went to Arnhem. Both are dead now but the families of these men are proud of the fact they had a father who was a "Paratrooper". Surnames were Oliver and Knight but no other info although I suspect Oliver was in 2 Para.

214

I have two stories that may trigger a memory or two. My platoon officer was Lt Richard Spender during the Tunisian campaign. I recall going out on patrol with him and remember the green feather in his hat and his black thorn walking stick. We came back through our lines into a French sector. They appeared shocked to see him playing a flute in the lead of a very weary bunch of Paras coming in from the enemy lines. He would read us poetry he had written and I think he was different from any other officer I served with. I really can see him now, he had little tufts of a beard on his face, a real character and a brave man. He was killed in action.

After the war I joined the Palestine Police and was in Tel Aviv during the 'problems' between the Paras and the local residents. In my group there was a couple of SAS and couple of ex-Paras. We had to round up a few rather wayward lads who were sort of shooting the place up. One I arrested turned out to be someone I knew from the old battalion. We spent some time talking over old times and later several of the ex-Para Palestine Police had an evening out with some of the old comrades.

George Stubbs . . . . *better the Golden Ball in Nottingham*

YOU ASKED me what was I doing on D Day? I can distinctly remember being on 'stag' at Easton Hall on the night of 5 June. Dozens of aircraft flew over during my 2 hours of duty. Although it was dark they were plain to see with their navigation lights on.

After breakfast A coy marched over to HQ and when they returned I was told the news. We were not very pleased to hear that the 6th Div had been given the task instead of us.

We all remember the various ops we were briefed for and suddenly cancelled but it looked like 'IT' when we went down to Down Ampney and slept under canvas on the 'drome'. Once again it was cancelled and we went on five days leave. Then came the call for Arnhem, just the 1st Div, early September, then that was cancelled. I remember being in Nottingham with Archie McAuslan on Friday 15 September and arriving back at camp on Saturday morning to be told we were CB and the operation was on again with 2 US Divs. We were ready and left on Sunday morning. That evening I was digging in on the Rhine embankment in the shadow of an almighty bridge with Archie. He said 'Christ, I wish I was in The Golden Ball instead of here,' that is where we were just a short 48 hours previously.

Two days later Archie was dead, killed in the house on the corner, East of the Bridge.

Bill Bloys . . . . *tells of an unfortunate story teller*

IN THE past 45 years and many pilgrimages I have come across twenty men who claim they were the first man on the bridge and another twenty who were last off the bridge. Most of them claim to have been attached to the Second Bn and could not remember if it was day or night, Sunday or Monday, or how many AFVs they knocked out. I will remind them of a story Father Egan told. After the war he was in London when a man in a red beret stopped him and asked for the price of a meal, two shillings. "What Bn were you with?" said Father Egan, "Second sir" came the reply. "Who was your CO?". "I can't remember" said the man. "Who was your Padre?" Father Egan said. "I did not see him sir, he was C of E and like you Father I am RC". "This is not your lucky day" replied Father Egan, "you are speaking to the Padre of 2 Para, come and see me at the church at 1300 hours".

So remember you story tellers, always check up to see to whom you are telling your story.

Dave Brooks . . . . *joins Bruneval Pilgrims*

AN ELEVENTH hour invitation, enabled me to fly to Bruneval on Sunday 14 June 1992 with 2 Para and 11 Bruneval veterans, I felt very privileged to be invited.

I met the main body at Lyneham airfield at 4.45am. Some of the Bruneval veterans were well looked after at Aldershot the night before and the night after, two of them travelled over by helicopter and others had joined the 50 strong sea party.

After a full English breakfast in the RAF dining room, it was time for the serious business, C Coy 2 Para formed the majority of the jumpers, they had already been briefed.

Prior to entering the hangar to draw chutes they were given their jumping orders, these orders seemed to be exactly the same as those given to qualified para's 50 years ago. We were able to mingle with the soldiers and chat to them.

Time came to board 2 Hercules, these are huge by comparison with the wartime planes, they are the functional workhorses of the air, not all that comfortable, and very noisy. The men were to exit 16 at a time, from 2 side doors. As we approached the DZ we were invited to stand on the ramp at the rear a few feet from the doors. The doors are not opened until needed. Tension time was here. I took note of how these young men combat that, some sitting silent, some chatting animatedly and some pretending to be asleep, but when the time came they went like young lions, there was an air of supreme efficiency from them and the RAF dispatchers.

We were taken from the aerodrome to the Beach memorial, in good time to see 2 Para march on, and a magnificent sight they were.

From the memorial we were taken to the ruins of the Radar station on top of the cliff, where veterans gave their accounts of the raid to the young men of today who serve in a Coy now called Bruneval, a feature of the day was the rapport between young and old.

Then followed a first class barbecue in a field at La Poterie, the 2 Para

216

Captain John Timothy in 1985 presented a wall plaque to the youth centre at Worth Matravers, Dorset, where the Radar equipment from Bruneval was first examined by the scientists. Photo: G. Gatland. MBE.

advance party did us proud, we had plenty of time to chat with old friends and our successors, commemorative medals were presented to Bruneval men by Jean-Claude Pinet, Curator of the museum at Le Havre.

Time came for the airborne party to depart for the flight home, a final pass was made over the historic DZ. Some of us were invited on to the flight deck as we approached the English coast, the navigating officer pointed out places of interest as we flew over. I was given the navigators seat for the landing, and had a good view of the leading Hercules touching down like some huge bird. Those of us not returning to Aldershot, said our goodbyes. A memorable day, paying due tribute to the Regiments first battle honour, a proud one for veterans John Timothy, Mac Forsyth, Jack Grafton, Jim Calderwood, Frank McCausland, Bill Addie, Andrew Young, 'Geordie' Johnstone, John Judge, Tom Hill, and 'Sticky' Wood, all 2 Bn. Stan Halliwell RE, Bob Dawson RN, and Donald Peveller and Charlie Cox RAF. A day made possible by the efforts of Major James Bashall and his men; by the RAF; by Major Steggles. I am grateful to them all, it is right that we should remember the sacrifices made during World War 2 and the young comrades who now occupy a 'small corner of a foreign field'.

Norman Deller .... *takes off on horseback*

I REMEMBER Lionel Pickering. He was probably the only man in 1st AB Div to wear an 'Argentina' shoulder title over his wings and Pegasus. He and I were good friends, and at Colsterworth we both had our feet

217

under the table with the local butcher, a Mr & Mrs Wright, who owned the horse that Lionel used to exercise.

Eventually Lionel suggested that I should ride the horse. ME, who had never been on a horse in his life, and so one evening Lionel brought the horse all saddled up into Back Lane and with great difficulty I mounted it and waited to get a few expert tips. To my horror Lionel shouted out in Spanish and smacked the beast on the rump and off I went at the gallop, holding on for dear life. Along Back Lane I went, into the High Street and headed towards the Great North Road. I was shrieking 'whoah', having visions of Dick Turpin's ride to York and wishing I had the Colonel's hunting horn, not to 'tallyho' but to sound a warning to any unlucky individual who might be coming towards me. Fortunately the horse swerved through an open gate and into a field. There looming in front of me was 'Beechers Brook' in the shape of a very high hedge, I closed my eyes and waited to become 'airborne' but the horse baulked and came to a stop. I got off and walked back to Colsterworth leading a well exercised horse and rubbing my sore and bruised thighs and backside, and when I saw Lionel I didn't give him time to speak either in English or Spanish, for I let fly at him with some Anglo-Saxon expletives which relieved my feelings in respect of his ancestry and all horses in general.

After being taken POW I lost touch with him, but received a letter in 1947 saying that he was back in Argentina and had married, I replied but there was no further correspondence.

During the Falklands crisis, Lionel was often in my thoughts. Not knowing how Argentinian conscription worked, I often wondered if Lionel had a son or grandson who may have gone to the Falklands and possibly fought against the 2nd Para Battalion. Coincidence is a strange thing.

John Hey . . . . *our visitor from Holland*

MIJNHEER JOHN A Hey who compiled the Arnhem Roll of Honour was invited to be our guest at the Reunion Dinner. He writes:

Dear friends, I like to say that those days at Stoke Rochford Hall have left on me a great impression. In the past I have attended the Reunions of other Regiments but this one really was the best. When talking with you and your comrades, the experiences of both the living and the dead formed – inevitably – a unity and all this was so recognisable to me. For me the culminating point was the church service on Sunday: Dave Brooks reading out the names of those who failed to return, the lament of the piper outside, the atmosphere of the building, the "We Remember Them" of the congregation, unforgettable... I never had so strong a feeling during a Remembrance Ceremony that it seemed the dead were physically present. Is that the pure remembrance?

218

Please convey my gratitude and best regards to all for the hospitality, friendship and support during these remindful days. It has been a privilege to have been among those 'who made one act an epic for all time'.

General Gale .... *when asked about Arnhem stated chances are slim*

DURING AN interview in 1971 at the Airborne Museum the Curator Major G Norton asked General Gale his opinion of the Arnhem operation. General Gale stated that the contents were not to be disclosed until after the participants death.

In it he said, General Browning had asked his opinion of the plan and he replied: "The whole division have to be landed on or close to the Bridge to be certain of success, or at the very least; a coup de main drop of a parachute brigade to hold the Bridge until the main force arrived. Without such a drop the chances of success were slim. When Browning asked what he would do if he had to accept the plan (of dropping 11kms to the west) Gale replied, "I would resign."

The above is taken from the review in Pegasus of General Deane Drummond's recently published autobiography, Arrows of Fortune.

Don Smith .... *Not so Friendly Fire*

DURING MONDAY 18 Sept 1944 I and others of 4 and 5 platoon B Coy, were with Major Crawley and Capt Hoyer-Millar in the police station overlooking the west side of the Bridge. 4 platoon Commander Loopy Levien, Brooks, Patterson, Elleray, Gockell, Ward and two others could not breakthrough the German perimeter defences, these were eventually taken prisoner at Bakkerstraat. During the evening we were briefed for a patrol onto the Bridge to take prisoners. The patrol was led by Capt. Hoyer-Millar with Sgt Carrier, Cartledge, Stott, Izzard, Moon, Wood, Logan, Cole, CSM Scott.

At dusk we made our way along the road which was at right angles to the Bridge. We occupied the house directly adjacent to the Bridge, previously occupied by A Coy. (The house shown in Alan Fearnley's painting). We assembled and finally left the house at about 22.00 hours, we approached the Bridge via the steps to the parapet. I was sent northwards along the Bridge to search for anyone in or around the burning armoured cars, which I must add, were exploding all the time. The remainder of the patrol charged across the Bridge eastwards, they took about 12 or so very frightened Germans, from some slit trenches, prisoner.

I in the meantime proceeded about 50 yards and saw an officer under a burning armoured car, he was waving a white handkerchief. I called him out and took him back to the parapet.

We assembled all the prisoners and started down the steps, when, suddenly we were fired upon by a bren gun from the house opposite.

Capt Hoyer-Millar shouted 'will the stupid bastard who is firing the effing bren gun cease immediately'. The remainder of us shouted 'Whoa Mohammed' to ensure he knew that we were friendly.

Luckily there were no casualties, we managed to round up all the prisoners and get them back in the house and put them in the cellar. In 1991 I met Francis Hoyer-Millar at Stoke Rochford and reminded him of this patrol. We have a deep feeling of respect for the man, who made boys into men.

General Frost . . . . *writes about that extinct Yellow Lanyard*

THE FIRST Commanding Officer in January '42 issued every member of the 2nd Parachute Battalion with a yellow lanyard to be worn on the left shoulder. It was not long before parachute rigging lines were plaited and dyed with Mepacrine, issued in Africa. After several post war amalgamations of Battalions the lanyard was discarded.

It was deliberate War Office policy that the newly merged battalions represented all the battalions formed during the war and not just the original three battalions. However, this is easier said than done and I am proud to think that the present 2 Para like to think of themselves as the direct descendants of the old.

Norman Dellar says: My own specimen nestles in a 1914 Princess Mary's Christmas tin dreaming of the days when it was part of a parachute, severed, plaited and immersed in golden liquid to be proudly worn on my left shoulder. It travelled around the Mediterranean area quite happily but in September 1944 it was taken POW and in an unusual but proud way let its owner down.

I was not interrogated until arriving at Stalag 12a (Limburg) and was asked for number, name and rank, and remembering those well fed German and Italian POW's in England added "I was a farm labourer." I refused to give my Unit and the fat, bespectacled Jerry ordered, "take off your smock" I did and in a triumphant voice he said, "you vear the yellow lanyard, you are the second Bn, ve know all about you". We travelled to 4B and to 4F, Muehlberg and Zwickau. 'Lanyardii' was never confiscated, it never occurred to them that it consisted of 30ft of silk cord, useful for escape purposes if the occasion arose.

In 1945, after ex-POW leave we were posted to 2 Bn at Bulford and in March 1946 to Palestine. In Haifa we amalgamated with 3 Bn in December 1947 and 'Lanyardii' was taken down and posted to the kitbag.

I wonder if some high thinking CO will ever read his Bn history thoroughly and decide that 'Lanyardii Mepicrinus' must once again take its rightful place on a proud left shoulder. 'Lanyardii' we salute you, you are neither extinct nor forgotten.

Arthur Letchford . . . . *with Battle in mind*

ELEMENTS OF nature have no precedence over men at war, fought in field, forest, on the street, down alleyways, byways, house or barn.

The venue of battle does not give exception to anything or anyone, fatigue is succeeded with sight of death and the fear of it.

The cleft between cowardice and heroism is paper thin with self preservation hovering above conscience of men.

The tide of battle will ebb and flow in defence and attack.

Men will fall, some will die, acts of courage happen all the time, a medic will tend the wounded, the Padre will comfort the dying.

Officers will lead their men from the front.

Sergeants and Corporals will go forward with them.

Excitement does not have a real place in war and the glory is false.

Discomfort of sweat and cold, hunger, thirst, and fatigue goes unnoticed perhaps that is because one is too aware of death being nearby and the prominent factor.

Discomfort is temporary, death is forever.

May 1943, Lt Col JD Frost, DSO, MC, being congratulated by General Eisenhower having been decorated with the DSO at a special ceremony in the field.   Photo: IWM.

CHAPTER TWELVE

A Tribute to our Colonel

ALTHOUGH WE always spoke of 'General John' he was to us, the members of his wartime Battalion, 'The Colonel'. He was very well respected by all ranks and will ever be remembered as the survivor of four difficult wartime parachute operations.

He more than shared all our fears and hardships and ended, as most men of his Battalion, wounded and suffering the indignity of surrendering his arms to the enemy. Seven months in a Prisoner of War camp were to follow.

He was the President of our Para 2 Club and fairly regularly submitted an article for publication in our Newsletter. As a tribute to John Frost, I include a selection of his writings where he looks back with pride on the achievements of his wartime Parachute Battalion.

General John sends this message:

When we are gone let Para 2 Club go too!

ONCE AGAIN the members of the Para 2 Club enjoyed a most successful reunion in the environment that we have come to know so well. Our committee are to be congratulated on the way in which improvements are achieved as the years go by. The great stately mansion which housed so many of us during the war is a fitting venue for our dance, and the dinner arrangements can hardly be bettered. Few of us will forget Padre Brian Dougall's address in the Church, and we must ensure that we have him again. I hope that everyone will have noticed the performance of our bugler, Jack Grafton, for I do not believe that any regular from the Regiment could have played better.

Whilst our Honorary Secretary was reading the list of the names of the fallen, we were firmly reminded of the whole object and purpose of our club which was that we, who had fought together in World War 2, should meet together again. I feel sure that that is what our old erstwhile comrades would like to know.

It is always tempting to try to expand on success and bring in others to share our pleasure in each others company, but other means exist to enable us to celebrate with other generations if we so wish. Indeed we all ought to belong to the local branches of the PRA and give them our full support. But, the Para 2 Club is for those who were brought together by very special events, unique to World War 2. I was glad that such was the firm decision taken at the AGM. Let this now be accepted without any further argument. When we are all gone, let the Para 2 Club go too.

Through no fault of our own, many of us were made prisoner during the war and May 1945, brought back to us our freedom. Next to life itself, freedom is the most important thing and for many of us the merry month of May is a time to rejoice and be thankful.

However, one event marred the enjoyment for many of our members at this years reunion and that was the inexcusable gatecrashing of our evening by an uninvited party of German tourists, purporting to be members of the German Parachute Association. The Secretary of the 5th Regimental Association had applied to attend with 37 German people and had been firmly told that they could not be received owing to lack of accommodation available. Nevertheless, the party came to Stoke Rochford Hall. Their leader demanding an official welcome.

Despite the lack of welcome, the party remained, and came again uninvited to our service the next morning. The service is of course a memorial to those who were killed by Germans. It is utterly incongruous that a party of German tourists should force themselves upon us at such a time. Whereas we can share our sorrows with a small number of ex enemy warriors, whose skill at arms and latent chivalry are known to us, to be subjected to such presumption as was displayed is more than this old soldier can accept.

I have written to Colonel Witzig, the President of the German Association, and to Herr Hambuch, President of the 5th Regiment's Association, explaining that we are a private organisation whose members are able to invite only limited numbers of guests for obvious reasons. I trust that all our members will respect the wishes of the majority more meticulously in future, giving no encouragement to those who would flout them.

An address given at the Imperial War Museum

Market Garden – an Unrepentant Advocate

IT WILL be presumed that those listening to the address will be familiar with the background of operation Market Garden and so this is by no means an account of the events. Ever since the battle took place all those years ago, one has been hearing about the 'Failure of Arnhem'. Indeed there was a failure in that the main road bridge was not held until the 2nd British Army could cross the Lower Rhine over it. The main purpose of my talk was to list the reasons.

Firstly the planning was based on false information. Although the presence of the 2nd SS Panzer Corps in the Arnhem area was known to many, this vital information was withheld from 1st Airborne Division and indeed the relieving 30 Corps. Secondly the Air Forces planners misinterpreted the suitability of the terrain near the bridge for a parachute drop or a glider landing. Moreover they quite wrongly accepted the reported strength of the enemy flak, but worst of all, insisted that it was impracticable to fly two sorties to Holland from the nearby airfields in the UK on one day.

Lt Gen Browning, GOC of the Airborne Corps, insisted on bringing his HQ into the battle area where it could do no possible good and used up the lift of a fighting unit. Moreover he selected for his location the Groesbeek Heights, which are not really a worthwhile tactical feature, and insisted that the 82nd US Airborne Division make this a priority task, whilst ignoring the one thing that really mattered which was the bridge at Nijmegen. It was the failure to capture this that spelt the doom of the 1st Airborne Division at Arnhem. It was barely defended by the enemy at all when the Americans came, yet they had to leave it until it was indeed fully defended.

Even after it was finally captured, although we were holding on to Arnhem bridge only by our eyelids, efforts made by nearly all elements of the 2nd British Army to relieve us were half-hearted and failed. In contrast, the German reorganisation after their defeat in Normandy was extraordinary. In the space of two weeks they had built a new army. It was all made up with bits and pieces but it fought just as well if not better than our own. Their generalship was dynamic, as opposed to phlegmatic. At this particular time, Winston Churchill and his CIGS were away from the UK in Canada and maybe our own Generals were having a few off days. There were obviously a lot of tea breaks.

Meanwhile 1st Airborne Division, and the Polish Parachute Brigade were virtually destroyed. Their task had been to take and hold the Arnhem Bridge for a few hours and they had done this for four days and then continued to resist for several more. There were other adverse factors, including the weather and the non-function of so much of our radio. In fact it would take a whole book to list all the things that went wrong. However supposing that the whole division had been landed on the first day and supposing that small coup-de-main forces had been introduced to take both Arnhem and the Nijmegen bridges and supposing that the two thousand fighter bombers available had been on call. Supposing that through proper organisation the remarkable Dutch Underground had been brought in, and had been encouraged to rise in Amsterdam and Rotterdam armed with weapons from our now redundant Home Guard.

Furthermore supposing our Generals had been as active as the German counterparts and supposing Boy Browning had kept his HQ in the UK and flown over in a Lysander to visit each division. He could have put the Polish Brigade in where it was really needed and completely turned the scales with the 52nd Lowland Division which was never used. Whilst if the Field Marshal Montgomery had momentarily

Bill Bloys, General John Frost, David Brooks and the author at the Imperial War Museum when the General gave his lecture 'An Unrepentant Advocate of Market Garden'. Photo: IWM.

ceased from plaguing his immediate superior and acted like a Rommel to galvanise his desultory army group, they could have been up to, not only to neutralise the Ruhr, but capture the great port of Rotterdam as well.

Therefore I am an unrepentant advocate of the whole conception and will ever remain so. Nothing will ever detract from the quite splendid battle fought by all the units of 1st Airborne Division whilst it might not be unfair to claim that the performance of those who captured and held the north end of the main Arnhem bridge was without parallel.

Reflects on the Regiments 50th Anniversary

THE MAIN thought in my mind when attending the 50th Anniversary Service at St Paul's Cathedral was how wonderful it was that our Regiment had not only survived the war but had become so immeasurably stronger ever since. When we began all those years ago, I think many of us thought that our parachuting might be something of a gimmick, a wartime measure which would have no practical purpose in peacetime, instead of which we have seen the Regiment fully confirmed as a major regiment within the infantry and able to carry out duties of every sort in every part of the world, rather better than any other Regiment.

We who served during the war are sometimes inclined to think that our part was so very much more important than the parts played by our successors. But when one looks at all the various conflicts, rebellions and small wars which our successors have been involved in, it certainly gives one food for thought. However one of the main items in that service was the presentation of all the colours to the High Altar. This was a most moving ocasion and when they were saluted by the mass trumpeters, I think very few of us can have found it easy to suppress tears of pride.

As a Battalion we are indeed unique in that two of the Regimental honours, Bruneval and Oudna, were earned entirely by members of the battalion which played a very large part in the granting of three more. At

226

Tamera, we were the only battalion in the brigade that was in the battle from start to finish, which included the original defence, the withdrawal and the final counter-attack.

In Sicily we held the all-important high ground on which the remainder of the brigade were able to rally when they had been told to break up into small parties and make their own way to the rear. Lastly, the battalion's part in the battle of Arnhem needs no further comment from me.

On the Death of the Battalion's Padre

THE REVEREND Father Bernard Egan MC was one of the first arrivals at Hardwick Hall in 1941 when the 1st Parachute Brigade was forming and was one of the first members of the Brigade to qualify at Ringway RAF Station. He felt then, as he always did, that part of his job was to set an example. Parachuting clergy were considered to be rather an oddity in those early days. Some of the uninitiated were inclined to question the necessity for their journeys. Little did they know. He came to 2 Para just after being with the 1st Battalion during their epic struggle for Djebel Mansour during the Tunisian Campaign in early 1942. We were in what was thought to be a quiet sector of the line which we called "Happy Valley". Whilst here we were attacked by an Italian Alpini Regiment which resulted most successfully for us. This almost pleasant episode was followed by the bitter and prolonged battle of Tamera on the Northern Sector where the battalion needed all the support and comfort only a Padre could give. After surviving this with us he felt he wanted to stay and almost became Battalion property. Not very proper really because there were three padres within the Brigade, each of different denominations, and they had to serve all three Battalions and stay with each in turn.

However, Father Egan went on to the Battle of the Ponte Primasole in Sicily with us and here he won his MC for outstanding devotion to duty in the face of the enemy. He was always a 'cool customer' and so he continued. Then on to Italy and back home to the UK. We settled down in Lincolnshire to prepare for our share of the war on the Continent. Difficulties now arose through the continuing attachment of the RC priest to one particular battalion, for the physical distances between them caused problems. We for our part, a predominantly Anglican community, sometimes forgot that he was a Roman but his own hierarchy could and would not.

He was badly wounded during the battle at the bridge at Arnhem where our Battalion was destroyed and when I saw him he felt that he had not long to live, but three months later we found ourselves in next door beds in the officers' hospital at Obermaasfeldt, for I became wounded too. By then we had both had our wounds operated on for the second time and, with the absence of modern drugs these had to be swabbed out twice daily. A painful business and I so well remember our argument as to whether it was best for the orderly giving the treatment to come to us at the beginning of his round or at the end. I wanted to get it over as quickly as possible but he felt that, hearing others suffering first, strengthened him to bear the pain too.

We met from time to time when the war was over, but most particularly I remember giving away the prizes on sports day at the prep school where he was the headmaster. This was at Edge Hill, Wimbledon. I have never seen an establishment with higher standards in every degree. It was nice that he should have Major John Lane, an old 2 Para officer, as his bursar at that time. I lost sight of him during the years that he was headmaster at Donhead Girls School in Dorset, then suddenly he was a bedridden patient in the Hospital of the Holy Cross in Haslemere. He was in a nice room overlooking the gardens.

On the 8th of July 1988, he was buried in the RC Cemetery at Wimbledon after a magnificent service in the Church of the Sacred Heart at Edge Hill. This had been the place of worship for the school of which he had been the headmaster several years before. The service was conducted with all appropriate pomp and ceremony, accompanied with quite lovely singing given by the choirs of his former schools, matched perhaps by the quite perfect calls sounded by the bugler our Regiment had provided.

Seven members of the Para 2 Club were at the graveside of the Padre who had officiated for so many of our numbers all those years ago. It was nice to be told that his diaries showed that he considered that the best years of his life were those he spent among us.

Jack Grayburn's Arnhem Victoria Cross

ON SUNDAY 20th September 1987, on behalf of the Regiment, I had the honour of receiving the Victoria Cross which had been won by Lieutenant Jack Grayburn at the battle of Arnhem. This had most generously been loaned by his son and will be displayed in the museum at Aldershot. The family came to the annual Arnhem service in the Regimental Chapel and afterwards saw a march past by colour guards from the 3rd Battalion, parties from the Regimental Depot and the Aldershot PRA. Then at a simple ceremony in the officers mess the presentation was made.

The son was so like the father that I was strongly reminded of the young officer who was so unassuming, gentle and perhaps ordinary that he was not a person one would expect to be so outstanding in the battle. However perhaps it is always men such as he who have the inner strength to do what we would all wish to be able to do. Despite wounds with the resulting shock and pain, the deprivation of every solace, the continuous enemy bombardment and the threat of being engulfed in flame, he fought on from his battle position until relieved by death. There were of course many others who did likewise, but no one so exemplified the spirit of the Battalion so well as Jack.

His Appreciation of a Fighting Man

Lieutenant Colonel DOUGLAS CRAWLEY, OBE, MC

WITHOUT HAVING all the facts, I cannot attempt a full obituary of such a gallant, able and hitherto indestructible old soldier as Douglas Crawley. Let these words serve as an appreciation of one of the finest fighting men the Regiment ever had.

In our first action in Tunisia he was blinded, some forty miles inside enemy territory and led back across most difficult country to our own lines. Fortunately he recovered his eyesight and was back with the battalion in the front line as soon as he was fit. In our last desperate battle against the Witzig Regiment he was again badly wounded and evacuated. By this time he had established a reputation as a resolute and skilled platoon commander. Always cheerful and debonair, every job he was given would be done to the letter. The effect of his wounds kept him away for some time but he was back to command B Company well before the Battle of Arnhem, when after three days and nights of intensive fighting he was wounded yet again with inevitable capture.

His decorations for gallantry only barely reflect his conduct in battle. He was imperturbable in trouble and great fun to be with at all times. All our sympathy goes out to Doreen and the family whose happiness has been shattered. His old friends and comrades will miss him greatly but will always be thankful that they knew him.

The Pilgrimage Speech in Arnhem 1989

FEW OF those who left England in September 1944 ever expected that the battle we were about to fight would become so famous. Most thought that the war was almost over, few of us had ever heard of Arnhem but it seemed to be as good a place as any to be in at the end of hostilities. We were told that the opposition would not amount to more than one Brigade, supported by a small number of tanks, but that there would be a considerable amount of flak.

The whole object was to capture and hold the bridges so that the British Army could cross the great rivers in Holland and pass on to surround the Ruhr. It was considered that without this vital production centre, the Germans could not continue in the war. It seemed to all of us to be a splendid concept. We had been made ready to undertake many other missions since the landings in Normandy, all of which had been cancelled and now we were more than anxious to get into action.

Many accounts have been written and I am sure that all will be aware of most of the difficulties we encountered and of the disastrous outcome of our venture. However it is still sometimes said that the Germans had been forewarned. This is far from being the case, in fact Field Marshal Model, the German C-in-C, was forced to leave his lunch and bolt for safety. We have met Major General Heinz Harmel, GOC of the 9th

Panzer Division, and he confirms that our arrival came as a complete surprise. But Model's presence enabled him to galvanise the enemy into action and obtain all the support that could possibly be made available.

It was terrible to have to witness the destruction of so much of this lovely city. The fine old churches and most other buildings around us were reduced to smouldering ruins. Even above the thunder of the guns and the rattle of musketry, I will always remember the crackle of the burning timber as house after house caught fire. There was no darkness for the flames provided constant light. Although we could hear the noise of battle towards Oosterbeek, there were no sounds from the South towards Nijmegen from whence we expected deliverance. After four days of fighting with all the anti-tank and nearly all the small arms ammunition spent, half our numbers killed or wounded and no water at all, we at the bridge, when our last bastion caught fire, had to evacuate the wounded and prisoners who would otherwise have burnt to death in the cellars. The Germans gave us all possible help but the short truce necessary enabled them to improve their positions and in the morning they were able to overwhelm those who tried to fight on. The rest of the Division fought on for several more days under the magnificent leadership of General Roy Urquhart, but with the main bridge back in German hands, there could be no future in the original concept of operation "Market Garden", 2,000 survivors withdrew across the river.

However, much had been achieved and half of the Netherlands liberated. The Allies were well poised for the next stage of the offensive, which resulted in the ultimate victory. During the course of the battle no two peoples can have been brought closer together than the Dutch and the British. So many of you gave us all that you possibly could and often at a terrible cost. We all felt dreadful guilt at so falsely raising your hopes and doing things which resulted in so much destruction and suffering. Yet from you we have received only thankfulness, hospitality and love.

Just as you did your utmost to help us during and after the battle, so you have continued to welcome and entertain us ever since. It is ironic to think that the Polish Nation on whose behalf Britain had declared war in 1939, and whose soldiers fought so valiantly beside us in 1944, are still the ones who have not gained their freedom. Let us all hope and pray that with a new spirit motivating the Russian Government and people, it will be not be long before the Polish friends are truly free to be with us as and when they wish.

President Reagan speaks of John Frost

AT THE Guildhall, London on the 3rd of June 1988, President Reagan spoke on the Subject of Freedom.

During the course of his speech he referred to General Frost and his Battalion at Arnhem.

> Operation Market Garden it was called ... A Battalion of British paratroopers were given the task of seizing the bridge deep in enemy territory at Arnhem ...

> Some years ago a reunion of those magnificent veterans was held in New York, a Dutch newspaperman Henri Knap gestured toward General Frost.

> Look at him, still with that black moustache, if you put him at the end of a bridge, even today, and said keep it, he'd keep it!.

– The President of the United States of America

Group Captain Lord Cheshire VC OM DSO DSC
sends his congratulations and regards

14th February, 1992

Major General J D Frost CB DSO MC

My Dear General,

I have just heard that the 50th anniversary of the Bruneval Raid falls on the night of the 27th/28th February and I feel that I cannot let this occasion go without sending these few lines to express something of the admiration I have always felt for C Company and the others who took part in that remarkable operation.

The first I actually learned of it was when we in the Dambusters were given the job of simulating a dummy D Day invasion force heading East of the Seine and I can well remember the impact it made upon us. How in the face of the unexpected opposition that you ran into you managed to extricate the radar operator himself – or was it two of them? – as well as the essential equipment and get it down the cliff face and into the pick-up submarine I really don't know. Our own op on the night of 5th/6th June 1944 could never have succeeded as it did had we not been able to test out the window sizes and the tactics on the radar set itself, and that is quite apart from the help it gave the boffins in developing window as a whole. We wartime aircrew have a great deal for which to thank you and those under your command and I know that I speak in the name of everyone when I say: Congratulations and a happy and meaningful anniversary ceremony. My own thoughts, I assure you, will be with you that evening.

Warm regards

Yours sincerely

Cheshire

Major General John Dutton Frost CB DSO MC
December 1912-May 1993

A much admired Commanding Officer and General

Appendix A

LOCATION OF OVERSEAS CEMETERIES AND MEMORIALS

LHAV	:	St Marie Cemetery, Le Havre, France
MEDM	:	Medjez-El-Bab Memorial, Tunisia
MEDC	:	Medjez-El-Bab Cemetery, Tunisia
BEJA	:	Beja War Cemetery, Tunisia
MASS	:	Massicault War Cemetery, Tunisia
ENFI	:	Enfidaville War Cemetery, Tunisia
TABA	:	Tabark-Ras-Regel War Cemetery, Tunisia
BONE	:	Bone War Cemetery, Algeria
LREU	:	La Reunion Cemetery, Bejaia, Algeria
DELY	:	Dely Ibrahim War Cemetery, Algeria
CATA	:	Catani War Cemetery, Sicily
CASS	:	Cassino Memorial Plaques, Italy
SANG	:	Sangro River War Cemetery, Italy
NAPL	:	Naples War Cemetery, Italy
MORO	:	Moro River Candian War Cemetery, Italy
OOST	:	Oosterbeek War Cemetery, Holland
CANH	:	Canadian War Cemetery, Holten, Holland
ENSC	:	Eastern General Cemetery, Enschede, Holland
OVER	:	Overloon War Cemetery, Holland
GROS	:	Groesbeek War Memorial, Holland
BECK	:	Becklingen War Cemetery, Germany
BERL	:	Berlin War Cemetery, Germany
RHIN	:	Rheinberg War Cemetery, Germany
NKG	:	No Known Grave

Extract from the address given by Padre AA Buchanan at the first Airborne Forces Memorial Service held at St Martin-in-the-Fields, London on 17th September 1945.

> ‘ Those of our number who did not return have passed on to us a trust. They charge us to hand down to the world the Airborne spirit, the fellowship, the daring, the selflessness, the Christian spirit. In fifty years time gliders might be obsolete, parachutes might be obsolete, please God war might become obsolete. The Airborne spirit must never become obsolete. ’

The Most Reverend Alan Buchanan DD was Chaplain to the 1st Airborne Division at Arnhem where he remained with the wounded and was taken prisoner.

BRUNEVAL

28 Feb 1942	3252284	Rfm HDMcD McINTYRE	LHAV
28 Feb 1942	5347681	Pte AW SCOTT	LHAV

NORTH AFRICA

29 Nov 1942	6089276	Sgt A PRENTICE	ENFI
1 Dec 1942	129439	Major HF CLEAVER	MASS
1 Dec 1942	64263	Major PR TEICHMAN	MASS
1 Dec 1942	65704	Lieut HKA CECIL (Hon)	MEDM NKG
1 Dec 1942	176950	Lieut KMcL MORRISON	ENFI
1 Dec 1942	2824086	Sgt D GRIEVE, MM	ENFI
1 Dec 1942	6144156	Sgt LW HOLMES	MEDM NKG
1 Dec 1942	3053379	Sgt W MacFARLANE	MEDM NKG
1 Dec 1942	5989943	Cpl SJ DUNCAN	MASS
1 Dec 1942	1498851	Cpl SH LYON	MASS
1 Dec 1942	2929484	Cpl RR SCOTT	MEDM NKG
1 Dec 1942	3523175	LCpl N ASHCROFT	MEDM NKG
1 Dec 1942	6200382	LCpl FC BERRYMAN	MASS
1 Dec 1942	3184752	LCpl JB DIAMOND	MEDM NKG
1 Dec 1942	2934514	LCpl HC MATKIN	MEDM NKG
1 Dec 1942	3249226	LCpl ML METCALFE	MEDM NKG
1 Dec 1942	2991875	LCpl DB MURDOCH	MEDM NKG
1 Dec 1942	5989499	Pte R ASTLEY	ENFI
1 Dec 1942	4349855	Pte T BOWES	MEDM NKG
1 Dec 1942	6144255	Pte EJ BROOKES	MEDM NKG
1 Dec 1942	5629070	Pte CG COOMBES	ENFI
1 Dec 1942	893484	Pte J DICKSON	MEDM NKG
1 Dec 1942	3191045	Pte E FALCONER	MASS
1 Dec 1942	5254696	Pte JL FLETCHER	MASS
1 Dec 1942	4698148	Pte E HARRISON	MEDM NKG
1 Dec 1942	2818294	Pte A HERON	MEDM NKG
1 Dec 1942	1797700	Pte SA HUGHES	MEDM NKG
1 Dec 1942	6139264	Pte G JENKINS	MEDM NKG
1 Dec 1942	4972542	Pte G JONES	MEDM NKG
1 Dec 1942	7017607	Pte HC LUCAS	MASS
1 Dec 1942	2052215	Pte W WAIN, MID	MASS
1 Dec 1942	5830656	Pte H YOUNG	MASS
1 Dec 1942	7265566	Pte J ROSE, RAMC	MASS
3 Dec 1942	174279	Lieut EBC CHARTERIS, MC	MASS
3 Dec 1942	2040689	Pte JG SPILSBURY	MEDC
6 Dec 1942	5247949	Pte T WORLOCK	DELY
14 Dec 1942	6402208	Pte FD HERBERT	MEDM NKG
15 Dec 1942	2764356	Pte A BROUGH	MEDC
27 Dec 1942	7013652	Sgt W CRAIG	MEDC
27 Dec 1942	6213700	LSgt W BROWN	MEDC
27 Dec 1942	106807	Pte H GUNN	MEDC

234

29 Dec 1942	5671972	Pte J CHURCHILL	MEDC
7 Jan 1943	4396735	Pte J BRAMLEY	BONE
3 Feb 1943	2765542	Pte S DOUGLAS	MEDM NKG
4 Feb 1943	168721	Major R ASHFORD, MC	ENFI
4 Feb 1943	2821897	Capt M MOORE	ENFI
5 Feb 1943	3319063	Sgt T MAGUIRE	MASS
26 Feb 1943	3250870	Pte G CODACK	MEDC
27 Feb 1943	7013578	Sgt JP DOWEY	DELY
27 Feb 1943	4750216	LCpl H FIRTH	MEDC
8 Mar 1943	22962	Major G ROTHERY	MEDC
8 Mar 1943	33827	Capt ERW RADCLIFFE	TABA
8 Mar 1943	6469672	Cpl WH REEVES	TABA
8 Mar 1943	6353808	Pte AGB BACON	TABA
8 Mar 1943	6153695	Pte GW BIGSBY	TABA
8 Mar 1943	5341080	Pte E DONALD	TABA
8 Mar 1943	6030158	Pte JA JACKSON	TABA
8 Mar 1943	5949933	Pte GW MARTIN	TABA
8 Mar 1943	6148291	Pte JW MILES	TABA
9 Mar 1943	5825158	Cpl AG CLOUTING	BONE
9 Mar 1943	11268236	Pte WC LAMBIRTH	TABA
10 Mar 1943	3655432	LSgt W ANDERSON	TABA
10 Mar 1943	4616277	Pte LJ CARROLL	TABA
10 Mar 1943	6354985	Pte ST DANGERFIELD	TABA
10 Mar 1943	1580292	Pte AM STEVENSON	MEDM NKG
11 Mar 1943	2991585	LCpl W CLARK	MEDM NKG
11 Mar 1943	2991663	Pte GR BURNS	TABA
11 Mar 1943	5437817	Pte J BYNG	TABA
11 Mar 1943	4033294	Pte JH SOUTHERN	TABA
11 Mar 1943	6153399	Pte GH WICKWAR	TABA
14 Mar 1943	3246796	Pte G McDONALD	TABA
15 Mar 1943	4698437	Pte M ALLSOP	TABA
5 Mar 1943	6025122	Pte RW BIXBY	TABA
15 Mar 1943	5835428	Pte RW HOWARD	TABA
15 Mar 1943	3963170	Pte E YOUNG	TABA
17 Mar 1943	6850553	Cpl JB DEE	TABA
17 Mar 1943	4278926	Pte C WILSON	TABA
18 Mar 1943	5835408	Pte EF SAMSON	MEDM NKG
18 Mar 1943	2060214	Pte J SCRUTTON	TABA
18 Mar 1943	6853721	Pte RE SMITH	MEDM NKG
27 Mar 1943	66860	Major MM WARDLE	TABA
27 Mar 1943	184635	Capt RWS SPENDER	TABA
27 Mar 1943	326757	Sgt CJ HUNTLEY	TABA
27 Mar 1943	3317778	Sgt JE JACKSON	MEDM NKG
27 Mar 1943	6148273	Sgt PE LENDERYOU	TABA
27 Mar 1943	6140645	Cpl TA GAY	MEDM NKG
27 Mar 1943	4133938	LCpl L McGRATH	MEDM NKG
27 Mar 1943	3962130	Pte I ADAMS	MEDM NKG

27 Mar 1943	11251923	Pte BC ARLISS	TABA
27 Mar 1943	6853425	Pte JG BEDDO	MEDM NKG
27 Mar 1943	6853947	Pte HW DAVIS	MEDM NKG
27 Mar 1943	7047374	Pte J FRIEL	MEDM NKG
27 Mar 1943	4275517	Pte M HERWOOD	MEDM NKG
27 Mar 1943	6353221	Pte JJ HINES	MEDM NKG
27 Mar 1943	6029683	Pte CT HOY	MEDM NKG
27 Mar 1943	4279453	Pte H McARDLE	MEDM NKG
27 Mar 1943	6403167	Pte M McCARTHY	BEJA
27 Mar 1943	2765647	Pte RJ MacDONALD	TABA
27 Mar 1943	5890923	Pte RD PAGE	TABA
27 Mar 1943	4618408	Pte FEG SELMAN	BEJA
27 Mar 1943	6354176	Pte RA STARK	MEDM NKG
5 Apr 1943	6029658	LCpl J AYERS	TABA
5 Apr 1943	6030160	Pte GA CAUNT	TABA
15 Apr 1943	2762175	LCpl J BOND	LREU
15 Apr 1943	5112861	Pte G BELLAMY	BONE

SICILY

14 Jly 1943	7020108	Pte K COCHRANE	CATA
14 Jly 1943	4456733	Pte M COLLINSON	CATA
14 Jly 1943	1655860	Cpl HWA COPPARD	CATA
14 Jly 1943	6409524	Pte JF DILLON	CATA
14 Jly 1943	112918	Lieut GM DUNKELD	CATA
14 Jly 1943	5948775	Cpl JF GAUGHT	CATA
14 Jly 1943	6853735	Pte AHT GREENHAM	CATA
14 Jly 1943	4925742	Pte RB HAYNES	CATA
14 Jly 1943	2889238	Pte WY HENDERSON	CATA
14 Jly 1943	156264	Lieut JC HORNER	CATA
14 Jly 1943	6148535	Pte NE JONES	CATA
14 Jly 1943	4756696	Pte H LOCKWOOD	CATA
14 Jly 1943	192704	Sgt I McWILLIAM	CATA
14 Jly 1943	4031549	Sgt D NORRIS	CATA
14 Jly 1943	4698769	Pte H SCOTT	CATA
14 Jly 1943	4979617	Pte H SEAL	CATA
14 Jly 1943	7021979	Pte J SHANNON	CATA
14 Jly 1943	6148064	Pte SB SMITH	CATA
14 Jly 1943	13094689	Sgt GA WARE	CATA
14 Jly 1943	4698229	Cpl R WHITTLE	CATA
14 Jly 1943	5682898	Pte J WILSON	CATA
14 Jly 1943	4343755	Pte J BROOKBANKS	CASS NKG
14 Jly 1943	886011	Pte JA FULLER	CASS NKG
14 Jly 1943	3663875	Pte EC PENNINGTON	CASS NKG
17 Jly 1943	2059716	Cpl HC DODD	CATA

ITALY

19 Apr 1943	2879732	Pte J SMITH MID	NAPL
8 Sep 1943	5044457	Pte FW BROOKES	CASS NKG
14 Sep 1943	79683	Pte TG HANDS	CASS NKG
30 Sep 1943	66800	Capt JC SHORT	MORO
20 Jan 1944	7021134	LCpl F COLLINS	SANG
28 Jan 1944	6351452	Cpl FW MARTIN	CASS NKG

ARNHEM

17 Sep 1944	174425	Lieut PH CANE	OOST
17 Sep 1944	6856184	Pte TA GIBSON	OOST
17 Sep 1944	5511524	Pte C GRONERT	OOST
17 Sep 1944	5511523	Pte T GRONERT	OOST
17 Sep 1944	935393	LCpl W LONEY	GROS NKG
17 Sep 1944	1630172	Pte WL PARKER	OOST
17 Sep 1944	2657936	Pte TA PRATT	GROS NKG
17 Sep 1944	7684046	Cpl EH ROGERS	OOST
17 Sep 1944	2065867	Pte NW SHIPLEY	GROS NKG
18 Sep 1944	3196639	Sgt W BURNS	GROS NKG
18 Sep 1944	1553167	Pte WF CREW	GROS NKG
18 Sep 1944	5126342	Pte G DAVIES	OOST
18 Sep 1944	1435154	CSM D MEADS	OOST
18 Sep 1944	4756150	LCpl E ORBELL	OOST
18 Sep 1944	5682985	Pte J PRINCE	OOST
18 Sep 1944	4468347	Pte JR SMITH	CANH
18 Sep 1944	93375	Major DW WALLIS	OOST
18 Sep 1944	886001	Pte PM MURRAY	OOST
18 Sep 1944	6349647	Pte EH COLE	OOST
18 Sep 1944	6029477	Pte WH REEVE	OOST
19 Sep 1944	1539601	Pte A COCKBURN	OOST
19 Sep 1944	14397305	Pte B BLISS, RAMC	OOST
19 Sep 1944	2044354	Pte J HIGGINS	GROS NKG
19 Sep 1944	5342680	Sgt W McCREATH	GROS NKG
19 Sep 1944	14409111	Pte W ROUGHSEDGE	GROS NKG
19 Sep 1944	2060433	Pte WJG RUSSELL	GROS NKG
19 Sep 1944	14534710	LCpl CR WADDILOVE	GROS NKG
20 Sep 1944	148629	Lt C BOITEUX-BUCHANAN, MC	OOST
20 Sep 1944	3055038	Pte D FRASER	OOST
20 Sep 1944	149002	Lieut JH GRAYBURN, VC	OOST
20 Sep 1944	6351076	Pte RWA MOON	GROS NKG
20 Sep 1944	5498235	Pte RS PURNELL	OOST
20 Sep 1944	2879697	Cpl AA RATTRAY	OOST
20 Sep 1944	4699009	Pte J SIMPSON	OOST
21 Sep 1944	14418022	Pte HJ BATTRICK	OOST
21 Sep 1944	5053340	Cpl FW DODDS	GROS NKG
21 Sep 1944	5835386	Pte GE ELLINGFORD	GROS NKG
21 Sep 1944	5672142	Cpl FS NICHOLLS	GROS NKG

21 Sep 1944	2991530	Cpl J RUDDY	OOST
21 Sep 1944	123505	Major FR TATE	OOST
21 Sep 1944	7013959	Sgt S POWER	OOST
21 Sep 1944	4342669	WO II WW SCOTT	OOST
22 Sep 1944	2934817	Cpl F BARNETT	OOST
22 Sep 1944	3134185	Pte AH McAUSLAN	OOST
22 Sep 1944	268968	Lieut AJ McDERMONT	OOST
22 Sep 1944	1440687	Sgt J THOMSON, MID	OOST
23 Sep 1944	7957298	Pte GE MAY	OOST
23 Sep 1944	14302633	LCpl S ALLEN	ENSC
23 Sep 1944	7017277	Pte GE McCRACKEN	ENSC
23 Sep 1944	5827349	Pte WJ PAGE	OOST
25 Sep 1944	14434095	Pte F ALLMAN	OOST
25 Sep 1944	14529484	Pte LD SADLER	GROS NKG
25 Sep 1944	5780347	Sgt BE THOMPSON	OOST
14 Oct 1944	176460	Lieut RB WOODS	BECK
16 Oct 1944	3131990	Pte CM FITTOCK	BERL
20 Oct 1944	2080216	Pte RW STOKES	OOST
27 Oct 1944	6021874	Sgt M KALIKOFF	RHIN
9 Feb 1945	14221053	Pte LC GEMMELL	BECK
21 Mar 1945	6211062	LSgt E RIDDLE	GROS NKG
17 Apr 1945	406828	Pte G FITZSIMMONS	BERL
7 May 1945	4699060	LCpl PGHW BADGER	OVER

DEATHS IN ENGLAND

Place of Burial

30 Jan 1942	2888206	Pte RK MOSELEY	Chesterfield
16 Feb 1942	838479	LCpl J DUCKETT	Blackburn
9 Oct 1942	200246	Lieut PDH STREET	Tidworth Military
9 Oct 1942	2879660	Pte DJ REID	Barry, Angus
9 Oct 1942	5341084	Pte LAG SHELLEY	Great Dunmow
7 May 1944	6354006	Pte BC DOGAN	Bexley Heath
27 Jun 1944	5339494	Sgt J BARDWELL, MM	Consett, Durham
28 June 1944	2041829	Pte HW BALL	Crick, Nrthants
28 Jun 1944	10631907	Sgt AE PARRY	West Bromwich

DIED OF WOUNDS RECEIVED AT ARNHEM

25 Apr 1947	5946661	Pte AJ WRIGLEY	Cardington

DEATH ON SS STRATHMORE en route Algiers and buried at sea

9 Nov 1942	4973360	Pte J HANDFORD	Brookwood Mem.

> *"They shall not grow old as we that are left grow old*
> *Age shall not weary them nor the years condemn*
> *At the going down of the sun and in the morning*
> *We will remember them"*

Appendix B

OFFICERS WHO SERVED THE 2ND BATTALION

List of Officers who served between its formation in September 1941 until September 1944.

Commanding Officers

Lieut Colonel EWC Flavell, MC, promoted Brigadier April 1942.
Lieut Colonel GP Goften Salmond, (joined Bn 1.42), relinquished command through medical condition October 1942.
Lieut Colonel JD Frost, (9.41) POW September 1944.

The Commanding Officer was responsible for accepting or rejecting all Officers in his Battalion. Officers were posted for a variety of reasons the most common being promotion to another Parachute Battalion.

I have marked those I know to have been POWs and where they were taken. T = Tunisia, S = Sicily and A = Arnhem.

Those names not thus marked quite probably were wounded and discharged or returned to their original unit.

Majors:

A Pearson, (9.41) posted 1Bn
MRJ Hope-Thompson, (9.41), posted 4 Bn
RG Pine-Coffin, (9.41) posted 3 Bn
PR Teichman, (9.41) KIA T
JG Ross, (10.41) POW S
HF Cleaver, (9.41) KIA T
R Ashford, (9.41) KIA T
R Murdock, (8.43)
JAC Fitch, (8.43), posted 3 Bn
K Mountford, (9.41) POW S
DE Crawley, (4.42) POW A

V Dover, (8.42) POW A
JHS Lane, (4.43) POW S
PJ Albury, (7.43) posted
D Dobie, att 3.43 with 3 Bn
JWB Marshall (1.43)
MM Wardle, (1.43) KIA T
G Rothery, (2.43) KIA T
RTH Lonsdale, (5.43) posted 11Bn
AD Tatham Warter, (10.43)
DW Wallis, (1.44) KIA A
FR Tate (1.44) KIA A

Captains:

DB Rendell, (9.41) POW T
J Timothy, (9.41) POW A
SE Panter, (9.41) POW A
RL Stark, (9.41) POW A
R Read, (1.42)
J Measures, (6.42) POW T
RS Johnson, (9.41)
RWS Spender, (9.41) KIA T
JC Short, (1.42) KIA T
JD Brayley, (4.42) posted
EM Kinsey, (2.43)
ER Elliott, MBE, (11.42)

J Rann, (11.42)
G Turnbull, (10.42)
ERW Radcliffe, (12.42) KIA T
D McLean, (7.43) POW A
AJH Rutherfoord, (11.42)
AM Frank, (5.43) POW A
FE Kite, (8.43)
M Moore, (8.42) KIA T
RC Morton, (8.43) POW A
FK Hoyer-Millar, (3.43) POW A
MD Willis, (8.43)

Lieutenants:

M Willcock (9.41)
PDH Street (9.41) Killed (10.42)
P Naoumoff (9.41)
M Callaghan (9.41)
CE Jackson (9.41)
EBC Charteris (10.41) KIA *T*
C FitzPatrick (9.41)
HW Wilks (9.41)
J Gourley (9.41)
Blewitt (10.41)
NE Wilson (10.41)
Livesey (10.41)
CD Boiteux Buchanan (1.42)
  KIA *A*
K McL Morrison (1.42) KIA *T*
PB Jessop (1.44)
Hon HK Cecil (4.42) KIA *T*
JT Parker (QM) (4.42)
IS Alexander (4.42)
P Young, att. for Bruneval
J Playford (8.42) POW *T*
AL Tannenbaum (2.44) POW *A*
AJ McDermont (4.43) KIA *A*
JH Grayburn (4.43) KIA *A*
MK Dunkeld (2.43) KIA *S*
JC Horner (6.43) KIA *S*

W Tite (4.43) CSM (9.41) POW *S*
JG Blunt (4.43) POW *A*
RB Woods (6.43) KIA *A*
MPH Barry (6.43) POW *A*
DJ Pye (6.43) POW *S*
DN Grove (6.43)
RH Levien (6.43) SGT (9.41) POW *A*
JG Reidy (6.43)
GFW Ellum (6.43) CQMS (9.41)
A Roberts (7.43) posted Brigade
DM Douglass (8.43) POW *A*
R McEwan (8.43)
C Stanford (7.43) POW *A*
PH Cane (8.43) KIA *A*
TO Bird (8.43)
JHA Monsell (9.43) POW *A*
WN Dormer (1.44) POW *A*
EL Russell (9.43)
A Russell (1.44) POW *A*
DEC Russell (2.44) POW *A*
JG Prudy (   )
JT Ainslie (3.44) POW *A*
RA Vlasto (2.44) POW *A*

2nd Lieutenant

JSC Flavell (6.44) POW *A*

Officers attached to the Battalion

Chaplains:

Captain Reverend ME
  MacDonald (9.41) POW *T*
Captain Reverend Watkins,
Brigade Chaplain (3.43)
Captain Reverend BM Egan
  (2.43) POW *A*

Royal Engineers

Captain D Vernon POW *A*
Captain P Stainforth POW *A*

Medical Officers:

Captain Isherwood, RAMC (9.41)
Captain J McGavin, RAMC
  (1.42) POW *T*
Captain RR Gordon, RAMC,
  (4.42) POW *A*
Captain JW Logan, RAMC,
  (8.43) POW *A*
Captain Wright, RAMC (9.44)
  Brigade MO POW *A*

Royal Artillery, Field Observation Officer:

Captain V Hodge, (7.43)

The Battalion had three Regimental Sergeant Majors during this period.
RSM T Cassidy was the first, soon followed by RSM WE Tite (later Lieut).
Acting RSM Macleod Forsyth took over and when CSM GA Strachan had
recovered from his Bruneval wounds he came out to Africa as RSM.

Appendix C

Honours and Awards for Bruneval 1942

MILITARY CROSS
53721   Major John Dutton FROST, *Cameronians*
174279   Second Lieutenant Euan Basil CHARTERIS, *KOSB*

MILITARY MEDAL
2748467 Sergeant Gregor McKENZIE, *Black Watch*
2824086 Sergeant David GRIEVE, *Seaforth Highlanders*

MENTIONED IN A DESPATCH for distinguished services
129341   Lieutenant Peter A YOUNG, *East Surrey Regt*
1871780 Corporal S JONES, *Royal Engineers*

CROIX DE GUERRE with GILT STAR
2751640 Company Sergeant major Gerald Alexander STRACHAN,
         Black Watch

During the Parachute raid on the RDF installation at Bruneval on the night of 27-28 February 1942 this Warrant Officer displayed courage, efficiency and devotion to duty of a high order. As Company Sergeant Major he was accompanying Company HQ and the reserve on the withdrawal to the beaches. The party came under heavy fire from the defences on the far side of the beach and CSM Strachan was severely wounded through the stomach. In spite of this, this Warrant Officer continued to assist his Company Commander in clearing the enemy from the beaches and in organising the embarkation. Both before and during the operation this WO displayed outstanding qualities of leadership and courage. His courage after he was seriously wounded was beyond all praise.

ROYAL AIR FORCE *on attachment to 2 Parachute Battalion*

MILITARY MEDAL
955754   Flt Sergeant Charles William Hall COX

King's Birthday Honours, June 1942

CERTIFICATE FOR GOOD CONDUCT
2751640 Company Sergeant Major Gerald Alexander STRACHAN
         Company Quarter Master Sergeant GWE ELLUM
(Later Commissioned in the Field, N Africa)

Honours and Awards for North Africa 1942-43

DISTINGUISHED SERVICE ORDER
48661   Brigadier Edwin William Conquest FLAVELL, MC
53721   Lieutenant Colonel John Dutton FROST, MC
88111   Major John Graham ROSS
188966   Captain James Watt LOGAN, RAMC

BAR TO MILITARY CROSS
Major Ronald R GORDON, MC, Medical Officer 2nd Battalion

MILITARY CROSS
168721   Major Richard ASHFORD
108192   Major Douglas Edward CRAWLEY
183734   Lieutenant John Desmond BRAYLEY
164821   Lieutenant John TIMOTHY
167154   Captain Ronald Leslie STARK
180657   Lieutenant Dennis Bassey RENDELL

DISTINGUISHED CONDUCT MEDAL
2748467   Sergeant Gregor McKENZIE

BAR TO THE MILITARY MEDAL
2754054   Sergeant James Low SHARP, MM, (MM, France 1940)

MILITARY MEDAL
2979279   Company Sergeant Major Macleod FORSYTH
5771257   Sergeant William CLOVES
2989834   Sergeant William FLEMING
1695912   Corporal Thomas David GRIFFITHS
          Corporal J HOLT, Medical Corporal RAMC
5339257   Private Matthew McALLISTER
4752311   Private William Ewart McDERMOTT
5780288   Private David Scott MILLER
2885157   Private Francis WELSH

MENTIONED IN A DESPATCH for distinguished service
167154   Captain Ronald Leslie STARK, MC
183734   Captain John Desmond BRAYLEY, MC
2052215   Private W WAIN
          Private WILKINSON

Foreign award by the French Government in exile.

CROIX-DE-GUERRE
Sergeant HEYHOW
Corporal WRIGHT, MM
Lance Corporal THIRKELL.
Three A Company NCO's attached Chasseurs d'Afrique for patrol duties.

by the President of the United States of America:

AMERICAN SILVER STAR
67178   Captain Andrew Joseph Hawksley RUTHERFOORD

Honours and Awards for the Invasion of SICILY 1943

DISTINGUISHED SERVICE ORDER
691129   Major Richard Thomas Henry LONSDALE, MC

MILITARY CROSS
113514   Captain Victor DOVER
165617   Captain Stanley Charles PANTER
99817   Captain Anthony Mutrie FRANK
          Captain Bernard M EGAN, Chaplain to the 2nd Battalion
          Captain V HODGE, RA, attached FOO

MILITARY MEDAL
2047962   Sergeant Frederick WRIGHT, Croix de Guerre
5339494   Sergeant John BARDWELL
4124109   Corporal Neville ASHLEY
5884314   Private Dennis BETTLE
3659183   Private William HALL
6351370   Private Dudley STEMP
2583477   Corporal Thomas WILSON attached 2 Battalion, RC of Signals

Decorations for successful escapes from POW camps.
For conduct in POW camp and for returning through enemy held territory in Italy after duty with prisoners.

MEMBER OF THE BRITISH EMPIRE
88111   Major John Graham ROSS, DSO
180657   Captain Dennis Bassey RENDELL, MC

BAR TO THE MILITARY CROSS
164812   Captain John TIMOTHY, MC

MILITARY CROSS
148624   Lieutenant Clifford Denis BOITEUX-BUCHANAN

MILITARY MEDAL
          Private W Cook

MENTIONED IN A DESPATCH for distinguished service
2989237   Sergeant TA LAUGHLAND
2879732   Private James SMITH, Parachute Regiment, Army Air Corps
A posthumous award, for POW murder.

Foreign award by the Union of Soviet Socialist Republics

ORDER OF THE RED STAR
2979279   Company Sergeant Major Macleod FORSYTH, MM
          posted Argyle and Sutherland Highlanders, Italy.

There were only 23 Red Stars awarded during the 1939-45 conflict and this was number eight. His Military Medal was won in North Africa.

Sergeant McKenzie's citations

MILITARY MEDAL
2748467   Lance Sergeant Gregor McKENZIE, Second Parachute Battalion.

During a raid on the French coast at Bruneval on the night of Friday February 27th and Saturday February 28th 1942 this NCO was in charge of a small party whose duty it was to deal with the enemy guarding the radio weather station. This task was done most successfully. Throughout the operation he was conspicous for his leadership, enthusiasm and in particular the determination with which he carried out the task. He showed great gallantry under fire.

DISTINGUISHED CONDUCT MEDAL
2748467   Sergeant Gregor McKENZIE

On 30th November 1942, during operations by the 2nd Battalion Parachute Regiment in Tunisia, this NCO was a platoon Sgt of a company which was ordered to attack and occupy the landing ground at Oudna. When the landing ground was reached the company was attacked by five heavy German tanks. This NCO pressed on in spite of all opposition with a party of ten men, made a thorough reconnaissance of the landing ground and then brought his party back. On the following day the platoon was in position in the hills called Djebel Sidi Bou Hadjeba when the battalion was heavily attacked. Sgt McKenzie in spite of heavy fire from artillery, mortars and machine guns and regardless of his personal safety moved about encouraging his men and held the position to the end. His conduct, gallantry and leadership were an example to his men and of the highest standard.

Honours and Awards for Arnhem 1944

The King has been graciously pleased to approve the posthumous award of the
VICTORIA CROSS to
149002   Lieutenant John Hollington GRAYBURN,
          2nd Battalion The Parachute Regiment
For supreme Courage, Leadership and Devotion to Duty.

Lieut Grayburn was a platoon commander of the Parachute Battalion, which was dropped on the 17th September, 1944 with the task of seizing and holding the bridge over the Rhine at Arnhem.

The north end of the bridge was captured and, early in the night, Lieut Grayburn was ordered to assault and capture the southern end with his platoon. He led his platoon onto the bridge and began the attack with the utmost determination, but the platoon was met by a hail of fire from two 20mm quick firing guns and from the machine-guns of an armoured car. Almost at once Lieut Grayburn was shot through the shoulder. Although there was no cover on the bridge and in spite of his wounds, Lieut Grayburn continued to press forward with the greatest dash and bravery until casualties became so heavy that he was ordered to withdraw. He directed the withdrawal from the bridge personally and was himself the last man to come off the embankment into comparative cover.

Later his platoon was ordered to occupy a house which was vital to the defence of the bridge and he personally organised the occupation of the house.

Throughout the next day and night the enemy made ceaseless attacks on the house, using not only infantry with mortars and machine-guns, but also tanks and self-propelled guns. The house was very exposed and difficult to defend and the fact that it did not fall to the enemy must be attributed to Lieut Grayburn's great courage and inspriing leadership. He constantly exposed himself to the enemy's fire while moving among and encouraging his platoon and seemed completely oblivious to danger.

On 19th September, 1944 the enemy renewed his attacks, which increased in intensity, as the house was vital to the defence of the bridge. All the attacks were repulsed, due to Lieut Grayburn's valour and skill in organising and encouraging his men, until eventually the house was set on fire and had to be evacuated.

Lieut Grayburn then took command of elements of all arms, including the remainder of his own company, and reformed them into a fighting force. he spent the night organising a defensive position to cover approaches to the bridge.

On 20th September, 1944, he extended his defence by a series of fighting patrols, which prevented the enemy from gaining access to the houses in the vicinity, the occupation of which would have prejudiced the defence of the bridge. This forced the enemy to bring up tanks, which brought Lieut Grayburn's position under such heavy fire that he was forced to withdraw to an area further north. The enemy now attempted to lay demolition charges under the bridge and the situation was critical. Realising this, Lieut Grayburn organised and led a fighting patrol, which drove the enemy off temporarily and gave time for the fuses to be removed. He was again wounded, this time in the back but refused to be evacuated.

Finally, an enemy tank, against which Lieut Grayburn had no defence, approached so close to his position that it became untenable.

He then stood up in full view of the tank, and personally directed the withdrawal of his men to the main defensive perimeter to which he had been ordered.

He was killed that night.

From the evening of September 17th until the night of September 20th, 1944, a period of over three days, Lieut Grayburn led his men with supreme gallantry and determination. Although in pain and weakened by his wounds, short of food and without sleep, his courage never flagged. There is no doubt, had it not been for this officer's inspiring leadership and personal bravery, the Arnhem Bridge could never have been held for this time.

BAR TO THE DISTINGUISHED SERVICE ORDER
53721   Lieutenant Colonel John Dutton FROST, DSO, MC
69129   Major Richard Thomas Henry LONSDALE, DSO, MC.

DISTINGUISHED SERVICE ORDER
75060   Major Allison Digby TATHAM WARTER

SECOND BAR TO THE MILITARY CROSS
168812   Major John TIMOTHY, MC, posted to 1st Battalion

BAR TO THE MILITARY CROSS
108192   Major Douglas Edward CRAWLEY, MC

MILITARY CROSS
85212   Captain Francis Kinglake HOYER-MILLAR

DISTINGUISHED CONDUCT MEDAL
7357051   Sergeant John Frederick WEATHERBY attached Medic RAMC

MILITARY MEDAL
4622101   Sergeant Herbert Wright CARRIER
14411425 Private Robert Alfred LYGO

MENTIONED IN A DESPATCH for distinguished service
99817   Captain AM FRANK
189329   Lieutenant JA RUSSELL
6469336   Sergeant AE JACKMAN
1440687   Sergeant J THOMPSON
728080   Sergeant J WALLACE
3857088   L/Sergeant J HAMILTON
14362066 Private RW PEATLING

Foreign Decorations; conferred for Arnhem by HM Queen of the Netherlands

BRONZE LION
167154   Major Ronald Leslie STARK, posted 1st Battalion
188966   Captain James Watt LOGAN, Medical Officer 2nd Battalion

by the President of the United States

DISTINGUISHED SERVICE CROSS
4617711   Corporal Robert PEARCE

SILVER STAR
99817   Captain Anthony Mutrie FRANK

14362066 Pte. PEATLING, R.W.,

     You will undoubtedly be very pleased to hear that your diary has turned up, having been found at the house of a Dutch Farmer – namely H. Van Esveld, Dwarsqiafweg 5, Essen, BARNEVELD by an officer of the 1st Canadian Division.

     I am taking care of it pending your instructions as to where you would like it to be sent.   Your dedication is most appropriate and I am sure your wife and father will be most interested in your first class evasion.

     While waiting for your present address I have read it and must congratulate you.

M.I.9,
Room 327,
Hotel Victoria,
Northumberland Avenue,
LONDON, W.C.2.

5 August 1945.

Lieut.-Colonel, G.S.

Reproduced are Awards for Arnhem submitted by the Battalion to Division for approval.

Sixteen Officers were recommended for awards and five were approved as submitted, two were given foreign awards and one a lesser award.

Twenty nine Other Ranks were recommended for specific awards only one was granted, one was given a foreign award and seven a lesser award.

When one considers the tributes paid and the sacrifices made, the awards do appear to be on the mean side.

Number	Rank	Name	Initials	Unit Recommendation	Div Recommendation	Date Recd.
461711	Lic (H/Cpl)	Pearce	R.	M.M.	U.S. D.S.C.	Oct 44
35721	A/Capt (A/Lt Col)	Frost	J.D. (BSO MC)	Bar to DSO	Bar to DSO	4 Dec 44
165617	W/Lieut (T/Capt)	Panter	S.C. (MC)	Bar to MC		4/12/44
85212	W/Lieut (T/Capt)	Hoyer-Miller	F.	MC	MC Dutch Bronze Helben	4/12/44
188966	W/Capt	Logan	J.H.	MC		4/12/44
94824	W/Lieut (T/Capt)	McLean	B.	MC		4/12/44
7013959	Sjt	Power	S.	DCM		2/12/44
45884	Pte	Lygo	R.A.	DCM	MM	2/12/44
193514	Sjt	Meade	A.	M.M.		2/12/44
6920723	Pte	Norton	L.M.	M.M.		2/12/44
6203748	Cpl	Dell	E.	MM		2/12/44
1359998	Pte	Newell	C.	MM		2/12/44
265726	Lt/Lieut	Vlasto	R.A.	Mention		2/12/44
315210	2/Lt	Flavell	J.S.C.	Mention		2/12/44
180226	Lt/Lieut	Dormer	Wm McK.	Mention		2/12/44
6148830	Pte	Harding	H.A.G.	Mention		2/12/44
123505	W/Capt (A/Maj)	Tate	F.R.	Mention		2/12/44
5259896	Sjt	Price	W.	Mention		2/12/44
6852122	Sjt	Kinsey	S.	Mention		2/12/44
6979513	Pte (L/Cpl)	Hannan	G.F.	Mention		2/12/44
72808	Sjt	Wallace	J.	~~Mention~~ MM	Mention	2/12/44
269244	W/Lieut	Blunt	J.G.	Mention		2/12/44
5778739	Sjt	Dennis	R.	Mention		2/12/44
11289	W/Lieut	Monsell	J.H.A.	Mention		2/12/44
899440	Cpl	Scopes	G.C.	Mention		2/12/44
5381521	Pte	Miles	J.E.	Mention		2/12/44
856061	Pte	Watkins	J.G.	Mention		2/12/44
5770303	Cpl	Orris	E.C.	Mention		2/12/44
4025583	Pte (L/Cpl)	Powell	C.	Mention		2/12/44
75060	A/Capt (T/Major)	Tatham-Warter	A.D.	DSO	DSO	Oct 44
149002	W/Lieut	Grayburn	J.H.	V.C.	V.C.	27/10/44
99817	W/Lieut (T/Capt)	Frank	A.M. (MC)	Bar to MC	U.S. Silver Star	Nov 44
108191	W/Capt (T/Maj)	Crawley	D.E. (MC)	Bar to MC	Bar to MC	1/7/45
189339	W/Lieut	Russell	J.R.	MC	Mention	1/7/45
7357051	W/Sjt	Weatherby	J.F.	DCM	DCM	1/7/45
4622101	W/Sjt	Carrier	A.W.	DCM	MM	1/7/45
4649336	W/Sjt	Jackman	A.E.	MM	Mention	1/7/45
1440687	W/Sjt	Thompson	J.	MM	Mention	1/7/45
5046367	Pte (L/Cpl)	Bayliss	G.H.	MM		1/7/45
4616630	Pte	Kelly	D.	MM		1/7/45
3055067	W/Sjt	Campbell	H.	MM	Mention	-
3857088	W/Cpl (L/Sjt)	Hamilton	J.	MM	Mention	-
2931605	Pte	Aitcheson	J.J.	MM		-
4128981	Pte	Ralphs	W.J.	MM		-
1139775	L/Cpl	McCreath	L.A.	MM		-

Glossary

AWOL	Absent without Leave		KRs	Kings Regulations
Arty	Artillery		KIA	Killed in Action
APO	Army Post Office			
Adjt	Adjutant		LO	Liaison Officer
A/L	Air Landing (glider)		L/Cpl	Lance Corporal
A/Tk	Anti-tank		LZ	Landing Zone
AMN	Ammunition		LMG	Light Machine Gun
Bde	Brigade		MM	Military Medal
Bn	Battalion		MID	Mentioned in Despatches
			MC	Military Cross
CFA	Chassuers D'Afrique		MG	Machine Gun
CO	Commanding Officer		Mc	Motor Cycle
CP	Command Post			
Cpl	Corporal		NIH	North Irish Horse Regiment
CQMS	Company Quartermaster Sergeant		OR	Other Rank
CB	Companion of the Most Honourable Order of the Bath		OP	Observation Post
			OC	Officer Commanding Company
Coy	Company			
			PFA	Parachute Field Ambulance
DLI	Durham Light Infantry		POW	Prisoner of War
DR	Despatch rider			
DJ	Djebel (desert undulation)		RASC	Royal Army Service Corps
DCM	Distinguished Conduct Medal		RDF	Radio Direction Finder
			RV	Rendezvous
DSO	Distinguished Service Order		RE	Royal Engineer
			RTU	Returned to parent Unit
DZ	Dropping Zone		RSM	Regimental Sergeant Major
FAAA	First Allied Airborne Army		Sgt	Sergeant
FOO	Field Observation Officer		Spr	Sapper (Engineer)
FDL	Forward Defence Line		SL	Start Line
FSP	Field Security Police		SD	German Secret Service
FOP	Forward Observation Post			
			TCV	Troop Carrying Vehicle
GOC	General Officer Commanding		TOO	Time of Origin
G1098	Army form for Ammunition			
			Wef	With effect from
HQ	Headquarter		WD	Wounded or War Dept
			WS18	Wireless set Number 18
ID	Identity Disc			
IO	Intelligence Officer		2ic	Second in Command

Bibliography

Airborne Forces, Second World War 1939-1945,
  Lt Col TBH Otway, DSO. Imperial War Museum, London 1990.

History of the Second Battalion The Parachute Regiment from its
  formation to the Battle of Arnhem, Captain D McLean,
  Gale and Polden, Aldershot 1946.

Prelue to Glory, Group Captain M Newman, OBE DFC,
  Sampson Low, Marston & Co, 1947.

The Bruneval Raid, George Millar, The Bodley Head Ltd, 1974.

A Drop Too Many, Major General John Frost, CB DSO MC,
  Cassell Ltd, 1980.

Pegasus Journal, Browning Barracks, Aldershot.

Honour to the Airborne, David Buxton, Elmdon Publishing, 1985.

Detour, Lieut JER Wood, MC, The Falcon Press, SW1, 1946.

Who Was Who during the Battle of Arnhem, C van Roekel,
  Airborne Museum, Oosterbeek, 1992.

Public Record Office, various, Kew, London.

The Royal Hussars Regimental report – Arnhem map.

The Airborne Forces Security Fund

The Airborne Forces Security Fund is open to all British Airborne soldiers, Gunners, Sappers, Medics etc as well as The Parachute Regiment/The Glider Pilot and Special Air Services Regiments.

If you served with British Airborne Forces from 1940 onwards, or are the dependant of one who so served, you qualify for assistance.

Increased demands upon the Fund

The Security Fund has been hit by rising demand in three ways
(a) the problems of old age, which as a young force we had not previously experienced to any degree
(b) the problems caused by successive recessions of which the 1990's is now perhaps the longest and, potentially, the most damaging in respect of claims upon the Fund
(c) a reduction of income as interest rates and dividends on investments have slumped. The increase of unemployment and of reduced business profits have also hit the pockets of many of the Fund's supporters.

The Trustees are most grateful to those who continue to support the Fund to the best of their ability. The need to increase the funds to meet the known and anticipated demands into the next century remain as important as ever.

If you are one of the lucky ones to be able to help the Fund then donations, legacies and the like are always most welcome.

Please send to:
The Controller
Airborne Forces Security Fund
Browning Barracks
Aldershot, Hampshire GU11 2BU